Skateboarding, Power and Change

"For all skateboarders and anyone with a passing curiosity about skateboarding, this book is a must read. Beautifully written and illustrated, and drawing upon interviews with a diverse group of changemakers, *Skateboarding, Power and Change* is a highly accessible, engaging and thought-provoking analysis of the 'ethical turn' in skateboarding. Written by two skateboarding academics, it offers powerful and moving insights into the various ways skateboarders are changing the world. Highly recommended."
—Holly Thorpe, *Professor of Sport and Gender in Te Huataki Waiora/School of Health at the University of Waikato, New Zealand*

"Willing and Pappalardo address one of the great new developments in skateboarding—its increasing capacity to face matters of race, ethnicity, gender and sexuality, and to effect new modes of active change. Combining erudite analysis and sensitive reflection with numerous interviews of key change-makers in the skate community, they surface multiple voices, nuances and routes forward. An impressive, provocative and timely study."
—Iain Borden, *Author of Skateboarding and the City: A Complete History (2019) and Professor of Architecture and Urban Culture at the Bartlett School of Architecture, University College London*

D1286200

Indigo Willing • Anthony Pappalardo

Skateboarding, Power and Change

palgrave
macmillan

Indigo Willing (iD)
Griffith University
Brisbane, QLD, Australia

Anthony Pappalardo
Independent researcher
Brooklyn, NY, USA

ISBN 978-981-99-1233-9   ISBN 978-981-99-1234-6   (eBook)
https://doi.org/10.1007/978-981-99-1234-6

This Palgrave Macmillan imprint is published by the registered company Springer Nature Singapore Pte Ltd.
The registered company address is: 152 Beach Road, #21-01/04 Gateway East, Singapore 189721, Singapore

Preface

Preface Illustration by Adam Abada

Somewhere on this planet, someone is experiencing their first moment of joy riding a skateboard. They could be new to skateboarding and they could have done something as simple as pushing down the street or carving below the coping of a ramp. It probably feels amazing and, in their minds, it also feels like an equally enjoyable and cool moment to share.

However, once that same action and motion is done around others or even documented on film, the feeling can change drastically—both positively and negatively.

In our minds, the feeling of skateboarding is pure. Doing something you have never done or doing something familiar with control and style feels great—it is a personal achievement that cannot be measured. Once that personal creativity becomes public, as in once others see you perform creativity, the entire process changes. We become aware of our posture, how our clothes look, or even how our fingers form odd poses when we attempt a trick.

But in skateboarding—in the form of skateboarding everyone at all levels pursues—even the most critical folks want to see you succeed. We cheer the beginner who drops in on a ramp for the first time successfully or does their first kickflip. There is a shared excitement in knowing that that person who just did that thing felt the same thing you did once and will again and again, as long as you ride a skateboard. Yes, it comes with warts, ribbing, off-hand comments, unwanted advice, and even harassment but the collective consciousness of skateboarding is one that is not only positive but communal, despite its differences.

Everyone is chasing fun and fun comes in different forms. Fun can be personal and purposely isolated. It can also be fostering community and create spaces that allow people to express themselves freely. Fun can be documenting the act of skateboarding, even if the one behind the lens is at a lower skill level than those in front of it. And yes, it can be a lot of fun writing about this feeling and thing too.

In a sense, documenting skateboarding is also as difficult as writing a song, and as with many, sometimes they just happen organically when no one is watching, but with a kind of magic that can happen when it is shared. What makes skateboarding so different from any sport or even most artistic endeavors is the relationship between the people doing it and the people watching it. Most professional athletes will not be rooting for their opponents to succeed against them. They do not fist bump when someone blocks their shot or strikes them out on a baseball diamond and no one is immediately elated for a victor who someone sprints past a finish line, fractions of a second before them. Skateboarding succeeds collectively; the challenge is getting everyone to understand that we do not succeed equally.

For our research, we developed a type of "skateboarders' mindset" which incorporates outlooks from our lived experiences as skaters and professional experiences as writers and researchers. Writing about skateboarding can be hard, no matter how much we believe we know it and love it. There is a need to be tenacious as if getting a skate trick and experiencing many trials and errors. You also need to be humble and stubborn and face inner fears and tough calls, and in the end, you have to "commit." And like skate tricks, there is always room for progression and "next tries."

With this skater's outlook in mind, our book does not aim to be a definitive history of skateboarding, nor an exhaustive look at people who have been leaders or involved in areas of social change. Rather, we see our work as an open-ended, mixed, and creative skate session, where skaters to skaters, we can look at our different skills and goals, "hype" each other up, gain and share tips, and do it for the shared love of skateboarding and sharing knowledge about it than to be competitive with our peers.

Our approach is also informed by our pre-existing knowledge that there is often a lot going on in the minds of skateboarders but not always an abundance of opportunities to share that, either on the board or off the board. We hope to open a window and provide a platform for the thoughts, goals, and motivations of skateboarders, which we aim to access by hearing how our peers talk about their experiences, perceptions, and opinions.

This book presents the journeys of over 42 people, from first becoming skateboarders to their lives as change-makers today, led by their passion for skateboarding, a curiosity, and a willingness to take risks, be creative, test things out, learn by trial and error, and keep going from a driving desire for progression. As part of this, we also acknowledge that we are positively influenced by generations of skateboarders before us. Our exploration ahead is founded upon the belief that there is a deep value in continuing to build knowledge today, sharing ideas with each other now, and laying down more building blocks for those who will follow us all in the future.

Nathan, QLD, Australia   Indigo Willing
New York City, NY, USA   Anthony Pappalardo

Acknowledgments

One of the catalysts for this book was our both being a part of the "Pushing Boarders" skateboarding conference in Malmö, Sweden in 2019. The week-long event of panel talks, skating sessions, film, and art exhibitions brought together academics, skate journalists, professional skateboarders, industry figures, skate organizations, and skaters from creative fields and non-profits. Dr. Indigo Willing was a panelist on the "University of Skate: Support Your Local Academic" panel and Anthony Pappalardo was a co-chair with Hannah Bailey on the "Editor's Note: Brutal Notes from Skate Journalism" panel. Adam, our creative and insightful book illustrator, was also one of the speakers in Malmö and gave a reading at a night devoted to literary works hosted by author Professor Kyle Beachy. Along with learning about each others' work at "Pushing Boarders," we met many of the skateboarders who we interviewed for this book or who were influential to us in terms of connecting with others and certain themes and issues we now explore. Accordingly, we extend our thanks to the team who organized "Pushing Boarders"— Dr. Sander Hölsgens, Dr. Thom Callan-Riley, Dr. Chris Lawton, and Dr. Dani Abulhawa.

From the global skateboarding community, we also wish to thank Douglas Miles Senior and Douglas Miles Junior from the Apache Skateboards team from San Carlos Reservation and Whiteriver for sharing some of their experiences and expertise in their own and in the broader world of skateboarding. We are also thankful to Adam Abada for contributing his artwork, and all the remarkable and generous individuals we interviewed for this book, who are listed in the Appendix.

We also wish to thank skateboarders who read drafts, gave feedback, or helped with skate knowledge in other ways before and during the writing of this book, including Dr. Paul O'Connor, Professor Iain Borden, Darren Kaehne, Nick Hayes, Dr. Mikko Piispa, Scott Shearer, Di'orr Greenwood, Cecely Todacheenie, Yulin Olliver, Adam Gray, Zane Foley, Dead Ramones Zine, Julianna McDuffie, Professor Sandy O'Sullivan, Ariel Stagni, Adelina Ong, Imke Leerink, Ian Smile, Ian Browning, Andreas Trolf, Nic Dobija-Nootens, Andrew Murrell, and others. Much appreciation also to Sarah Huston and Bradley Ehlers for permission to use their artwork and designs as thank-you gifts we sent to interviewees for their participation. Additional thanks go to academics at Griffith University Sport and Gender Equity Network and Griffith Centre for Social and Cultural Research, and in particular Dr. Adele Pavlidis, Professor Simone Fullagar, Dr. Ben Green, Dr. Ben Duester, and Professor Andy Bennett.

We are also appreciative of people who connected us to potential interviewees and research topics or who reached out to possibly be involved with this project. We were unable to include as many people as we hoped for in this exploration and especially with so much going on in the US and abroad from 2020 onward. However, we look forward to other opportunities to engage with and work with more people in the future and especially now that travel restrictions are easing.

A special shout-out also goes to #SkateTwitter people, consisting of fellow skaters on Twitter, for being a type of DIY and punk "brains trust," providing fun, good-natured, and generous advice on a broad range of topics. Social media can be a harsh and critical space to discuss skateboarding, yet the people using the #SkateTwitter hashtag are mostly welcoming and have created a space to enjoy the magic of being "die-hards," "skate-lifers," or "skate nerds" and just having a good laugh together.

In our personal lives, Indigo wishes to acknowledge the traditional owners of where she lives and works, the Jagera/Yuggera, Yugerabul, and Turrbal Peoples, Meanjin. She is thankful to her soulmate and lifelong partner plus her family for all their love, support, and acceptance. This includes accepting all the late nights she was up writing, helping her do numerous trips to the local stationery store to get paper and ink, and having to stay out of view during video interviews at all hours due to doing research across international time zones. She is also eternally thankful to individuals in her skate crew and others in skate scenes who inspire constantly, including Evie Ryder, Izy Duncombe, Sarah Huston, Amanda France, Emanuele Barbier, Enni Kalilainen, Kirby Clark, Tessa Fox, Tora Waldren, Peach Sørensen, Gabriela Levy, Jack Connor, Dr. Jessica Forsyth, Miljana Miljevic, Lily Turek, Alex Blyth, Riley Pemberton, Brooke Manning, Vivi T, Kane Stewart, Pat Gemzik, Josh Sabini skaters from Coops, Paddo, Fairfield, and treasured friends she's made through skating from around the world. Last but not least, much gratitude to Nanja van Rijsse, Templeton Elliott, Scott Moreton, and all those who shared cute cat and puppy videos and "cat reports" while she was in writing hibernation.

Anthony's acknowledgments unfold across a brief timeline of praise. He recalls starting skating in the late 1980s and all the folks who lent him an old board, pair of trucks, wheels, or even a kingpin to keep him rolling. For him, skateboarding has always been about the people devoted to sharing the feeling of skateboarding and whose vision for the culture of skateboarding is about advancing the whole. Our stories and needs are so personal, but it is the people who use their resources, platform, and relationships to work for the greater good of skateboarding and who have always resonated with him.

He would also like to acknowledge the following people who not only pushed him to pursue writing but to find his voice to tell the stories of skateboarding, especially the ones that are vastly ignored. Anthony would like to thank Hannah Bailey, Lance Dawes, Thomas Dupere, Amy Ellington, Cairo Foster, Norma Ibarra, Andy Jenkins, Ben Kelly, Vern Laird, Aaron Meza, Ian Michna, Yullin Oliver, Alyasha Owerke-Moore, Walker Ryan, Jim Thiebaud, Nora Vasconcellos, Alex White, Mark Whiteley, and Lucas Wisenthal.

Contents

About the Authors and Illustrator

Indigo Willing holds a PhD in Sociology from The University of Queensland and has been a research fellow at Griffith University. She is a parent and a community volunteer who started skateboarding aged 41. At the time of writing this book, she has been skating for over ten years. Her co-authored and solo-authored writings are published in academic peer-reviewed journals such as *Sociology, Young, Sport and Society*, and *Leisure Studies*, edited books, and skate media including Yeah Girl, *Quell Magazine*, and *Skateism*. She has also co-edited with Jenny Wills and Tobias Hubinette the book *Adoption and Multiculturalism* (2020).

Indigo is the co-founder of the We Skate QLD group (@weskateqld) which was originally called Girls Skate Brisbane (GSB) and launched in 2016 on the land of the Turrbal, Yugarabul, and Yuggera Peoples in Meanjin Brisbane. We Skate QLD was chosen to be the group's new name in July 2020 to recognize the expanding demographics of its participants and staff, including racial, ethnic, age, and gender-diverse skateboarders, as well as supportive allies. The group holds skate events, inclusive competitions, mentoring projects, and art initiatives and has been awarded a Pushing Against Racism Community Grant as well as one from Relationships Australia to promote skating to youth. Indigo is also the co-founder and project leader of The Consent Is Rad (https://consentisrad.wordpress.com), an international campaign launched in 2019 at the "Pushing Boarders" in Malmö, Sweden. Consent Is Rad has a no naming, shaming, or blaming policy and is committed to raising awareness and educating the skate community about consent. The campaign was awarded second place in the Skate Rising Awards for social projects in 2021 and equal first place in the Skate Like a Girl Awards for social projects in 2023.

Anthony Pappalardo started skateboarding in the late 1980s and has remained active in the community, writing, authoring, creating digital content, and producing books for several outlets and brands. He has co-authored two books about subculture titled *Radio Silence: A Visual History of American Hardcore Music* (2008) with Nathan Nedorostek and *Live… Suburbia!* (2011) with Max G. Morton. His work has been published in *Thrasher Magazine*, *ESPN*, *Huck Magazine*, *High Snobiety*, *Vice*, *Skateism*, *Jenkem Magazine*, and several other publications including *Slap Magazine* which he contributed to from 1995 to 2002.

Anthony also publishes his own work on substack *Artless Industria* https://anthonypappalardo.substack.com, a newsletter where he explores personal writing and industry happenings and also tackles topical issues within skateboarding. He is also a lifestyle, sport, and youth culture expert and a digital strategy professional, working on campaigns and marketing projects for several global clients. One of the recent social campaigns in skateboarding he has worked on is the Skaters Vote project (https://www.skatersvote.com), a non-profit created with the goal of encouraging skateboarders in the US to register to vote. In 2020, Skaters Vote created a campaign with Tony Hawk, Mark Gonzales, and several other traditional and non-traditional skateboarders directed by Colin Read which became a Vimeo Staff Pick and was considered for several awards.

For the illustrations for this book, we collaborated with **Adam Abada**, who is a skateboarder who was born in New York City, is based in LA, and has been drawing and illustrating for as long as he can remember. A filmmaker by trade, he draws from observations in the world around him and over time is learning how to inspire contemplation, thoughtfulness, and second looks. His artwork includes the Skaters Vote campaign and is also featured in several skate magazines and platforms and he is also a contributing writer for *Quartersnacks*.

1

Skateboarders Are Taking a Stance

Chapter 1 Illustration by Adam Abada

© The Author(s), under exclusive license to Springer Nature Singapore Pte Ltd. 2023
I. Willing, A. Pappalardo, *Skateboarding, Power and Change*,
https://doi.org/10.1007/978-981-99-1234-6_1

Introduction

Skateboarders are taking a stance, and this book is dedicated to exploring who these individuals and collectives are; what drives them to challenge, redistribute, and reimagine power; and what key changes have they now brought to life. We are also inspired by Jim Thiebaud, a senior figure and "lifer" in skateboarding, who when asked about what skateboarders could do in the face of discrimination and exclusionary attitudes in skateboarding urged skaters to "take a fucking stance" (quoted by Schwinghammer in *Solo Magazine*, 2018). Thiebaud is a significant part of skateboarding history as a professional skater in the 1980s, and then in the 1990s, as co-founder of *Real Skateboards* with Tommy Guerrero (also a legendary figure as one of the key members of Powell Peralta's *Bones Brigade* team). Thiebaud is now a figurehead of *Deluxe Skate Distribution,* or as it is better known, *DLX.* It is in this latter role that he lays out a new kind of figure in skating that is part-punk provocateur and part ethical entrepreneur. This includes in 2022 when *DLX* brought queer-run skate company *There Skateboards* into its fold who defy and move aside the long-term stronghold of hyper-masculinity and heteronormativity in skateboarding. In short, he points to a type of skateboarder who has the drive to use their ability to shake up the top-end of the skate industry. He states:

> I catch a lot of hate when we do political things here at *DLX.* I get text messages and comments about, "You are ruining skateboarding!" or "Keep politics out of skateboarding!" I fully don't understand that. When we started *Real*, it was to try and do really great shit with and for skateboarding. And it was always acknowledging the fact that this platform of skateboarding gives you this really loud voice to try and do great shit, to try and help people, to try and change the world. (quoted in Schwinghammer 2018)

The term "taking a stance" also has a double meaning for skateboarders, referring to how they stand on, push, or direct their board and also what they fight for. We argue skateboarding is experiencing a kind of "ethical turn" or new "ethics of skateboarding" where skaters are no longer forced to "shut up and skate" and instead are actively taking a stance for a range of people and social issues that many have always done, but with more energy and urgency post-2020 following the momentum of the *Black Live Matter* movement.

The research questions guiding our exploration are: What type of people are leading social change in skateboarding? And, what lived experiences of skateboarding and personal outlooks, as well as strategies and skills, do they develop and bring into their activities focused on social change? Our goals are also to gain insight into their perceptions, feelings, and reflections on what taking a stance involve, and where others can help or hinder their efforts. Furthermore, we aim to explore what lessons can be drawn from their stories to keep creating change now, and in the future for skateboarding.

How we see our worlds and our lives suddenly changed in the year 2020, especially in the United States (US) with the explosion of protests sparked by the *Black Lives Matter* movement. Police brutality and many other injustices toward Black Americans sparked a wave of street marches, civil protests, and awareness campaigns on a domestic and world scale not seen since the Civil Rights Marches and anti-Vietnam War Protests of the 1960s–1970s (Berger 2020; Buchanan et al. 2020). In addition, the global COVID-19 pandemic which also came to world attention in 2020 brought about unprecedented and unforeseen impacts, including lockdowns, widespread illness, and a spiraling economy.

The unforgettable beginning of this decade was also identified as also producing a gendered phenomenon (Thorpe et al. 2022) with women, non-binary, transgender, and gender-diverse people of various sexualities carrying additional losses and burdens. This was also compounded in ways for Black, Indigenous, or People of Color (PoC) people and other barriers that are intersectional (Crenshaw 1991). Yet as a range of things once taken for granted in "normal" life was being turned upside down, some of the most striking responses were the emergence of energized forms of critical reflection about the uneven power relationships in society, and the need to push for forms of individual and collective resistance.

A pandemic, the death of George Floyd, and an upcoming presidential election were just a few of the things that have called Americans to action this year. But while some called 2020 the apocalypse, others said it is a much-needed look in the mirror. (Rosenblatt 2020)

The social momentum from such remarkable phenomena included Black, Indigenous, and People of Color (BIPoC) people and other marginalized groups raising their voices and increasing the pressure on those in power to respond to calls for justice, representation, compensation, equity, and inclusion. This sense of urgency for society to do better was led by Black people, but their efforts were joined by other populations such as First Nations peoples challenging ongoing colonialism, Asians attacked from COVID-19-related racism, and Latin and Hispanic people facing hardline treatment in the name of US border security, such as being detained en masse and deported. Issues such as racism and racial privilege, which are often downplayed, evaded and seen as divisive, impolite, and uncomfortable by dominant groups (Bonilla-Silva 2012; Frankenberg 1993) were being more openly discussed by ordinary people, activists, and people with considerable power and influence, as well as on social media and traditional media (Rosenblatt 2020). In short, a culture of "calling people out" for various injustices as well as "calling people in" to become allies and part of a social change was moving to center stage.

Far from skateboarders in the US being removed and unaffected by the events of 2020 onwards, a myriad of social issues in skateboarding that has long existed but is often thrown into the shadows or dismissed as peripheral has also been brought to light. This includes attention to First Nations skateboarders (Miles Snr 2022) and Black skateboarders in an effort to address colonialism, anti-Blackness, and racism (such as Brown 2022; Garcia Marquez 2021; Lanza 2020; Jefferson 2020; Williams 2021; Williams 2022). There is also increased attention to many other forms of discrimination and exclusion in skateboarding, such as gender discrimination (Atencio and Becky 2011; Thorpe and Ahmad 2015), sexual violence, and "rape culture" (Abulhawa 2021; Consent is Rad 2021; Delardi 2021; Doyenne Skateboards 2022; Pappalardo, 2020a, 2022; White and Ebling 2019; Willing 2020), and transphobia, and homophobia (Abulhawa 2021; Dupont and Beal 2021; Geckle and Shaw 2022; Willing 2020). Efforts by individuals and groups for the right to use public space to skate, achieve pay parity in competitions, and calls to redistribute and reimagine forms of power in the skate industry have also gained support and momentum (Chiu and Giamarino 2019; Cianciotto 2020; Vivoni 2009).

As these growing points of protest indicate, skateboarding is not a utopian space of equality and inclusion. Yet, as there are no set rule books, forcible restrictions, or governing body on what skateboarding entails, this also keeps it flexible and with a fluidity that allows it to be open to various forms of change and progression. Rather than viewing this as "just how things are" we find guidance in Michael Foucault's (1982) seminal work on how power operates not just from above but can also be harnessed from below. What his insights can bring to skateboarding is a sharper awareness that there are always multiple "truths" and perspectives at play, and always within relationships of power that can be budged, radically shift, overturned, retract, or pushed forward.

As we discuss in more detail in future chapters, the types of skateboarders we interviewed for this book range from energetic and emerging activists to seasoned advocates, and some would also resist and defy such labels. We use the term "change-makers" to broadly refer to people in skating who are taking a stance, who want to change the game, and who may do so at the level of communities, industry, the arts, media, and broader social and cultural life. Valuable insights and pathways can be revealed from talking to people who overcome challenges, and wherever the love of skateboarding takes hold as the driving force and motivation for change. We also hope the conversations and knowledge we all generated together are able to shed light on collective and often shared processes that promote feelings of connection, growth, learning, recognition, and social purpose in skating.

Our motivation to write about skateboarding is because we love it and as skateboarders, we felt inspired to explore how, as a community, we can be aware of how we sometimes can neglect, exclude, and harm each other, and to now think together about ways we might improve. Our study is focused on the US, which is the most well-known "home" of skateboarding and also has the largest industry presence globally (Borden 2001, 2019). In the next chapter, we reflect on the tendency of studies of skateboarding to be biased toward Western skateboarding. We acknowledge our own study as not offering a more global view, yet we also emphasize the need to not see the US in isolation from the rest of the world either (McDuie-Ra 2021a, 2021b; Willing 2021). The influence of skateboarding in the US internationally is sometimes absent, only partial but in many countries appreciated and influential (McDuie-Ra 2021c).

There is a need to understand that skateboarding, wherever it occurs, will exist within relationships of power with various complex entanglements, uneven relationships, and hierarchical dynamics between individuals, groups, communities, and the skate industry (Abulhawa 2021; Beachy 2021; Delardi 2021). As future chapters will reveal, in the US various breakthroughs, advances, and exciting moments exist that have advanced the culture and brought joy to the skate community. Even so, we are wary of a simple romanticization of the culture of skateboarding, and through our exploration note how harmful practices, biases, and privileges have also been at play. Moreover, despite our own respect and admiration of many outstanding skateboarders throughout the history of skateboarding, we are also careful to avoid perpetuating an unhelpful hero worship of skaters.

At the same time, we argue there is a boom in "change-makers" in skateboarding who are pushing for positive social change, from traditionally spatially oriented activism to addressing a wider variety of social issues, inside their own culture and beyond. The aim of this chapter is to introduce the context with which our inquiry emerged and our approach to the research. We outline the sociological and qualitative approach our study adopts to generate a more in-depth knowledge of what kinds of people are involved in bringing about social change, the types of values they hold, typical challenges they face and strategies they roll out, and what advice they offer for now and in the future. Our discussion in this chapter is presented in four themes and sections: 1) The Sociology of Skateboarding, 2) Skateboarding Researchers as "Insiders" in the Culture, 3) Methodological Considerations and Processes During a Pandemic, and 4) Chapter Summaries.

The Sociology of Skateboarding

This section introduces some of the key definitions and frameworks that will guide our qualitative and sociological exploration of skateboarding, power, and change. We draw on various concepts and theories from the discipline of sociology and other relevant areas in the social sciences such as urban planning. To begin, we use the term "skate culture" as a useful umbrella term to refer to the physical, financial, social, and cultural dimensions of skateboarding. Paul O'Connor (2020), a skateboarder and sociologist, argues that beyond types of tricks, and preferences of terrain and spatial uses like "street," "vertical" or "vert," and "transition", there is no neat or singularly correct way to define what skateboarding is about. We can observe for instance that it is recognized as being a sport, subculture, a lifestyle, a commercialized venture, a competitive action sport, and even more things depending on how people relate to it (Atencio et al. 2018; Beal and Wilson 2004; Borden 2001; Lombard 2010, 2016; Snyder, 2017; Schwier and Kilberth 2020; Wheaton 2010, 2013; and Williams 2022). The idea of "being a skateboarder" can also be an embodied identity and a lifelong commitment (Beachy 2021, O'Connor 2017, Salusuo et al. 2016, Toffoletti et al. 2018, Willing et al. 2019, 2020). Yet across these multiple purposes and meanings, the concept of a "skate culture" remains a useful doorway to explore the social, physical, affective, spatial, economic, and cultural world of skateboarding. We are also guided by O'Connor's own outlook that:

> Skateboarding is a sport, that is also a lifestyle, a subculture, a philosophy, and an art form. As a qualitative ethnographer and sociologist, I find it simplest to define and explain skateboarding as a culture. In practicing skateboarding one embodies a particular way of viewing the world and engaging with it. Skateboarding becomes a part of human software, a field of communication, understanding, and symbolism. (O'Connor 2020: 9)

The kind of skateboarding that we explore in our book is the type that O'Connor (2020: 12) explains "largely conforms to the practices of street and park or transition skateboarding." We acknowledge other forms exist, such as freestyle, longboarding, artistic dancing, and fingerboarding, but want to concentrate on the quite specific histories, practices, cultural symbols, and meanings attached to the type of skateboarding O'Connor identifies. Street skating and transition skating are most commonly seen in magazines such as the influential *Thrasher* and formerly *Transworld*, and in events like *X-Games* and *The Olympic Games*. Street skating adopts elements of the built environment like stairs, ledges, parking curbs, and rails, and transition skateboarding is practiced on "vert" (skating on vertical ramps), mini-ramps and half pipes, pools, and bowls.

Skateboarding and urban studies scholar Duncan McDuie-Ra in his study of skateboarding in Asia (McDuie-Ra 2021b) and skateboarding videos (McDuie-Ra 2021c) argues that the physical relationship skateboarders have with the terrain they skate leads to them having a specific logic and outlook on the world that is grounded "from below" and also creates a special connection between skateboarders that is able to transcend international and cultural differences. In a sociological study of older skateboarders by Indigo (Willing et al. 2019) and her colleagues Andy Bennett, Mikko Piispa, and Ben Green also adopt Sarah Thornton's (1996) concept of "subcultural capital," which entails a type of power and insider status that only can arise from displaying symbols and having knowledge about a scene that is shared, specific, and carries social status.

Sociologist Gregory Snyder (2017: 61) who is a part of the LA skateboarding scene further assists with why the type of skateboarding we aim to explore warrants a certain level of defining and distinction from other types as:

> Skating has a very strict set of rules of interaction that are always changing according to who the rule makers are. The rule makers' power comes not from a privileged racial, class, or ethnic position, but from their skateboarding prowess and position within the industry, combined with their likability. And knowing the rules is part of being a member of the subculture.

Max Harrison-Cadwell (2019) then assists our study to unpack the term "core," which is an aspect of skate culture where these informal rules and forms of subcultural knowledge are used to identify and have control over what skating trick styles and symbolical things such as dress style are coded as being authentic, superior, and "cool." The "core" skate culture is something that can keep skateboarding unique and give it a sense of a community through peer-to-peer recognition, affirmation, and support. While Harrison-Cadwell (2019) notes that definitions of what is "core" are always subjective, he explains that the following are generally recognized: "1) core is an aesthetic, based on clothing and trick selection, 2) core is about supporting skater-owned brands and shops, and 3) core is just about sincerely loving skateboarding and building a community around it." Problems arise however when skaters "core" skating is hierarchical over other styles and tastes and used as a form of gatekeeping and exclusionary boundary maintenance.

O'Connor (2020: 10) argues that "skateboarding is now so widely understood as prosocial that the veneer of subversion and antisocial behavior has largely been removed. In short, social changes and transformations in skateboarding over the years have seen skateboarding grow from a subculture to a culture." While we wholeheartedly and enthusiastically support and embrace his conceptualizing of skating as a culture and those anti-social elements can be conflated, we depart from his proposal that skateboarding is no longer subversive. In future chapters, we point to various forms of activism and creative interventions that aim to challenge the status quo and create social changes within and outside of skateboarding. We also still align with researchers such as Snyder (2017) and writers such as Harrison-Cadwell (2019) that point to how subcultural knowledge can still create "rules" so people conform to "core" skateboarding. Yet older sociological understandings of subcultures can indeed be too rigid and require some contemporary reflection.

Subcultures were originally perceived as an identity, lifestyle, and set of activities largely taken up by outsiders, misfits, and rebels as an act of resistance, and these ideas have also often applied to the culture of skateboarding (see discussions by Borden 2001, 2019, Snyder, 2017, Yochim 2010). It was also traditionally believed subcultures were mostly made up of participants having working class and/or other marginalized backgrounds, who choose subcultures after being rejected by dominant groups, and in doing so, might find a sense of status, but one that often is only symbolic and stylistic, and does not result in tangible changes or shifts in power.

Variations of skateboarding culture certainly harbor many of those classic subcultural social and stylistic traits. As skateboarders ourselves, which we will discuss in a later section here, we identify with some of these traits. However, our insider status also inspires us to provide a more nuanced and fuller picture of the lives and outlooks of our peers and ourselves. Moreover, today, scholars are careful to emphasize more nuance is needed beyond the frameworks available in classic theories of subcultures (Hebdige 1979; Hodkinson and Deike 2007; Muggleton 2000). This push for a widening view also builds on post-subcultural theorists (such as Bennett 2011, Muggleton and Weinzierl 2003) who argue that classic subcultural theory can be reified, and instead emphasize the importance of context, individual reflexivity, and diverse biographies including class, and more fluid rather than hard lines of belonging.

The traditional sociological categorization of skateboarding as exclusively a "youth culture" also requires adjusting. No longer just a toy for kids that people always give up for more "responsible" adult pursuits, studies of the life course of skaters demonstrate skateboarding appeals to a wide age range that includes middle-aged skaters and older (O'Connor 2017; Salusuo et al. 2016; Willing et al. 2019, 2020). This also complements scholars who argue skateboarding for many can more holistically be framed as a "lifestyle" (Wheaton 2010, 2013; Salusuo et al. 2016) and an example of a positive and inclusive "active aging" (Willing et al. 2019). O'Connor (2017) adopts the concepts of "temporal capital" and Sarah Thornton's (1996) concept of "subcultural capital," which draws on the work of Pierre Bourdieu (1984), to highlight how different types of knowledge as capital can allow older skateboarders to still maintain a sense of identity and status in skateboarding (also discussed by Snow 2012). Building on this work, sociological studies of things such as videos of older skaters also assist us to understand some of the ways older individuals can nurture, construct, and "keep up" particular outlooks, knowledge, and identities as skateboarders, even while their hours of commitment may be compromised and skills may decrease (Willing et al. 2019).

In skateboarding, power does not exclusively exist only from the top, and outside of the reach of marginalized and minority skateboarders. Drawing on studies of skateboarding (Atencio et al. 2018; Delardi 2021) and action sports (Pavlidis and Fullagar 2016; Thorpe 2008) that build on Foucault's framework, power can be seen as something that reverberates, and can oscillate up and down, charge through, and electrify skate culture sparking incremental steps to larger transformations at every level. For instance, Pavlidis, and Fullagar (2016: 85) in their study of power and affect in roller derby provide further insight stating, "power is not some unified, central, sovereign 'thing'…power is not centralized…It is the nuanced exchanges between people, the effects produced through these relations and individual orientations towards these effects that tells us more about power."

Power can also serve to normalize the idea that things such as negative stereotypes are ahistorical and natural rather than arising from beliefs, discourses, and positionings that can shift across time and need to be contextualized. In our journey throughout this book, we argue that there are always dynamics of power, even in worlds as joyful and fun as skateboarding, that can work to "other" (Said 1991) less privileged populations and situate them as inferior. Skateboarders who struggle for power can also internalize negative attitudes and be complicit in their own marginalization or others (Sharp and Threadgold 2020). Of relevance to this research is how individuals resist and defy formations of power that act to erase, upheave, push out, and marginalize skateboarders across social classes, genders, sexualities, race and ethnicity, ages, and abilities. We also pay attention to when uneven situations of power and hierarchical relationships are reimagined, re-configured, redistributed, and shared in skateboarding, from the ground up and "from below" (McDuie-Ra 2021b).

Our goal is to draw attention to what we see as a boom in "change-makers" currently taking prominence in skateboarding who are pushing for change and are trying to shift and share power across a variety of social realms and issues, both inside the culture and beyond. Our approach is to explore what kinds of people are involved, what types of values they hold, the typical challenges they face and strategies they roll out, and what hopes and advice they offer for the future.

Australian geographer Nicholas Nolan (2003: 324) states that in many ways "skate culture still promotes an ideology of male superiority" (also see the critique of hegemonic masculinity in Connell 1995, and in skateboarding in Yochim 2010). Yet research on Korean skateboarding by Sander Hölsgens (2021) illustrates some distinct differences even within how masculine culture is performed at skateparks, with less aggressive forms seen in his ethnography of the skate scene in Seoul. Additionally, things like equal gender participation, something not yet achieved in the US, are seen in documentaries such as *Learning to Skate In a War Zone (If*

You're a Girl) which is directed by Carol Dysinger (2019) about skateboarding in Afghanistan and received an Academy Award in 2020 for the best short film. Interestingly, the award followed the US production of *Minding the Gap* directed by skateboarder Bing Liu (2018) and featuring himself alongside his friends from childhood, skateboarders Keire Johnson and Zack Mulligan. Liu's film which was nominated for an Academy Award in the same category in 2019. In Liu's film, problematic forms of masculinity and how they can affect men skaters' mental health and even promote violent behaviors are explored. It also illustrates the benefits of men communicating and sharing their emotions with each other.

Our study of skateboarding in the US can assist with breaking up myths and stereotypes that skateboarding is only for White, heterosexual boys and men (Atencio and Becky 2011; Dupont 2020). As we shall illustrate, skateboarders are represented by various genders and a spectrum of sexualities including women, non-binary, intersex, transgender and gender-diverse, lesbian, gay, bisexual, and queer people, plus racialized groups such as Indigenous, Black (African American and Black immigrants), Asian, Latin, and Hispanic peoples, and others. We also offer insights into how White, heterosexual, and cisgender people (who identify with the gender assigned to them at birth) can resist reproducing exclusionary practices and can work to be allies.

We also explore forms of "alternative masculinity," which is a positive and reflexive form of masculinity able to be fostered in skateboarding due to its more transgressive and progressive traits, as firstly argued in the context of skateboarding in the earlier work of anthropologists and skate researcher Becky Beal (1995). We also position our research lens over skaters who may harness being subversive and transgressive (Beal 1995; Nolan 2003; Wheaton and Beal 2003; Yochim 2010), convivial and community-minded (Ahmad and Thorpe 2020; Chiu and Giamarino 2019; Pappalardo 2020b), open to commercialism (Lombard 2010), or have a subcultural "entrepreneurial dynamic" (Snyder, 2017: 146). We identify and explore how all these traits can assist skateboarders to facilitate and contribute toward improving how skateboarders relate to each other, the well-being of others, and the environments they share.

In our exploration ahead, we have a particular interest in the experiences, perceptions, and insights of "non-traditional skaters," which is not to say diverse skateboarders have not always existed and been a part of skateboarding. We turn to the work of feminist and skate scholar Carla Delardi (2021) who defines "non-traditional" skaters are those who have been pushed and excluded from "traditional" forms of power, influence, and representation. Delardi (2021: 77) also explains that "the "non-traditional" label was not imposed upon skateboarders by academics, journalists, or other outside observers and instead originated from within the community itself. She adds that:

> Rather than a distinction imposed by the dominant culture (and thus, a symbolic form of Othering), the moniker can be understood as a claim to autonomy and self-defined cultural identity. Although all labels have limitations and the potential to be overly homogenizing, the scope of identities encompassed by this categorization also makes a necessary move away from binary understandings of identity, be it gender, sexuality, race, age, or ability, leaving space for intersectional interpretations as well as a sense of flexibility. At the same time, it does not suggest that marginalization is experienced uniformly among those who identify with this group; attenuation towards issues of access and privilege are, in fact, part of the fabric of this community. (Delardi 2021: 77)

When we refer to categories of identity it is important to emphasize that we do not see them as static or biologically determined. In contrast, we view skateboarders and their various identities as socially constructed (Bergman and Luckmann 1966), open to negative labeling (Becker 1963, 2018), types of impression management (Goffman 1959), subjectivity and positionality (Foucault 1980, 1982), and performativity (Butler 1990, 2006). The social constructionist standpoint does not deny that things such as gender and race do not exist, but rather, such categories are not fixed, and are shaped by things such as social beliefs which shift across time and context. Scholars of racism for example (Frankenberg 1993; Goldberg 1997; Williams 2021; Yochim 2010) emphasize how in Western nations like the US, identities that are racialized are set within a racial hierarchy that privileges White identity and forms of whiteness which position White people and Western culture as normative, "neutral," and superior, while reifying and stereotyping non-Whites.

We are also guided by the work of Sandy O'Sullivan (2021: 1), a nonbinary and Indigenous scholar who resists what they call the "colonial project of gender" which attempts to restrict categories of gender to male and female only. Through the colonial project, everyday language, discursive, legal, and political practices, and representations of gender refuse to recognize or respect the rights of populations who are transgender, nonbinary (and who use they/them pronouns), and gender non-conforming. The effect is one of gender-diverse people being ridiculed, rejected, and "intentionally erased" (O'Sullivan 2021: 2).

In drawing attention to "non-traditional" skaters, we set out to present a much richer window onto "the culture" of skateboarding, while also enabling individuals who push for change to be better acknowledged, understood, reached out to as guides and mentors, and also able to receive further support. Additionally, due to the range of individuals that we introduce and interview for this book, we also aim to highlight how many kinds of people with differing traits and lived experiences can bring about change rather than only elite, professional, and high-profile skateboarders. This includes skateboarders who are also often behind the scenes doing work, in Do-it-Yourself (DIY) scenes and belonging to grassroots networks. All kinds of skateboarders, including those with different bodies, abilities, and backgrounds, can bring particular strengths that are well suited for tackling social issues in skateboarding. Our objective is also to bring attention to their insights and the advice they share, providing a fresh window onto sometimes unrecognized guides and experts in the culture.

Skateboarding Researchers as "Insiders" in the Culture

It is neither surprising nor, we argue, a weakness that increasingly, studies about skateboarding are being produced by academics and writers who are skateboarders themselves. While skateboarding studies is a comparatively new field of research, many lifelong skaters as well as more recent ones have academic or journalistic backgrounds. High-profile breakthrough figures include Professor Iain Borden and Professor Ocean Howell (also a former professional skater), whose disciplinary areas span architectural and urban studies. And by looking at the staff biographies in skate magazines from established ones like *Thrasher* to newer publications like *Skateism*, it becomes clear that most individuals who write about skateboarding are skateboarders.

These scholars now join a number of published authors who are skaters in fields such as sociology, geography, and the arts. Academics who are skateboarders include from creative arts, media and performance studies such as Dr Dani Abulhawa, Dr Ted Barrow, Kava Garcia Marquez, Cole Nowicki, Joel Lardner, Dr Adelina Ong, Dr Pollyanna Ruiz, Tom Critchley, Ben Dixon, Wyatt Cunningham and Andreas Trolf, literature such as Professor Kyle Beachy, philosophy, psychology and education such as Brian Ball, John Rattray, John Dalquist, Dr Jessica Forysth, John Thurgood, Dr Adam Walker, Professor Brian Glenney, and Dr Esther Sayers, sociology including Dr Ben Duester, Professor Duncan McDuie-Ra, Dr Paul O'Connor and Dr Neftalie Williams, gender and sexuality studies such as Dr Nida Ahmad and Dr Bethany Geckle, and conflict studies with Sophie Friedel. In urban studies, there are also Dr Luke Cianciotto, Maxwell Dubler, Chris Giamarino, Scott Shearer, and many others. Rather than being held as outsiders, skate researchers and academics are generally accepted by other skateboarders as "insiders" to the culture, and with their works supported and shared in "core" skate platforms such as *Jenkem Magazine* (Jenkem Magazine Staff 2019, Kerr, 2018) and *Thrasher Magazine* (Schmitz 2019).

The groundbreaking *Pushing Boarders* (https://www.pushingboarders.com) skate-themed conference event held in London, United Kingdom (UK), in 2018 and Malmo, Sweden, in 2019 has also assisted to foster more attention and connections for this new wave of skate researchers/writers and scholars, with its hybrid mix of panel talks, poetry, literary readings, and presentations by skateboarders in academia, media, industry, and the arts. It is also organized by skateboarders who are academics including Dr Sander Holsgens, Dr Dani Abhulhawa, Dr Thom Callan-Riley, and Dr Chris Lawton.

Our own backgrounds include both of us being skateboarders, with active ties to the culture and doing work on social projects within skate communities. Dr Indigo Willing is a sociologist, writer, and community volunteer. At the time of writing this book, she has been skating for over ten years. Willing is also the co-founder of the *We Skate QLD group* (@ weskateqld) which was originally called *Girls Skate Brisbane (GSB)* dedicated to recognizing women, non-binary, and gender-diverse skateboarders, as well as supportive allies. Willing is also the co-founder and project leader of The *Consent is Rad* (https://consentisrad.wordpress.com) international campaign. Anthony Pappalardo started skateboarding in the late 1980s in Salem, New Hampshire, and has remained active in the community, writing, authoring, and contributing to skate-centric books, and creating digital content. One of the recent social campaigns in skateboarding Pappalardo has worked on is the *Skaters Vote* project (https:// www.skatersvote.com), a non-profit created with the goal of encouraging skateboarders in the US to register to vote.

Some of the strengths of writers and researchers who are skateboarders include how our works are enriched by an often fine-grained, rich ethnographic style of detail, and in-depth insights shaped by our lived experiences and subcultural knowledge of skating, its history, and its social impacts (see discussion in Ahmad and Thorpe 2020, McDuie-Ra 2021b, 2021c). O'Connor (2017: 6) explains that "insider information in qualitative research on sports can be a powerful asset as it enables the researcher to fluidly understand technical and cultural terminology" (also see his discussion of Sparkes and Smith 2013). This reflects arguments in feminist research of action sport where having an "insider" perspective assists with conceptual development, access to and rapport with participants, and where transparency and reflexive discussions of the positionality of researchers are transparent (Ahmad and Thorpe 2020; Pavlidis and Fullagar 2016; Thorpe and Olive 2016; Thorpe et al. 2022; Toffoletti et al. 2018; Wheaton 2013).

Methodological Considerations and Processes During a Pandemic

Our research draws on a combination of qualitative sociological inquiry, journalism, and social critique, guided by theoretical frameworks developed by skateboarders and theorists of youth and subcultures outlined in previous sections. The methodology underpinning the research for this book also combines a bricolage of approaches drawn from the broader qualitative research literature (King-White 2017; Schwandt 2000) and thematic analysis (Braun and Clarke 2006). Our research also brings together sociological ideas from studies of action and lifestyle sports, gender studies, sports studies, and research on athlete activism (such as Ahmad and Thorpe 2020; Pavlidis and Fullagar 2016; Magrath 2022; Skinner et al. 2021; Sparkes and Smith 2013; Toffoletti et al. 2018).

While writing this book we also needed plenty of persistence and belief in the process, something as skateboarders we also build up from endless slams, and a will to get back up again until we get our tricks. Throughout writing this book from 2020 to 2022 Indigo was based in her home in Meanjin, Brisbane, Australia, while Anthony was living on the East Coast of the US. Both our lives and indeed the world were affected by various unforeseen and unprecedented upheavals and events. Challenges included our facing a range of physical, health, social, geographic, and climate-related issues as well as social and financial hurdles.

The emergence of a global pandemic in COVID-19 has been one of the most encompassing in sports research (Thorpe et al. 2022). Its impact included dealing with our own and our significant others' health, and care duties, months-long lockdowns, unstable economies, evaporating work opportunities, and international travel restrictions. Throughout this period, travel abroad from Australia was banned, making it impossible for both of us to be together in the US in person to do interviews. Restriction on domestic travel in the US due to COVID-19 was also an issue. None of these scenarios came even close to reflecting the envious image of writers by their desks enjoying predictable and comfortable environments conducive to writing streams of uninterrupted and tidy thoughts onto the pages.

A lot of other things have happened in the US, Australia, and overseas that had an impact and influence on our research. Protests as part of *Black Lives Matter* erupted on the streets in 2020 and deservedly commanded our and others' attention via attending rallies and online efforts to address anti-Blackness not just in policing but throughout US society and abroad. An explosion of COVID-related racism against Asians also made it unsafe for Indigo to move freely without fear due to having Vietnamese heritage and being of Asian appearance, and with the personal toll that weighed on her after being the target of verbal racial abuse once in the workplace and several times on the streets. Fires in 2020 and floods in 2022 also swamped whole towns and cities in heavy smoke and floodwaters in Australia, requiring forced pauses in activities and taking away time otherwise devoted to writing. And mega-events and competitions that we had anticipated being able to talk to skaters about were also affected by the pandemic, with some events delayed such as the *Olympic Games* in Tokyo moving to 2021, while others went online such as *Exposure Skate* 2021.

In seeking a way forward, we decided to have a consistent interviewing approach relying on using video calls to conduct all interviews, which have been used effectively in other recent research in action sports (Ahmad and Thorpe 2020). We conducted interviews with 42 individuals. We discuss our purposive and expert sample and their biographical information in Chap. 3. Our methods were based on qualitative research principles (Denzin 2001; Holstein and Gubrium 2003), using semi-structured and open-ended questions to keep flexible topics of interest to the participants and with interviews lasting around one hour. Our line of questioning was designed to elicit insights into things such as individuals' perceptions of skateboarding, what meanings they attached to it, their motivations for change, their values and intentions that guide them, and insights into their own self-knowledge and critical reflections.

We used a chronological approach in the interviews to create a coherent narrative and to better understand the interviewees' journey of going from newly formed skaters to change-makers in skateboarding. We began by asking when did people start getting into skateboarding. We then asked if it was very diverse and what might they remember about their own experiences in that time. Next, we focused on what kinds of experiences, mentors, or outlooks in the past shaped their desire to do social justice projects or related activities. We also asked interviewees about what challenges they face today and how they feel about the resources and strategies they have at hand. In each step, we framed these questions as looking for insights and advice they could offer to better educate or assist others in skating, including the next generation of skaters. Our concluding questions then focus on actionable changes they recommend being followed up on and what hopes they have for the future.

Our research for the book was not funded, and financial incentives did not shape our involvement or the participants who contributed to this research. Non-financial support was acquired via institutional and administrative resources at the *Griffith Centre for Social and Cultural Research* at *Griffith University* and we gained ethical clearance in 2021 (GU ref no: 2021/066). Safeguards for participants included their need to give informed consent before speaking to us for the research, and in the knowledge, their participation was voluntary and for the purpose of extending knowledge on how change happens in skateboarding. As a way to acknowledge that we appreciate their time and knowledge, we organized for each participant to receive printed or online gifts of artwork donated by artist Adam Abada and designer Sarah Huston from *Yeah Girl*. We also organized honorariums for some participants where specific cultural protocols, special expertise, and extra time requirements were a factor.

The interview transcripts which were our main research data were explored and analyzed using thematic analysis (Braun and Clarke 2006). We paid attention in the interviews to the perspectives, experiences, meanings, motivations, feelings, and values of the participants. This included looking for common patterns like lifestyle characteristics and experiences, values and ethics, resources and strategies, and hopes for skateboarding. The analysis was continually categorized and refined until main themes were developed and these will be introduced in future chapters that discuss our findings. To address issues of interrater reliability and bias due to familiarity or friendships with many of the interviewees, emerging insights during the analysis were checked with secondary sources in the media, relevant skate and academic literature, and conversations with other researchers who study skateboarding, youth, or subcultures. In the concluding section below for this chapter, we provide an overview of the chapters ahead.

Chapter Summaries

In this chapter we introduced the social context and era in which our research arose, the main aims and goals of our research, and why this warrants exploration. We also provided some sociological definitions and theoretical frameworks for exploring skateboarding as a culture. We then outlined key aspects of our research field, including that many researchers and ourselves are positioned as "insiders" in skateboarding. We also introduced our chosen methodology, which consists of a qualitative approach, purposive and expert sample, and thematic analysis.

In Chap. 2 we present a brief historical overview of skateboarding and argue that there have always been skateboarders with diverse backgrounds in skateboarding. However, we also map how their presence and contributions started to be overlooked and pushed to the margins as the culture of skateboarding evolved and grew into an industry. We also point to how a range of efforts are made by "non-traditional" skaters to challenge such erasure and hierarchies of power. Our aim is to generate a deeper understanding of how they make sense of their experiences. In doing so, we also reinforce the importance of this study which is to gain insights through skateboarders' own perspectives.

Chapter 3 introduces skateboarders as social "change-makers," which in doing so challenges traditional theories of subcultures and negative stereotypes of skaters as inherently anti-social, or that their acts of social resistance are only stylistic and symbolic. The discussion begins by outlining how mainstream sports provide strong examples of activists and athletes who challenge power and then some of their iconic counterparts in skateboarding. But rather than categorizing skaters under the label of activists, we introduce a range of typologies that assist us to understand some of the nuances and specific strengths and styles of these mostly under-recognized change-makers. We also include an overview of the backgrounds of the individuals we interviewed, which aims to illustrate how a wide range of people, rather than just professional and elite-level skateboarders are able to effect social change in skateboarding.

In Chap. 4 we move our attention to the formative experiences, outlooks, and values of skateboarders. We highlight their early, lived experience of transforming from being introduced to a skateboard to becoming a "skateboarder." We identify some of the intersectional issues that impacted their early journeys of identity and belonging. This includes various internal and external challenges that were more commonly faced by women and non-binary skaters. Even so, across genders, we can observe a shared commitment to skateboarding as a lifestyle, not just inspired by physical rewards but also social and cultural ones. Insight into the outlooks and values that skaters attach to skateboarding also provides a deeper understanding of the foundations of why and how they are change-makers.

In Chap. 5 we present a more extensive discussion of our interviews which is divided into three main parts. We focus on the critical thinking of skateboarders, which is revealed in their discussion of key challenges they face and how that leads to a range of strategies and actions. Areas explored include racism and decolonization, issues of equity in the industry, roles of skate competitions, skate media and creative areas, skatepark activism, and how skateboarders relate to each other within skate communities and with spaces in public and common spaces. Rather than being exclusive to skateboarding culture, many of the social issues they grapple with are seen in and are intertwined with wider society. As such, their insights on challenging social discrimination and structural inequality offer useful guides for not just skateboarding but also other youth cultures, subcultures, lifestyle and mainstream sports, and beyond.

Chapter 6 presents an overview of the wish lists, roadmaps, and recommendations that skateboarders hold for the future, including advice they wish to share with others wanting to effect change in the skateboarding community. For some, there is a range of changes that can be actionable now or in the near future, and with others, their focus is on goals that require a longer commitment, more resources, and planning. Their insights also address the need to build self-care and self-critique into the work they do. The discussion also reflects on how certain values and outlooks that skateboarders have developed across their lives as skaters, which were explored in previous chapters, continue to inform their hopes and advice for the future of skateboarding.

In Chap. 7, we conclude our exploration of skateboarding, power, and change with some final reflections on the implications and significance of this research, as well as offering recommendations for future research. This includes an emphasis on how change-makers consist of a range of individuals of various backgrounds who love and are committed to the culture and utilize particular strengths to address social issues they are concerned about. We then emphasize their need for additional and tangible forms of support, through things such as inclusion and representation, funding, and other resources.

References

Abulhawa, D. (2021) *Skateboarding and femininity: gender, space-making and expressive movement* London: Routledge.

Ahmad, N and Thorpe, H (2020) Muslim Sportswomen as Digital Space Invaders: Hashtag Politics and Everyday Visibilities, *Communication and Sport*, 1-20. DOI: https://doi.org/10.1177/2167479519898447

Atencio, M and Becky B (2011) Beautiful Losers: The Symbolic Exhibition and Legitimization of Outsider Masculinity. *Sport in Society* 14(1):1–16.

Atencio, M., Beal, B., Wright, M. E., and ZáNean, M (2018) *Moving Boarders: Skateboarding and the Changing Landscape of Urban Youth Sports*. Fayetteville, AR: University of Arkansas Press.

Beachy, K (2021) *The Most Fun Thing*. Grand Central Publishing.

Beal, B (1995). Disqualifying the official: An exploration of social resistance through the subculture of skateboarding. *Sociology of Sport Journal, 12*(3), 252–267. https://doi.org/10.1123/ssj.12.3.252

Beal, B & Wilson, C (2004) "Chicks dig scars": Commercialisation and the Transformations of Skateboarders' Identities. In B. Wheaton (Ed.), *Understanding Lifestyle Sports: Consumption, Identity, and Difference* (pp. 31–54). Routledge.

Becker, H (1963, 2018) *Outsiders: Studies in the Sociology of Deviance*, New York: Free Press.

Bennett, A (2011) The post-subcultural turn: some reflections 10 years on. *Journal of Youth Studies, 14*(5), 493–506. https://doi.org/10.1080/1367626 1.2011.559216

Berger, M (2020) The Pandemic is an Era of Protests — and Protest Restrictions, *The Washington Post*. Posted 3 October. Downloaded 18 July 2022: https://www.washingtonpost.com/world/2020/10/02/coronavirus-pandemic-demonstrations-protest-restrictions/

Bergman, P and Luckmann, T (1966) *The Social Construction of Reality: A Treatise in the Sociology of Knowledge*. Anchor Books.

Borden, I (2001) *Skateboarding, Space and the City: Architecture and the Body*. Oxford: Berg.

Bonilla-Silva, E (2012) The Invisible Weight of Whiteness: The Racial Grammar of Everyday Life in Contemporary America, *Ethnic and Racial Studies*, 35:2, 173-194, DOI: https://doi.org/10.1080/01419870.2011.613997

Bourdieu, P (1984) *Distinction: A Social Critique of Judgement and Taste*. Cambridge: Harvard University Press.

Braun, V and Clarke, V (2006) Using Thematic Analysis in Psychology. *Qualitative Research in Psychology*, 3(2), 77-101. https://doi.org/10.1191/1478088706qp063oa

Brown, A (2022) Honouring the Lineage of Black Skateboarders, *Nosesliders*, Posted 15 February. Downloaded 18 July 2022: https://nosesliders.substack.com/p/honoring-the-lineage-of-black-skateboarders?r=z8hv9

Buchanan, L, Bui, Q and Patel, J (2020) Black Lives Matter May Be the Largest Movement in U.S. History, *New York Times*. Posted 3 July. Downloaded 18 July 2022: https://www.nytimes.com/interactive/2020/07/03/us/george-floyd-protests-crowd-size.html

Butler, J (1990, 2006) *Gender Trouble: Feminism and the Subversion of Identity*, London, Routledge.

Crenshaw, K (1991) Mapping the Margins: Intersectionality, Identity Politics, and Violence against Women of Color, *Stanford Law Review*, 46(6): 1241-1299. 10.2307/1229039

Cianciotto, L (2020). Public Space, Common Space, and the Spaces In–Between: A Case Study of Philadelphia's LOVE Park. *City & Community*, 19(3), 676–703. https://doi.org/10.1111/cico.12454

Chiu, C., and Giamarino, C (2019) Creativity, Conviviality, and Civil Society in Neoliberalizing Public Space: Changing Politics and Discourses in Skateboarder Activism From New York City to Los Angeles. *Journal of Sport and Social Issues*, 43(6), 462–492. https://doi.org/10.1177/0193723519842219

Connell, R (1995) *Masculinities*. Cambridge, UK: Polity Press.

Consent is Rad (2021) Break the Cycle Campaign Consent is Rad x WKND Skateboards, *Consent is Rad* https://consentisrad.wordpress.com/break-the-cycle/

Delardi, C (2021) *Pushing Boarders, Creating Alternative Futures: Resistance and Radical Inclusion in the Production of Non-Traditional Skateboarding Culture*, MA Thesis, Gallatin School of Independent Study, New York University.

Denzin, N (2001) '*The Reflexive Interview and a Performative Social Science*', *Qualitative Research*, 1(1), 23-46.

Dysinger, C (2019) director, *Learning to Skate In a War Zone (If You're a Girl)*, A&E IndieFilms and Grain Media, USA.

Dupont, T (2020) Authentic subcultural identities and social media: American skateboarders and Instagram. *Deviant Behavior, 41*(5), 649–664. 10.1080/01639625.2019.1585413

Dupont, T and Beal, B (2021) *Lifestyle Sports and Identities: Subcultural Careers through the Life Course*. Milton: Taylor & Francis Group.

Doyenne Skateboards (2022) Ask: A Project About Consent. *Doyenne Skateboards*. Posted March 2022. Downloaded 19 July 2022: https://doyenneskateboards.com/blogs/archive-1/ask-a-zine-about-consent

Foucault, M (1980) Power/Knowledge: Selected Interviews and Other Writings, *1972-1977*. New York: Pantheon Books, 1980.

Foucault, M (1982) The Subject and Power, *Critical Inquiry*, 8(4) (1982): 777-795.

Frankenberg, R (1993) *White Women, Race Matters: The Social Construction of Whiteness*, University of Minnesota Press

Garcia Marquez, K (2021) Skateboarding into the Sun, Eds Callen-Riley, T and Holsgens, S, *Urban Pamphleteer #8 Skateboardings*, pp 32-33, Downloaded 18 July 2022: http://urbanpamphleteer.org/skateboardings

Geckle, B and Shaw, S (2022) Failure and Futurity: The Transformative Potential of Queer Skateboarding. *YOUNG, 30*(2), 132–148. https://doi.org/10.1177/1103308820945100

Goldberg, T (1997) *Racial Subjects: Writing on Race in America*, New York: Routledge.

Goffman, E (1959) *The Presentation of Self in Everyday Life*. Double Day.

Hebdige, D (1979). *Subculture: The Meaning of Style*. London: Routledge.

Hodkinson, P and Deike, W (2007) *Youth Cultures: Scenes, Subcultures and Tribes*, New York: Routledge.

Hölsgens, S (2021) *Skateboarding in Seoul: A Sensory Ethnography*. University of Groningen Press.

Holstein, J and Gubrium, J (Eds.) (2003) *Inside Interviewing*. SAGE Publications, Inc., https://doi.org/10.4135/9781412984492

King-White, R (2017) *Routledge Handbook of Physical Cultural Studies*. Routledge

Jenkem Staff (2019) 'Looking Into the World Of Skate Academia', review of skate research, Jenkem Magazine, Posted 14 October, 2019. Downloaded 18 July 2022: http://www.jenkemmag.com/home/2019/10/14/looking-inside-world-skate-academia/

Lanza, L (2020) Black Skateboarders Share their Experiences, *Jenkem Magazine*, posted 31 July. Downloaded 18 July 2022: https://www.jenkemmag.com/home/2020/07/31/black-skaters-share-experiences-skateboarding/

Liu, B (2018) *Minding the Gap*. Kartemquin Films, USA.

Lombard, K.J (2010). Skate and create/skate and destroy: The commercial and governmental incorporation of skateboarding. *Continuum: Journal of Media & Cultural Studies, 24*(4), 475–488. https://doi.org/10.1080/10304310903294713

Lombard, KJ (2016) *Skateboarding: Subcultures, Sites and Shifts*. London: Routledge.

Magrath, R (2022) *Athlete Activism: Contemporary Perspectives*. Taylor and Francis Group.

McDuie-Ra, D (2021a). The ludic lives of memoryscapes: skateboarding post-soviet peripheries. *Memory Studies, (20210222)*. https://doi.org/10.1177/1750698021995982

McDuie-Ra, D (2021b) *Skateboarding and Urban Landscapes in Asia: Endless Spots*. Amsterdam University Press

McDuie-Ra, D (2021c) *Skateboard Video: Archiving the City from Below*. Palgrave Pivot.

Muggleton, D (2000). *Inside Subculture: The Postmodern Meaning of Style*. Oxford: Berg.

Muggleton, D and Weinzierl, R. Eds. (2003). *The Post-subcultures Reader*. Oxford: Berg.

Miles Snr, D (2022), Desert Rider: Under the Hood–Douglas Miles (ep. 01), interview for *Desert Rider Series Installation*, Phoenix Art Museum, Downloaded 13 May. URL: bit.ly/UTH-Miles

Nolan (2003) The Ins and Outs of Skateboarding and Transgression in Public Space in Newcastle, Australia, *Australian Geographer*, 34(3), 311-327, DOI: https://doi.org/10.1080/00049180320001524 01

O'Connor, P (2017) Beyond the youth culture: Understanding Middle-aged Skateboarders through Temporal Capital, *International Review for the Sociology of Sport*, Preview Copy. 1-20

O'Connor, P (2020) *Skateboarding and Religion*. London: Palgrave

Salusuo, M, Piispa, M and Huhta, H (2016) *Exceptional Life Courses: Elite Athletes and Successful Artists in 2000s Finland*, Finnish Youth Research Society and Network.

O'Sullivan, S (2021) The Colonial Project of Gender (and Everything Else), *Genealogy*, 5(67): 1-9 https://doi.org/10.3390/genealogy5030067

Pappalardo, A (2020a) Skateboarding Needs to Listen. *Artless Industria*. Posted 6 August. Downloaded 18 July 2022: https://anthonypappalardo.substack.com/p/skateboarding-needs-to-listen

Pappalardo, A (2020b) Skaters Vote PSA: A Call To Vote From Birdman, The Gonz, & More by Colin Read. *Artless Industria*. Posted 28 October. Downloaded 19 July 2022: https://anthonypappalardo.substack.com/p/skaters-vote-psa

Pappalardo, A (2022) Gator, Mark Oblow and Apologies, *Artless Industria*. Posted Downloaded 17 July 2022: https://anthonypappalardo.substack.com/p/gator-mark-oblow-and-apologies

Pavlidis, A and Fullagar, S (2016) *Sport, Gender and Power: The Rise of Roller Derby*. London: Taylor and Francis.

Rosenblatt, K (2020) How 2020 Became the Summer of Activism Both Online and Offline, *NBC News*. Posted 26 September. Downloaded 18 July 2022: https://www.nbcnews.com/news/us-news/summer-digital-protest-how-2020-became-summer-activism-both-online-n1241001

Said, E (1991) *Orientalism*. New York: Penguin.

Schmitz, T (2019) Pushing Boarders Second Annual Skate Academic Conference. *Thrasher Magazine*. Posted 25 September. Downloaded 18 July 2022: https://www.thrashermagazine.com/articles/pushing-boarders-second-annual-academic-skate-conference/

Schwandt, T (2000) 'Three Epistemological Stances for Qualitative Inquiry: Interpretivism, Hermeneutics and Social Constructivism'. In *The Handbook of Qualitative Research*. (Eds, Denzin, N. & Lincoln, Y.). 2nd Edition. London: Sage Publications. pp. 189–213.

Schwier, J and Kilberth, V. eds (2020) *Skateboarding Between Subculture and the Olympics: A Youth Culture under Pressure from Commercialization and Sportification*. Columbia University Press.

Schwinghammer, S (2018) Jim Thiebaud Taking a Fucking Stance. *Solo Magazine*. Posted 18 August. Download 20 July 2022: https://soloskatemag.com/jim-thiebaud

Sharp, M and Threadgold, S (2020) Defiance Labour and Reflexive Complicity: Illusio and Gendered Marginalisation in DIY Punk Scenes. *Sociological Review*, 68(3), pp. 606-622. https://doi.org/10.1177/0038026119875325.

Skinner, J, Edwards, A and Smith, A (2021). *Qualitative Research in Sport Management.* 2nd ed. Milton: Taylor & Francis Group.

Snow, D (2012) Skateboarders, Streets and Style, in R White (ed), *Youth subcultures: Theory, history and the Australian experience (revised second edition)*, ACYS, Hobart, pp. 273-282.

Sparkes, A and Smith, B (2013) eds. *Qualitative Research Methods in Sport, Exercise and Health: From Process to Product.* New York: Routledge.

Jefferson, A (2020) Cover, Black Lives Matter Issue. *Thrasher Magazine.* September 2020.

Thornton, S (1996). *Club Cultures: Music, Media and Subcultural Capital.* Middletown, CT: Wesleyan University Press.

Thorpe, H (2008) Foucault, technologies of the Self, and the Media: Discourses of Femininity in Snowboarding Culture, *Journal of Sport and Social Issues.* 32. 199-229

Thorpe, H and Ahmad, N (2015) Youth, action sports and political agency in the Middle East: Lessons from a grassroots parkour group in Gaza, *International Review for the Sociology of Sport*, 50, 678–704.

Thorpe, H and Olive, R. eds. (2016) *Women in Action Sport Cultures: Identity, Politics and Experience*, London: Palgrave Macmillan.

Thorpe, H, Jeffrey, A, Fullagar, S, and Pavlidis, A (2022) Reconceptualizing Women's Wellbeing During the Pandemic: Sport, Fitness and More-Than-Human Connection, *Journal of Sport and Social Issues.* https://doi. org/10.1177/01937235221109438

Toffoletti, K, Francombe-Webb, J and Thorpe, T (2018) *New Sporting Femininities: Embodied Politics in Postfeminist Times.* Cham, Switzerland: Palgrave Macmillan.

Vivoni, F (2009) Spots of Spatial Desire: Skateparks, Skateplazas, and Urban Politics. *Journal of Sport and Social Issues* 33 (2): 130–49.

Wheaton, B and Beal, B (2003). 'Keeping it Real: Subcultural media and the discourses of authenticity in alternative sport. *International Review for the Sociology of Sport, 38*(2), 155–176. https://doi.org/10.1177/1012690203038002002

Wheaton, B (2010) Introducing the Consumption and Representation of Lifestyle Sports. *Sport in Society, 13*(7-8), 1057–1081.

Wheaton, B (2013) *The Cultural Politics of Lifestyle Sports.* London: Routledge.

White, A and Ebling, K (2019) Coping with Creeps: Concrete Action You Can Take, *Bigfoot Magazine.* Posted 18 September. Downloaded 18 July 2022: https://bigfootskatemag.com/coping-with-perverts/

Williams, N (2021) Understanding Race in Skateboarding: A Retrospection and Agenda for the Importance of Being Seen, Dupont, T and Beal, B (eds), *Lifestyle Sports and Identities: Subcultural Careers Throughout the Life Course*, London: Routledge, pp 284–296.

Williams, N (2022) Before the Gold: Connecting Aspirations, Activism, and BIPOC Excellence Through Olympic Skateboarding, *Journal of Olympic Studies*, 3 (1): 4–27. https://doi.org/10.5406/26396025.3.1.02

Willing, I, (2020) 'The Film Kids 25 Years On: A Qualitative Study of Rape Culture and Representations of Sexual Violence in Skateboarding'. *Young*, Special Issue on Skateboarding. Accepted 20 July, 2020. First published 6 November: https://journals.sagepub.com/doi/10.1177/1103308820966457

Willing I (2021) Book Review: 'Skateboarding and Urban Landscapes in Asia: Endless Spots' by Duncan McDuie-Ra. *Asian Anthropology Journal*. Preview version August, 2021: https://doi.org/10.1080/1683478X.2021.1968106

Willing, I, Bennett, Am, Piispa M and Green, B (2019) Skateboarding and the 'Tired Generation': Aging in Youth Cultures and Lifestyle Sports. *Sociology* 53(3):503–18.

Willing, I, Green, B and Pavlidis, P (2020) The 'Boy Scouts' and 'Bad Boys' of Skateboarding: A Thematic Analysis of *The Bones Brigade. Sport in Society*, 23(5), 832–846. https://doi.org/10.1080/17430437.2019.1580265

Yochim, E (2010) *Skate Life: Re-imagining White Masculinity*. San Francisco: University of Michigan Press.

2

Skateboarding Beyond the Looking Glass of Perceived Progressivism

I. Willing, A. Pappalardo, *Skateboarding, Power and Change*,
https://doi.org/10.1007/978-981-99-1234-6_2

Chapter 2 Illustration by Adam Abada

Introduction

Historically, skateboarding began as a highly undocumented activity, save periodicals and videos. Even in the current digital era where it is intensely documented in real-time on mediums such as social media, skateboarding history has many versions and with many voices and experiences often neglected. Unlike many formal sports or even subcultures such as punk or hip-hop, skateboarding's perpetual motion as a cultural, and physical, practice (Abulhawa 2021) can be caught up in the moment. What is meant by this is while there are plenty of homages and hero worship, and an endless push to share "never been done" (NBD) tricks, skateboarding has lacked critical reflection on its harder lessons and, in turn, important learning moments to improve its ability to be socially responsible and transparent and demonstrate accountability when problems and issues arise. At the same time, there has always been an openness for progression and change. As Jeff Grosso in the documentary *LBGT Queer Skateboarding—Love Letters to Skateboarding* stated, "we were the freaks, that's what drew us to skateboarding, and somehow we made it, we got through all that and made it all OK. So like, it just seems like it's our responsibility to make it okay for the next group" (Grosso 2020).

As we discussed in Chap. 1, our starting point is that skateboarding is a multi-tiered activity with many different scenes, styles, and aims, depending on the individual and their view of skateboarding. What we are interested in is not how it can be measured by metrics and points or a series of informal tests by skateboarding's "core" and elite created to gatekeep. Rather, we are interested in how its social and cultural dimensions operate within various power relations and with our aim to see how those dynamics are being changed to achieve more equity and inclusion in skateboarding. To assist our exploration ahead, in this chapter we foreground some of the key cultural moments and shifts, as well as conflicts and tensions that have arisen in its history while keeping in mind all knowledge can be contested. Importantly, the context of how particular knowledges are produced matters and always needs to be considered. Foucault (1982: 131), for instance, also draws critical attention to how "each society has its 'regime of truth', and its 'general politics' of truth" (also see Foucault 1978, 1979). Foucault also argues there are

the types of discourse which it accepts and makes function as true; the mechanisms and instances which enable one to distinguish true and false statements, the means by which each is sanctioned; the techniques and procedures accorded value in the acquisition of truth; the status of those who are charged with saying what counts as true. (Foucault 1982: 131)

Accordingly, we are not presenting a history of skateboarding as a distantly removed critique we play no part in or one of "heroes" and "villains." We see our historical overview, as providing snapshots of its flexible nature, contestations and contradictions, and some examples from the past of how social change happens. Also, as with other scenes, sports and subcultures, we see this as an exercise skateboarders need to do together so that we can collectively improve our communities and culture. A push for progress is not punishment, and while some of the benefits of change may be specific, we feel they can have a ripple effect and resonate outward to create environments of equity and inclusion that all can share. But alongside our encouragement for togetherness, we also recognize we do this from a specific moment in time, with our subjective understandings and that of the interviewees also informing the lenses and frameworks ahead.

In this chapter, we offer a historical look at skateboarding as a culture that certainly can be inclusive but is also not inherently progressive (Harrison-Cadwell 2019; Pappalardo 2019; Willing 2019). Instead, we argue skateboarding is like the physical practice of skating itself, being a mixture of wins and fails, leaps forward, stalls, steps backward and downplayed or under-recognized painful lessons, and always with room to practice to improve and to learn more to progress. As much as it is an individual activity, it is also communal and often dependent on its immediate environment—both physical and cultural. For example, there is a sense of joy and accomplishment wired into performing a trick, even if there is no one to see it, but there is also communal energy created and shared when people are pushing themselves and their abilities together.

In future chapters, we will explore how skaters make sense of issues in skateboarding and their motivations for changing how things have been. But in this chapter, we will take a historical overview of the foundations of skateboarding that is attentive to various dynamics of power, moments of erasure and issues of intersectionality, and key barriers that skateboarders have faced. We will also highlight breakthroughs and shifts that show history is not static and that people can make a difference which warrants a more in-depth study of what kinds of people are drawn to making a differenc, and what knowledge and insights they can offer for now and the future.

The California Scene and the Emergence of the Skate Industry

In a comprehensive history of skateboarding, Iain Borden (2001: 2) places its emergence and expanse from the 1950s but also states that in "representing the history of skateboarding, certain problematics necessarily remain unresolved." This includes that most accounts are American-centric and Euro-centric and that national, state, and regional differences exist, to which we also acknowledge ours is also constrained within. However, as we emphasized in Chap. 1, the scope of our study is purposely limited to the US. More globally informed insights in other studies will be a valuable addition to the overall body of literature. Another important insight from Borden (2001: 2) that supports our approach to offering a generalized historical overview is that "while being highly localized in its specific manifestations, [it] is part of a global network of approximately like-minded practitioners."

While home-crafted versions of what we know as a skateboard today existed long before their commercial introduction in the US, its roots were in Southern California, where surfers turned to skateboards as an outlet when waves were not ideal (Stecyck and Friedman 2000). This led to the influence of a loose yet aggressive approach to skateboarding, shaped by surfers mimicking the motions and actions they take to waves. As we shall see, the surfing culture was pivotal to skateboarding going from a leisure activity to some of its earliest various commercialized ventures.

Before we expand on links between skateboarding's origins in surfing, we add some important points of reflection when thinking about how diverse influences can quickly become omitted. This includes that, like surfing, skateboarding is another action sport and subculture that has been popularized in magazines and advertisements and by Hollywood as an activity taken up by mostly White, young, heterosexual males. Ho

(2021), for instance, describes the issue of narratives about the origins of surfing as, "imagine if the Hollywood version of yoga became an Olympic sport, and by default, overshadowed its roots in India, whitewashing the original cultural flavor into a white Californian trope."

Turning a critical eye over to skateboarding Douglas Miles Sr. founder of Apache Skateboards, in his interview with us adds: "We cannot expect a White run skate industry and brands that easily co-opted and appropriated Hawai'ian surfing to understand what it is like to be Native American and in the skate industry." In skateboarding, the style of Hawai'ian surfers influenced the *Dogtown* skaters, for instance (Stecyck and Friedman 2000), and Native skateboarders were also a part of early skate history (Cleophas 2021). What would become a more embraced image of skateboarding is what we might call a "subcultural flavor" that has also been whitewashed into stereotypes and tropes of White Californian boys and men skaters existing in a world where diversity barely registers (see Abulhawa 2021; Atencio et al. 2013; Borden 2001, 2019; Yochim 2010). The Hawai'ian skateboarding scene was also remarkably diverse, with figures such as Jaime Reyes, Johnny Kop, Christian Hosoi, Jef Hartsel, Bo Ikeda, Kale Sandridge, Dyson Ramones Rob Carlyon, Hunter Long, and Heimana Reynolds today.

As we shall see in our short overview here and in the chapters ahead, skateboarding has always been diverse. While an extensive in-depth study on how First Nations skaters, along with Black and People of Color (PoC) skaters, have all played roles in the earliest origins of skateboarding is outside the scope of our exploration, much-needed studies are emerging such as in the work of Neftalie Williams (2021) and others we highlight ahead. In the chapters to follow where we turn our attention to the perspectives of our interviewees, what we aim to do is speak to skateboarders from such populations about contemporary issues they address and how they perceive the culture of skateboarding in the present.

Our overview joins others in presenting narratives of skateboarding's transformation from a child's wooden toy to its multiple purposes today. Of note, Iain Borden (2001) has explored how in the 1950s the components of skateboards were drawn from child's scooters, roller skates, and surfing materials to its various board formations, social scenes, trick techniques, and spatial relations in terms of how skateboarders use the built environment today (Borden 2019). We begin our discussion in the 1960s when skateboarding was well and truly experiencing a boom and an industry rapidly emerged. Notable influences include several surfboard manufacturers. For instance, Jack's, Kips', Hobie's, Bing's, and Makaha Skateboards were introducing what were essentially scaled-down surfboards with wheels to the market (Arts Selectronic Staff 2020; Borden 2001). Shortly after the first skateboarding publication was launched in 1964. *The Quarterly Skateboarder* was founded by John Severson who is credited as being the first to approach documenting surfing as an art, rather than a sport. Later truncated to *Skateboarder Magazine* which ran from 1964 to 1965, then re-emerged in 1975, Severson's first published editorial stated:

> Today's skateboarders are founders in this sport—they're pioneers—they are the first. There is no history in Skateboarding—it's being made now—by you. The sport is being molded and we believe that doing the right thing now will lead to a bright future for the sport. Already, there are storm clouds on the horizon with opponents of the sport talking about ban and restrictions. (Stevenson 1964)

One year after skateboarding had its first publication, it had its first superstar. In 1965 sponsored skateboarder Patti McGee was featured on the cover of *Life Magazine* and she also appeared on several popular US television programs. Linda Benson was also the first woman to have her own "pro deck" with her name on it by Hensen Surfboards in 1964. Women began to be regulars and excel in skateboarding competitions. Skateboarding sales also experienced their first boom, with Makaha reporting $4 million in sales between 1963 and 1965 (Marcus 2011). However, by 1966, due to pushback by the media that the activity was dangerous, skateboarding was largely seen as too hazardous for children resulting in a massive drop in sales.

The introduction of polyurethane wheels in the early 1970s by Frank Nasworthy then returned skateboarding sales to experiencing significant growth. Before Nasworthy's innovation with his company Cadillac Wheels, skateboards were manufactured with metal or clay wheels and, to be fair, were much more prone to instability and stoppage due to terrain. The urethane wheel was softer and provided a more stable ride, opening up new possibilities as to where they could be ridden. The answer again drew from its roots in surfing.

As Borden (2001: 29) explains, "skateboarders in the 1960s-1970s were commonly surfers and used skateboards when the surf was flat. The suburban modernism of Los Angeles and other California oceanside cities allowed frustrated surfers to re-enact the sense of being on the sea, rolling down the tarmac drives and roads … as if they were an ocean wave." However, he continues that "early skateboarders also found other terrains, in particular the gently inclined banks" (Borden 2001: 31). Soon "skateboarders were finding more challenging terrains … Above all, Los Angeles … was the 'pool capital'" (Borden 2001: 33) with many gravitating to private backyards, schoolyards, drains, and ditches. As Snyder (2017: 54) also explains, "the cognitive map of Los Angeles covers an immense geographic expanse, but rather than 'staying local' in one's specific area like many Angelenos do, skaters go to spots that suit their needs, no matter where they exist."

While there is no definitive pioneer who can claim to take skateboarding to drainage ditches and pools, this style of skateboarding was a key development and highly popular in California. This transition from other terrains, such as roads and esplanades, is partly due to the coastal state's natural terrain and drainage needs, along with an extended drought in 1976 that led many people not to fill their home pools for years. As equipment progressed so did the actual skateboarding and by the mid-1970s private concrete parks were also being developed in California and later across the US to accommodate the burgeoning activity. It was also generating big business for construction companies with most costing $200,000 and some parks costing as much as $1 million. Borden (2001: 68) observes that "by 1982 over 190 skateparks had been built in the US across at least 35 states, of which over a quarter (48) were in California, 22 in Florida, and 16 in Texas."

The growth of skateboarding competitions in the 1970s is another important window into the evolving culture of skateboarding. In 1975 the Del Mar National Championships showcased where skateboarding styles were heading. The sea change was led by a group of skateboarders from Santa Monica called the Zephyr Team, who would later be the subjects of a documentary titled *Dogtown and Z-Boys* (Peralta 2001) and a film adaptation titled *Lords of Dogtown* (Hardwicke 2005). Merging surf-influenced maneuvers and an aggressive approach, the Zephyr Team's performances clashed with the more ballet or gymnastic approach others were talking to freestyle skateboarding as an almost act of defiance that resonated with the skateboarding community. More importantly, it introduced some of skateboarding's most significant names to the zeitgeist including Jay Adams, Tony Alva, Peggy Oki, and Stacy Peralta. Artist, designer, and photographer Craig Stecyk wrote about the team for *Skateboarder Magazine* as did photographer Glen E. Friedman, who along with Stecyk captured some of the earliest and most iconic images of the team's innovation.

One of those biggest trick innovations in this period was the frontside air, credited to Tony Alva in 1977. Before Alva's breakthrough, skateboarders had mostly carved the walls of pools and ramps or performed tricks on the edge or lip of these structures. Everyone saw the possibility, but Alva was the first to be documented maneuvering his board above pool coping. This innovation set off an era of vertical or "vert" skating as it is commonly referred to, which helped skateboarding's popularity. Yet the skate industry would face another massive industry collapse. However, it was also resilient, and skateboarding started to establish itself again as an industry.

During this time, sanctioned competitions were being developed with greater prize money and in 1977 outside sponsors such as Pepsi Cola would be one of the first corporations to sponsor a team. Skateboarders were concurrently developing a rich subculture that prided itself on having no set rules and an underground lifestyle of resisting authority, "jumping fences" and sometimes trespassing to find new spots, while its more palatable, "sporty," and leisure-based sides were gaining influence and shaping a market as well as paying market for private skateparks.

From Underground Subculture to Scene with Market Power

When we move our focus to before Alva's vert innovation and before pool skating and getting air, we again note how skateboarding was mostly a ground sport. There was freestyle, essentially a ground-based routine format, slalom and downhill luge racing, barrel jumping, carving on banks and sidewalks, and other niche forms, but it was not until it became a vert activity that a new discipline was unlocked that it captivated people by its sheer danger and defiance of gravity. While vert skating led to more interest and more concrete parks being built, it also created two problems: firstly, a barrier to entry and, secondly, the issue of liability.

The skateparks of the 1970s and 1980s were "pay to play," and while many locals found their way around exchanging money for access, this was not the case for most skateboarders, especially those just entering it. This is the first example of classism in skateboarding and also how it can change and, in a sense, "correct" itself to its original values of freedom and fun rather than corporate entanglements. Finding skateable pools was still possible for many skateboarders around the world, and homemade wooden ramps became an equalizer for those with an opportunity to construct one. It is an early example of the do-it-yourself (DIY) culture that continues to give skateboarders a way to gain power back in how they shape skate culture, not just by making physical obstacles to skate, but also by overcoming social ones preventing certain groups from skateboarding. The first creations of backyard ramps were often built with wood stolen from construction sites or cobbled together from discarded scraps. The concept helped democratize vert and transition skating (such as in pools, on ramps, and in bowls) by making it somewhat more accessible, at least to those with the space and resources.

In future chapters, we speak to skatepark advocacy groups and an urban planning scholar to understand some of the contemporary issues today and how skaters are working to build and freely activate more spaces. In many countries, we might also note that skateparks are viewed as something that should be free to access and with their maintenance and things like insurance covered by local governments the way that parklands and mainstream sports fields are (Willing and Shearer 2016). But the issue of liability, particularly in the past, was especially litigious for private parks in the US. While innovations in vert and transition skateboarding progressed the physical side of the culture, social, financial, and legal barriers were rapidly emerging. These restraints were in part due to the increased risk of injury that progressions in skateboarding were opening up, and with authorities controlling the spaces, skaters used seeing a need for safer equipment and attention to issues of liability for skateparks. The majority of skateparks also had minors as their major participants which also influenced the culture's tendency to embrace risk for progression.

By the early 1980s many once-thriving parks were shutting down, coinciding with a downturn in the industry and also increased insurance liability costs. While there is room for debate over discerning which of these factors was the major contributor to an industry-wide downturn, as parks closed and were demolished, skateboarding was once again forced underground. However, this time, there was a "core" group of dedicated skateboarders in place who had gained experience and networks to generate a range of creative responses to keep what they loved going and with room to keep expanding. In this period we find yet another example of where industry power can be seen as not all-encompassing and both elite and ordinary skateboarders as having agency and occasions to shift the culture in new directions.

As the shine and interest for skateboarding were simmering off for the general public and sponsors, and skateboarders were directing their energy toward backyard ramps, independent jams and community-run contests offered an outlet for the "die-hards." Pivotal to understanding this period is that skateboarding was also often stigmatized as deviant and not the more fashionable, prosocial, and career-making endeavor it is today (Borden 2001; O'Connor 2017). Skateboarding was a haven and sanctuary for people who did not fit in with mainstream sports and very often were also excluded in society due to their backgrounds or even just having independent attitudes (Peralta 2001, 2012). Ironically, the industry downsizing proved to be a cog in what would be skateboarding's next boom, sparked by vert skating's growing underground popularity and progression and rise in smaller companies owned by actual skateboarders.

Most notably Powell Peralta which was founded in 1978 by George Powell and Stacy Peralta and whose rise to being extremely profitable is explored in the documentary *The Bones Brigade* (Peralta 2012; Willing et al. 2020).

Along with their product innovation, Powell Peralta was adept at forecasting and marketing. They employed Craig Stecyk as de facto art director, bringing large-scale editorial ideas and conceptual thoughts on the language of skateboarding into the mix. Peralta himself was visionary in seeing the potential not only of vert and transition skating but also of street skating and introduced it in the first action sports video released to the public, *The Bones Brigade Video Show* (1984, featured in Peralta 2012). Video rapidly transformed skateboarding because before the first Powell Peralta video, any film or video coverage of skateboarding was sparse and often shown on television once and lost to the ether.

Powell Peralta's formation of *The Bones Brigade*, the formal moniker given to their team of sponsored skateboarders, initially comprised of teenage boys and young men. Peralta (2012) describes them as misfits who were also exceptionally gifted and would become famous for their pioneering skateboarding tricks but also marketable profiles, through advertisements and videos, which drove up board sales. This includes Tony Hawk, Lance Mountain, Rodney Mullen, Steve Caballero, Tommy Guerrero, and Mike McGill who were clean-cut and described as "boy scouts" by their rivals (Willing et al. 2020). Their contemporaries included Tony Alva's team with skateboarders like Christian Hosoi who were also technically gifted skaters, but had a "bad boy" image including wearing leather, dressing like "rock stars" and heavily partying (Willing et al. 2020). Hosoi's key rival was Tony Hawk and both would become major stars of the era.

Today, skate videos are integral to skate culture whether on social media, on a home screen, or at a film premiere at skate events (Dinces 2011; McDuie-Ra 2021; Willing et al. 2020; Yochim 2010), and this aspect of skate culture owes much to the influence of 1980s video productions. *The Bones Brigade Video Show*'s release coincided with an increase in sales in VHS and Betamax home systems, allowing anyone who owned or bootlegged skate videos to view them ad infinitum. Peralta's bet that showcasing street skating as a "thing" rather than a mode of transportation would later prove to be as powerful and forward-thinking as his introduction of the modern skate video. It is worth mentioning that Powell Peralta is still operating and thriving, along with contemporaries Santa Cruz Skateboards (founded in 1973) though the latter was formed by Richard Novak, Doug Haut, and Jay Shuirman, three surfers from Santa Cruz, California. Despite their surf origins, Santa Cruz has maintained its profile in skateboarding due to its relationships and rider input.

While Powell Peralta was innovating skateboarding and pushing its progress on video, two significant magazines would tell its story in print. *Thrasher Magazine* was founded in 1981 in San Francisco, California, by Eric Swenson and Fausto Vitello, primarily as a vehicle to promote their skateboard truck company Independent. From 1993 the magazine would be steered by the macho, gung-ho editor James Kendall "Jake" Phelps (1962–2019). Phelps was a "skaters' skater" who did much to hold up the culture and help it thrive and achieved an iconic status from his role. However, he also reflected the heteronormative and hyper-masculine values of many skateboarders of the time that could perpetuate problematic forms of gatekeeping that placed women and LGBTQIA+ people on the periphery.

Two years later another truck manufacturer, Tracker Trucks, owned by Larry Balma and Peggy Cozens, founded *Transworld Skateboarding* as an answer to *Thrasher*'s "Skate and Destroy" mantra. The magazine's first issue featured an editorial penned by Cozens titled "Skate and Create," intended to highlight skateboarding's creativity in a positive light, counter to the raw depictions and allusions to sex, drugs, alcohol, and nihilism *Thrasher* was putting forth (Lombard 2010).

With an energy and style akin to punk rock in its zine-esque newsprint presentation from the beginning, *Thrasher* leaned into their "fuck you" attitude, while *Transworld* became known for a more artful and "professional" approach to design and photography. Both sought to have the best content, yet how they presented it could not have been more polarized. These differences are also highlighted in a discussion by Amelia Brodka (2013) with *Transworld* editor Kevin Duffle and *Thrasher* editor Michael Burnett, in her documentary *Underexposed: A Women's Skateboarding Documentary*. Ultimately, *Thrasher* won the "content wars" by investing in additional platforms like the video content space in skate-boarding. In contrast, *Transworld* began scaling down due to a corporate acquisition and ceased printing the magazine in 2019. Both magazines had markets and content that reached and had an influence across the globe, and while each had its loyalists, the culture of skateboarding benefited from having two highly different titles devoted to their passion.

Demonstrating the flexible and shifting nature of skateboarding culture, as quickly as it was driven underground, a new crop of brands, publications, and organizations in the US grew in the 1980s and scaled globally. The 1980s were also a time when "the look" and aesthetic styles of skateboard graphics had changed dramatically, from hand-crafted designs that called back to surf culture over to icon/text-based graphics and multicolor graphics that employed anything from graffiti and comic book art to neo-psychedelia and loose painterly graphics (Borden 2019).

The graphics for skateboards were now a space to tell a story and choosing one meant choosing an identity, not just the more passive fandom of buying something with a person or brand's name on it. Some professional skaters (pros) who hardly had any coverage or success in contests could survive off the strength of a graphic sold on boards, clothing, and stickers. A leading example is Powell Peralta's *The Bones Brigade* merchandise. Each team member in *The Bones Brigade* was given a graphic that spoke to their personality and the videos marketed them as such and the public was highly receptive. As Peralta's (2012) documentary reveals, in the mid-1980s during their peak popularity, some riders were making as much as six figures a year as teenagers.

With skateboarding's latest wave of growth came new interest from Hollywood, which would spawn several motion pictures that featured or were centered around skateboarding. Chronologically, the most recognized and referenced movies were *Back to the Future* (Zemeckis 1985), *Thrashin'* (Winters 1986), *Police Academy 4: Citizens on Patrol* (Drake 1984), and *Gleaming the Cube* (Clifford 1989). The films featured men who were professional skateboarders for stunt and acting work to varying degrees, with Peralta involved in three and members of *The Bones Brigade*. The films did have some women, but as was normative in the era, the characters and narratives were primarily focused on masculine identities and heteronormative in their gender dynamics, where women that had roles were usually portrayed as love interests or girlfriends to the main characters and did not skateboard (Willing et al. 2020). However, *Thrashin'* not only featured some women skaters as on-screen extras, but the film's screenwriter has stated that the original idea for the movie was inspired by an article he read about the Hags, an all-women skate crew from West Los Angeles, some of whom appeared in the film. Additionally, the Hags' motto "Flow or Go Home" was spray painted on a wall that appears briefly in the film (Savage 2017).

Back to the Future was the most commercially successful of these films, becoming a blockbuster and part of the pop culture canon. Its relevance is that it was influential to people taking up skateboarding, and a branded *Back to the Future* "complete" skateboard (a retail term referring to buying a deck with wheels and trucks already put together which is popular with beginners) was released in 1985.

In this section, we have outlined some of the ways skateboarding advanced its physical culture with new tricks, its commercial growth, and its general exposure through new platforms and technologies. But we have also thrown light on a less linear journey in terms of being socially and culturally progressive. We have also highlighted some of the ways the industry and commercialized side of skateboarding such as in Hollywood films and locked in certain archetypes of masculinity and masculine codes within the culture that was hierarchical, and many of which would continue to be the most dominant portrayal and a window onto skateboarding throughout the 1990s.

In the next section we continue our historical overview with an interest in how skateboarding culture kept expanding and at times could be transgressive and progressive, but not always together in mutually affirming ways. We navigate the past carefully so as not to create a picture of the past being wholly negative or with marginalized skaters as completely powerless. Rather, we hope to shed light on the sometimes complementary, sometimes competing, and contested ways that skateboarding culture plays out amidst various periods and barriers.

Expanding, Transgressive and Progressive Horizons in Skateboarding

Apparent throughout these mainstream cultural dalliances into skateboarding is that it was being depicted in a very homogeneous manner filled with tropes and clichés. Along with the roles of women being noticeably absent, outside of being love interests, boys and men are restrained by a kind of "compulsory heterosexuality" and hypermasculinity in the form of big stunts and other coded behaviors that establish male dominance (Harrison-Cadwell 2019). This was echoed in many of the skate videos being produced in this era. Few brands were sponsoring or featuring women prominently in their ads or videos. The representation of diversity in terms of gender and sexuality was also largely absent, with the skateboarding industry also acting as a reflection of wider social discrimination, as discussed by queer, transgender, and non-binary skateboarders in Grosso's (2020) *Love Letters* video dedicated to their perspectives and experiences of skateboarding. This included anti-gay rhetoric and policies in the Regan era concerning things such as the AIDS epidemic and government-level opposition to equal rights that forced many to stay in the closet (Florêncio 2018).

Magazines and visual media rival the major influence of film and video on skateboarding culture (Borden 2019; Snyder 2017). And, unlike some of the more gender-inclusive magazine stories from the 1970s, *Thrasher*'s and *Transworld*'s coverage skewed toward being predominantly about men, making McGee's appearance on the cover of *Life* a distant outlier. As advertising page counts increased and brands outside of skateboarding bought pages in the magazine, there was an emphasis on commerce over exposing new and less marketable skaters. The marketing dollars were targeted toward men in skateboarding and the lifestyle that was being marketed as that of heterosexual men, and the audience was presumed to reflect these demographics. As Abulhawa's (2021) research on skateboarding and femininity explores in depth, women were creators of small grassroots and DIY media and especially zines in this period. Figures such as Lynn Kramer and Di Dootsen paved spaces for women skateboarders in print. *Womxn's Skateboarding History* (https://womxnskatehistory.ca)

founder Natalie Porter also provides a richly detailed documentation of women skateboarders in magazines like *Skateboarder* from the 1970s to the present, particularly on her Instagram account (@womxnsk8history). And in the "core" magazines, breakthrough moments did occur on rare occasions, including in 1988 when Cara-Beth Burnside became the first woman to be featured on the cover of *Thrasher*, followed by Jaime Reyes in 1994. However, it took *Thrasher* until 2017 to feature Lizzie Armanto, who was the third woman on the cover of the magazine. In 2021 Breana Geering was featured, and in 2022 Samarria Brevard was also given the cover page.

We highlight these moments in history, sometimes outside a linear or chronological trajectory, to point to how the seemingly subversive and underground side of skateboarding can also be complicit in the constraining commercialized and mainstreamed side. It can also marginalize minorities such as based on their gender or sexuality, repeating some of the exclusionary hallmarks usually associated with "jocks" in mainstream sports culture. Moreover, while cultural productions in skateboarding in the form of magazines like *Thrasher* and Hollywood films may be poles apart, each has also very often conformed to distinctly masculine and heteronormative conventions of skateboarding. In future chapters we talk to several women who run their media platforms, are editors of magazines, and are content creators to explore how they are balancing out who has the power to capture, shape, and advance the culture today.

As vert, park, and street skateboarding all began to expand at least creatively, skateboarding seemed primed to build off that momentum into the 1990s. However, several factors included a relatively brief recession in the US in March 1991, where the industry was centered, and skateboarding was once again evolving in ways that the industry had not prepared for or predicted. While a specific flashpoint moment to pin the skate industry is not easy to discern, it once again was contracting as it had done two major times before. In this period, street skating began overtaking vert skating in popularity, setting the dominos in place for another new wave of cultural progress. With many of the "core" brands dictating the direction, product, and look of skateboarding now entering close to a decade of operation, pro skaters such as Steve Rocco were seeing the economic industry downturn as a signal of change and that the industry had too much generational "oldness" in it. A former freestyle and street pro for Sims Skateboards, Rocco founded the first iteration of what would become World Industries in 1987, with former Powell Peralta skateboarders Rodney Mullen joining in 1988, and Mike Vallely into the company in 1989.

In this period the companies that had been dominating the market were Powell Peralta, Santa Cruz, Tracker, Independent, and Vision. Each had achieved significant things for skateboarding, but skateboarders' hunger for innovation, fun, and what's cutting edge always created room for newcomers and provocateurs. What World Industries lacked in financial capital it made up for with an impressive lineup of skateboarders and a knack for turning subversive ideas into highly effective marketing. Under its umbrella of teams and companies, this included pivotal figures in skateboarding such as Jessie Martinez, Mark Gonzales, Jason Lee, Natas Kaupas, Jeff Hartsel, and many others who pushed skating into new realms technically and who shape the culture on and off the board still today as iconic figures and within the industry. Lee, for example, would become a television and film star while also founding Stereo Skateboards in 1992 with Chris Patras.

Rocco was a key figure in demonstrating that skateboarders with certain clout, talent, and vision had the power to gain more attention from a rising market than the larger companies could. The World Industries approach was almost anti-commercial in its aesthetic, using conceptually playful gimmicks in their advertisements, ranging from one-page black-and-white satirical texts and no actual skateboarding to the "Nice Ad" which had a full blank window box in print and stated in small text below, "We had two ads we wanted to run this month, but they were deemed too offensive because we said a bad word and made fun of Powell." The latter was rejected by *Transworld*.

The World Industries advertisements ran in multiple spreads in *Thrasher, Poweredge,* and *Transworld.* Taking influence from Sun Tzu's *The Art of War*, he turned the tables on the industries "big timers," observing the marketing "rules" and promotional conventions and then breaking as many as possible. Under Rocco's direction, advertising images focused on things such as sex, and drugs, and wrapped up in plenty of satire. Most importantly, World Industries was speaking to skateboarders as "one of them" in contrast to the larger companies that were becoming hierarchical and communicating in a way that was "looking" down.

The brand's first video *Rubbish Heap* (1989) predominantly featured street skating, with irreverent bits of B-roll spliced in between the skateboarding and was mostly sans music. If street skating made skateboarding more accessible to people across the world, *Rubbish Heap* made video more relatable, feeling much more akin to what an ordinary kid with a camcorder would produce than the big-budget videos Peralta was making. Along with other skateboarding companies' productions like *H-Street* and *New Deal*, World Industries' videos were showing a grittier side of skateboarding. The Spike Jonze-directed *Rubbish Heap* certainly showcased its oddest folds, with shots of children swallowing worms and in-joke dialogue, for instance. At the same time, women were not as prominent in this world of innovation and discovery, with people like Saecha Clarke, Elissa Steamer, and Marisa Dal Santo being exceptions while many others were still on the periphery of how "core" street skating was documented (Abulhawa 2021; McDuie-Ra 2021; Yochim 2010).

Counter to Rocco and World Industries' mission to promote an "edgier" and transgressive side of skateboarding, in 1990 Nickelodeon debuted *SK8-TV*, a children's program about skateboarding developed by Peralta and Stecyk. Hosted by "Skatemaster Tate" and Matthew Lillard, then known as Matthew Lynn, the show was unable to resonate with skateboarders or the public alike and ran for only one season. This is even when it tried to engage with or co-opt aspects of the "core" culture, such as having several World Industries riders appearing on the show. The relevance here is that skateboarding has a style and attitude about it that gives it a sense of authenticity that is hard to fake, and even while mainstream may try to co-op what skaters do, it is not always successful or even convincing (Wheaton and Beal 2003).

As we have highlighted, originally it was vert and transition skateboarding that transformed from underground practice to appealing to a mass market and becoming profitable for corporations. When street-style skateboarding began to overtake in popularity, older professional skaters, particularly those from the 1980s, began to see their royalties decreasing. The major brands at the time—Powell Peralta, Santa Cruz, and Vision—were slow to pivot and were still producing products on a larger scale than most competitors. Small brands such as World Industries and New Deal however were more nimble, emphasized street skating, and presented it in a way closer to what was happening for ordinary skateboarders. Street skating, with (back then) openly available obstacles that were accessible, fresh, and fun, had an easier entry point than rarer and sometimes costly skateparks. And with this, skateboarders who were devoted to the older disciplines began to see a drop in their participants, media coverage, and profits.

In the 1980s, skateboard decks became artistic spaces to sell the culture's lifestyle of leisure and resistance to mainstream sports. What Rocco and World Industries' art department introduced in the 1990s was using a skateboard graphic as a place to introduce ideas, even sometimes with an intent solely to shock and sell products as a consequence. Along with their subversive print advertisements in magazines, the brands under World Industries including 101, Blind, Fuct, Plan B, and later Prime, used the "real estate" on the bottom and top of a skateboard to depict drug use, drunk driving, sexual encounters that could be highly misogynist in tone, accidental gun deaths, racial stereotypes, and other off-limits and taboo topics in skateboarding (Carayol 2014; Jenkem Staff 2014).

Whether the intentions were "bro" humor insulated by a time when masculine dominance was seen as normative, wildly satirical commentary that slyly challenged stereotypes, or done with no statement at all and was subversive for the sake of it, these graphics grabbed other companies' attention, spawning several lesser effective knock-offs of the style of graphics created by Mark McKee and Sean Cliver. Other small brands such as Real Skateboards found a way to be provocative in an entirely different way, using their graphics to address racism, Native American rights, and even Holocaust awareness through their graphics, art, and advertisements (Dobija-Nootens 2017). In future chapters, we argue that with an "ethical turn" in skateboarding, the strategies of more progressive brands have continued to evolve. Offering more insight, we speak with Tommy Guerrero and others about how they can play with iconography and satire or use more direct messages of activism as ways to adopt ethical stances for their brands.

The controversial tone and style that World Industries was pushing the limits with hit a barrier when *Transworld Skateboarding* refused to run an ad alluding to suicide, with which publisher Larry Balma also had a personal connection. Tension with *Transworld* and other magazines becoming increasingly cautious with content was one of the catalysts that resulted in Rocco starting his magazine in 1992 titled *Big Brother*. As World Industries' graphics and advertisements operated without caution, news of him having a print publication he had full editorial control over arrived with expectations he would push the subversive side of skateboarding to an even more risky, offensive, and provocative place.

Although the debut issue of *Big Brother* was non-controversial, if not lacking luster, it soon made waves with its subsequent issues with a mix of profanity, "low-brow" culture, blunt satire, and an energetic tone of recklessness. This includes publishing an article detailing how to commit suicide that drew national attention and later ran a piece by a then-unknown writer named Johnny Knoxville about self-defense where Knoxville tests several methods before shooting himself in the chest while wearing a cheap Kevlar vest. The magazine was eventually sold to Larry Flynt's publishing company and ceased production in 2004. David Carnie, a former editor at *Big Brother*, states, "*Big Brother* never had a proper funeral. It committed suicide, or Larry Flynt stabbed it in the back and it died. We never really got to do a last issue" (quoted by Gabert-Doyon 2016). However, under the ownership of Flynt's company, several skateboarding and prank-laden skit videos were released, including Knoxville's self-defense footage, laying the blueprint for what would later become the *Jackass* franchise (Thorpe 2007).

Big Brother's legacy was eclectic and not easy to pin down as to its ethical orientation and could be confusing to its readership despite its appeal to them. It was "transgressive without always being progressive," but at the same time, it could also sometimes achieve both (Kerr 2019). For instance, the magazine did have women writers and published a Black-themed issue and Asian-themed issue. Yet it also played up and perpetuated homophobic, sexist, and racist stereotypes through images and language in its content as a comedic strategy. In 2002, for example, the magazine featured Jarret Berry, who is a skateboarder and gay man, on the cover dressed in a cowboy hat and revealing leather chaps, mocking stereotypes but also with the magazine not overtly challenging them. In Chap. 5 we explore the idea of satire in more detail, turning our attention to how it can be used as a way to critique masculine dominance and educate men on how to challenge some of their own biases and habits that can harm others.

With its provocative style, *Big Brother* was charting questionable ethical terrain but was not aiming to be "acceptable" and, because of this, was able to be one of the only magazines to challenge the status quo of skateboarding upholding White masculine archetypes as its cornerstone. For example, World Industries sponsored Saecha Clark, one of the first women street skaters as well as employed Megan Baltimore, who later co-founded Girl Skateboards with Rick Howard, Mike Carroll, and Spike Jonze. Regardless of intention, *Big Brother* and World Industries championed street skating through a diverse roster of skateboarders of different backgrounds including races and ethnicities. They also established the brand Menace with Kareem Campbell, a professional skateboarder at World Industries who is also Black, and demonstrated how individuals in leadership roles in the industry can and should be more diverse. With only one skateboarder on its roster who is a White, cisgender man, Menace along with 60/40 team were some of the only street-centric skateboarding teams featuring almost all Black and PoC skateboarders.

We highlight World Industries as an example of how skateboarding can be transgressive yet also push the underground scene of skateboarding to the forefront and continue to differentiate it from mainstream sports. But this is not to paint them as a picture of how the subcultural side of skateboarding is inherently anti-commercial. The company was sold in 1998 for $29 million and provides a window into the complex, if not paradoxical, ways skateboarding and other subcultures maintain boundaries while also growing their commercial potential and mainstream audiences, often as a way of finding sustainable ways to do what they love. As skate researchers have observed (such as Lombard 2010; Snyder 2012, 2017), these kinds of entanglements can sometimes actually advance the culture even while at risk of diluting or exploiting it. Skateboarders' resistance and stances of opposition can also be flexible under late capitalism (Dinces 2011; Gazeres 2022).

Further Mainstreaming and a Continuing Culture of Resistance

In the following chapters of this book we explore contemporary issues and examples of social change, where our interest is mostly focused on the period just before and following the year 2020 when we started our research. In this section, we continue with an overview of skateboarding in the 1990s and onto the first two decades of the 2000s, paying attention now to institutional and grassroots cultural moments and uneven yet shifting power relationships had an impact on the culture. We begin by highlighting what can be seen as a successful push by corporations, with the active participation of elite-level skateboarders, to elevate the "cleaner," "sporty," and more marketable side of skateboarding. As we progress, we show that a culture of social resistance remains part of the identity and life force and source of vibrancy, innovation, and community-building in skateboarding as well.

Starting in 1995, sports network conglomerate ESPN introduced the X Games, a nationally televised action sports competition that introduced vert and street skating on a park course to new audiences, many of whom had not seen it at such an advanced level before. While far from the underground, it hosted some defining moments in terms of trick progression. For instance, during the 1999 Best Trick competition Tony Hawk completed what is known as the 900 trick on vert, a world first, which became part of the highlight reel and sports ticker indicating the significance of the moment but also the newsworthy status of skateboarding as a sport. Outside of skate celebrities like Hawk, such corporate-style "mega-events" were also able to bring financial windfalls to skateboarders who very often had to find multiple income streams.

The competitions were also exciting and generated collective joy like other sports. However, they did not have gender equality built into their structure, such as lacking inclusive divisions and pay parity for women, for instance, which fell short of Title IX's federal legislation for gender equality and sparked protests and a boycott (Wheaton and Thorpe 2019, 2021). In 2005 Cara-Beth Burnside, Jen O'Brien, and Mimi Knoop with X Games competitors such as Elissa Steamer and Amy Caron and with support by Drew Mearns refused to skate in protest of the huge difference in prize money and lack of coverage for women. It took until 2006 for them to reach some progress and was also the beginning of the Action Sports Alliance, which later became the Women's Skateboard Alliance (WSA). Equal prize money was achieved in 2008 (Browning 2020).

That same year marked the beginning of the *Tony Hawk Pro Skater* video game franchise, which was remarkably successful reaching a 1 billion profit since its release. The original versions were focused on fun and advanced the ways more people could engage with skateboarding, and broke new social ground by including the character of Elissa Steamer into an otherwise all-men line up of characters for the first two versions. As newer versions have been released, more skateboarding characters who are women have now been included such as Aori Nishimura and Lizzie Armanto, and a skateboarder who is transgender, Leo Baker, now features versions released in 2020.

Tony Hawk's series of video games may not have been the first skateboarding video game, but it remains the most successful. And, along with digital video cameras, websites, and message boards embraced by skateboarders in the 1990s, it ushered in the "digital era" for skateboarding. This followed on from the mid-1980s when *Thrasher* had set up a *Thrasher BBS* board to dial-up, perhaps the earliest example of skateboarding's digital presence c.1986. The magazine purchased the software from Tom Jennings, a queer skater and programmer, who created FidoNet, an international network of small-scale DIY bulletin board systems (or BBSs) run out of the homes of hackers and hobbyists.

In the transition from the 1990s to the 2000s, many other interesting cultural moments, pioneers, and provocateurs in skateboarding were to follow. Many would continue to reproduce masculinity that was not highly inclusive in terms of representing things like diverse genders and sexualities. At the same time, more transgressive projects and brands pushed the ways that skateboarding as a subculture and its commercialization could interweave, creating new spaces for subversive ideas and productions. This includes when MTV debuted a new series in 2000 created by the *Big Brother* "brain trust" of Jeff Tremaine, Spike Jonze, and Johnny Knoxville titled *Jackass*. The series started in the 1990s as a series of videos and is described by Thorpe (2007: 1) as helping to "produce and reproduce the fratriarchal cultures at the core of skateboarding, snowboarding, and other extreme sports." A fratriarchal culture differs from patriarchy as it is primarily about young men interested in freedom and "good times," an avoidance of responsibility except to a "brotherhood" and with status built on impressing each other (Thorpe 2007: 3). Purposely avoiding high-culture and enacting extreme physical dares and absurd pranks, the franchise connected with a wider audience and its three feature films have been highly profitable with the *Hollywood Reporter* (Abramovitch 2022) stating 2002's *Jackass: The Movie* grossed $80 million worldwide; 2006's *Jackass Number Two* $85 million; and 2010's *Jackass 3D* $172 million. Here skateboarders were changing highly commercialized cultural worlds, not the other way around.

Before X Games, contests in the 1990s did not have a huge cultural influence nor generate the celebrity status for skateboarders as was enjoyed in the 1980s by Tony Alva's team and *The Bones Brigade* in the decade before. Formed in 1981, the National Skateboarding Association (NSA) was recognized as the largest competitive organization in skateboarding, but by 1993 it was dissolved and World Cup Skateboarding (WCS) was created to replace it. Most contests in this period were treated more as community and industry gatherings rather than spectacles or a measure of "cool" or "cutting edge." But with significant money injected into them, it was X Games and later big events like the Dew Tour competition that opened up new revenue streams and new levels of exposure for skateboarders to much wider audiences (also see Wheaton and Thorpe 2019, 2021).

As we have now discussed, the mid-1990s and into the 2000s were also a time when skate companies, skate videos, and other forms of cultural growth from the street skateboarding scene brought in an authentic freshness and, tricks-wise, saw skateboarders pushing what they did on a board in ways that were as cutting edge as vert and pool skating was in earlier eras. This was an expansive era for creativity, with many cultural landmarks which still shape skateboarding today. Many angles are explored in excellent studies, such as in art, technology, and architecture by Borden (2001, 2019), skate videos by McDuie-Ra (2021), the rise of subcultural entrepreneurship by Snyder (2012, 2017), and others such as the memoir by Kyle Beachy (2021) with in-depth reflections of cultural milestones and figures.

In the remaining parts of this section focused on the 1990s to just before the present day, we focus our attention on interesting moments in the history of women, non-binary, and LGBTQIA+ skateboarders. Of particular interest are what social challenges they faced and also acts of defiance. These populations have not always been well-documented in skate studies, but a number of researchers have made considerable efforts to bring "non-traditional" skateboarders' history to light (with the earliest efforts including by Atencio et al., 2013, 2016, 2018; Beal 1995; Beal and Wilson 2004; Thorpe and Olive 2016; Wheaton 2013; Yochim 2010). Key to their findings is those past barriers include everyday micro-aggressions and biases in interactions at skateparks to more structural exclusions such as in skate media, competition divisions, and influential industry roles. In response, such exclusions have pushed "non-traditional" skateboarders to create their own spaces out of necessity and with positive social benefits. Their efforts join contemporary "non-traditional" skate-boarders' efforts today, including more exposure and presence by trans-gender, non-binary, and gender-diverse skateboarders and the LGBTQIA+ community (Delardi 2021; Geckle and Shaw 2020; Willing 2019).

Dani Abulhawa's (2021) in-depth study of constructions of femininity in skateboarding points to the women's skate scene having Patti McGee as one of the earlier icons and many other women in competitive skating, such as Thornhill Caswell. We can also note breakthrough figures such as Judi Oyama, who was sponsored by Santa Cruz, has some of her skate memorabilia in The Smithsonian National Museum of American History, was inducted into the Skateboarders Hall of Fame in 2018, and still com-petes today. Oyama remains an advocate of ensuring women's, non-binary and transgender skateboarders' history from her era is remembered. This includes peers of hers such as Vicki Vickers, Cindy Whitehead, Robin Logan, Kim Cespedes, Jana Booker, Leilani Glasheen, Peggy Turner, Kerry Germain, and Terry Lawrence. The prominent women from the 1970s and 1980s that we interviewed for this book are Peggy Oki, Cindy Whitehead, and Lynn Kramer. From this historical era women who were competitive skateboarders also worked behind the scenes and in creative fields such as Lynn Kramer, Di Dootsen with the

National Skateboard Review, and the late Bonnie Blouin who wrote for *Thrasher Magazine* in the 1980s.

Instagram accounts such as Womxn's Skate History (@womxnsk8history), Skaters of Color (@skatersofcolor), and Native Sisters Shred (@native.sisters.shred) are also continually bringing to light the contributions and accomplishments of women skateboarders in the US who are not always recognized, including Ellen O'Neal nee Deason, Laurie Turner, and Gina Esperanza, and Stephanie Person, the first Black woman to be a professional skater, and Crystal Solomon, also a Black woman who was one of the early sponsored street skaters. Amelia Brodka's (2013) documentary *Underexposed: A Women's Skateboarding History* also charts the rise of vert and street skaters from the 1970s to the 2000s, such as LynZ Adams Hawkins Pastrana, Cara-Beth Burnside, Mimi Knoop, Julie Lynn Kindstrand Nelson, Allysha Le, Elissa Steamer, Leticia Bufoni, Evelyn Boulliart, Amy Caron, Nora Vasconcellos, Vanessa Torres, Niki Williams, and Samarria Brevard. Brodka also interviews David Everly, who talks about his experiences in skateboarding as a transgender man.

Many of these figures are not just icons for their skateboarding, but also their work as social change-makers. For instance, in 1994 Cara-Beth Burnside made history for a second time following her *Thrasher* cover by releasing the first women's pro signature shoe with Vans. Also in 1994, Jaime Reyes became the second woman on the cover of *Thrasher Magazine*. With video emerging as a powerful medium, Elissa Steamer's debut part in *Welcome to Hell*, part of Toy Machine's full-length in 1996, was another watershed moment. Founded by Ed Templeton, a vocal advocate of gay rights since the early 1990s, Toy Machine was held in high esteem in skateboarding, and Steamer's inclusion juxtaposed her skating with other established pros. Her part in *Welcome to Hell* not only pushed women's street skating level but also challenged the antiquated ideas of how "women skated." As we previously highlighted, Steamer was also the first woman featured in Tony Hawk's video game franchise in 1999.

Independent zines and videos made by everyday skateboarders rather than just brands and corporations have also always been an integral part of skate culture, especially during the 1980s when the industry crashed, and in the 1990s they became a vital component for marginalized skateboarders. In 1996, Villa Villa Cola was established by sisters Tiffany and Nicole Morgan. Their strategy was to empower women skaters by giving them creative roles, which portrayed women's skating as something joyful, playful, and with a punk-like style of resistance, with one of their flagship videos being *Getting Nowhere Faster* in 2004 made with support from Element Skateboards and *411 Video Magazine*. The Villa Villa Cola creative team included Van Nguyen, Faye Jaime, Lisa Whitaker, Michelle Pezel, Jaime Sinift, Andria Lessler, and Rebecca Burnquist.

The studies by Steph MacKay and Christine Dallaire (2013) and MacKay (2016) also highlight the importance of media platforms such as Lisa Whittaker's The Side Project, which later became The Girls Skate Network, and Skate Like a Girl as other women and non-binary skater-led initiatives as an example of how a DIY approach was able to empower the community through representing what they do and what they are about on their terms. Mahfia created by Kim Woozy was also influential, and we speak to her in the following chapters about some of her more recent projects (Willing 2014, 2019). The content being created was fresh and resonated due to it having an authenticity that contrasted with how men's skate media had been portraying them. In the following chapters we explore what it is like for women and non-binary skater-run and focused platforms today through interviews with skateboarders involved with the editorial and creative side of The Skate Witches, Skate Like a Girl, Yeah Girl, and froSkate. We also speak with a former editor from *Skateism* which is a queer-run magazine and platform.

With women's presence and potential customer base for the skate industry growing in the very late 1990s and into the 2000s, "core" brands and independent companies started testing special lines and products for this market, with shoe brands such as Osiris and Etnies producing women's lines for the first time. In the following chapters we also talk to Kim Woozy about her efforts in Osiris to grow their women's market. We also speak to women-run emerging brands like Doyenne Skateboards and Proper Gnar that are also forging space within, sometimes defying, and transforming how the skate industry creates content and products, and also how it connects and communicates with its markets. An interesting theme we foreground now is that unlike how the "core" skateboarding culture that has largely been shaped and often gate-kept by men, women appear less concerned with the hardest or latest tricks as a measure of coolness and are more invested in what skateboarders and brands stand for. For instance, in an interview with Mimi Knoop about whether women had created their version of "cool," she agreed but also joked that

> I struggle all the time! I am still trying to figure out how to be cool … At a certain point, you just stop caring as much because it's exhausting to try and keep up with the cool factor … My advice would be to focus on having fun and being yourself, and be sure to always keep good-hearted, authentic people in your corner. (quoted in Willing 2019)

Another key development in the women's scene of skateboarding in the 1990s was the emergence of Rookie Skateboards, which was also co-founded in 1996 by Catharine Lyons and Elska von Hatzfeldt. With a raw aesthetic that challenged the skate industry's propensity of a "shrink it and pink it" marketing tactic in their women's product lines, the New York-based brand emerged with a distinct art direction and diverse roster. This includes Amy Caron, Sean Kelling, Lauren Mollica, Tino Razo, Jaimie Reyes, Jessie Van Roechoudt, Lisa Whitaker, and several others (Roechoudt and Quell Skateboarding 2021).

In the 2000s, Cara-Beth Burnside and Mimi Knoop would create Hoopla Skateboards, which was another pivotal women's-led skate company in 2008. The creation of Pink Widow Distribution in 2010 was also women-run, with icons such as Patti McGhee as figureheads, and housing women-focused brands Silly Girl Skateboards and The Original Betty. Lisa Whittaker launched Meow Skateboards in 2012 with skaters such as Vanessa Torres, Shari White, Amy Caron, Kristin Ebeling, and a new generation of "new gen" lineup of skaters from the US and overseas. As part of our discussion in the following chapters, we share some of the perspectives of Kristin Ebeling and Shari White, as well as other elite-level skaters such as Alex White and Amelia Brodka, as well as women with skate companies like Latosha Stone on what the scene was like for them and what advice they share to today's skateboarders.

In time, more "legacy" brands and "core" skate companies would start adding women to their teams, such as Lizzie Armanto joining Birdhouse in 2017, and Breana Geering being added to the Girl Skateboards team and going professional in 2021. The rising inclusion was often only one or two women in otherwise men-dominated teams. However, with these changes, Burnside and Knoop decided to conclude Hoopla and concentrate on other activities that empowered women. With the gate pushed open, many smaller, home-run, and DIY brands by women and non-binary, as well as LGBTQIA+, skaters have been created. Pave the Way Skateboards (2017) which was co-founded by Tara Jepsen and Miriam Klein Stahl, for instance, was the first queer-focused skateboard company and was later joined by queer-owned brands such as Jeffery Cheung's Unity (2017) and There (2020) and Leo Baker's skate brand Glue (2021).

From the early 2000s, the skateboarding industry also became mostly focused on meeting product demands due to skateboarding's experiencing another wave of interest that combined its "core" market, new consumers, and mainstream culture. In particular, skateboarding shoes were permeating into the tastes of the youth market and music cultures. As part of this shift, shoe companies and brands with shoe lines would accumulate a new level of profit and power. For example, shoes such as the Osiris "D3 2001" and the Supra "Muska Skytop" were adopted by several musicians including Fred Durst, Tom DeLonge, Jay-Z, Lil Wayne, and Kanye West, resulting in a rise in sales and higher visibility of skateboarding fashion.

One of the key discrepancies in power that accompanied this rise in sales, which included consumers of diverse racial and ethnic backgrounds, was the lack of substantial power held by Native, Black, and PoC skateboarders in industry roles and team spots (Brown 2022; Grimes et al. 2011; Williams 2021). This is not to say these skating populations were not getting team spots or seen in videos and magazines. However, their presence could often be token and in environments that were not always pro-actively anti-racist. In terms of moving past gatekeepers and acquiring success, notable exceptions include Stevie Williams and Troy Morgan of The Kayo Corp who founded Dirty Ghetto Kids (DGK) which would go on to be highly popular and profitable. As noted earlier, Kareem Campbell was pioneering in co-founding brands in the 1990 s, including Menace which would later become City Stars, as well as Axion Footwear. Ron Allen was also pivotal, co-founding Life and later American Dream

Inc., whose graphics, designed by Alyasha Owerka-Moore, often used iconic Black Power imagery as well as images of several Black civil rights leaders. Sal Barbier not only had several successful signature shoes starting in 1993, but he also co-founded 23, Aesthetics, and Elwood Clothing and continues to produce products under his name. And as we shall highlight in Chap. 5, a range of others went on to have careers that continue to expand with commercial collaborations inside and outside skating based on their achieving iconic status (Thrasher Staff 2020).

Native skateboarders, also referred to as First Nations and Indigenous skaters, like surfers (Cleophas 2021), have also often been positioned on the margins in terms of representation by those portraying the "core" skateboarding culture. Both Indigenous (O'Sullivan 2021) and non-Indigenous scholars (Borden 2001) agree Native skateboarding is beginning to be recognized in curatorial spaces but that their contributions have not always been strongly reflected. *The Ramp It Up: Skateboard Culture in Native America* exhibition curated by Betsy Gordon held in 2014 at the Smithsonian National Museum of the American Indian, for instance, represents a past effort to showcase these diverse populations of skateboarding and some of their overshadowed history (Briggs 2018; Gordon et al. 2022).

Breakthrough figures include Steve Saiz, one of the first professional skaters of Native American descent whose first pro model featured Native-inspired art. Saiz currently works as an artist, repurposing skateboard decks and infusing them with Comanche iconography. Todd Harder has also been influential and is the founder of the First Nations Skate Jam, an annual event that is held to coincide with the Gathering of Nations Powwow in Albuquerque, New Mexico. And Terry Lawrence, who was a vert champion in the 1970s has recently become an important voice for young people in the LGBTQIA+ skate community (Barbier 2020). The Native skate scene is now a growing and diverse one, spread across different nations, geographies, and languages in the US including Diné Navajo Nation skateboarders Di'orr Greenwood (Willing 2019) and Cecely Todacheenie (Willing 2020a).

In future chapters, we continue to focus on Native skateboarding and through our interviews, Douglas Miles Sr. of Apache Skateboards who has been elevating Native skateboarding for over 20 years, and his son Douglas Miles Jr. of Indellica Skateboards and the Apache Passion Skate

Project, discuss their work. Miles Jr. is also a professional skateboarder who has collaborated with brands such as Etnies and Red Bull plus also worked with The Skatepark Project (formerly The Tony Hawk Foundation) who we also interview through speaking to Alec Beck.

In his in-depth and comprehensive reflections on racism, Neftalie Williams' (2021, 2022) research outlines how pervasive it has been in skateboarding and the challenge of it being acknowledged. The wider momentum and impact of the 2020 Black Lives Matter protests and calls for action brought the issue to the forefront across multiple realms of American society, including in subcultures and sports. In the following chapters we contribute to Williams' call for researchers to explore how racism can be challenged by speaking to Native, Black, and PoC skateboarders who discuss the contemporary issues they face and strategies they roll out to de-colonize skateboarding and combat racial and ethnic discrimination.

With corporatized skateboarding competitions and big brands enjoying more influence and profits than ever before, those with an eye on the Olympic Games were taking note and particularly of the audience demographics being attracted. Focusing their efforts on bringing it to the Summer Olympics, the first significant push was in 2002 when the International Skateboarding Federation (ISF) was formed. Following on, efforts to get skateboarding considered for inclusion were made for the 2012 Games, and more attempts were made in 2007. The bids started to gain more momentum and were able to leverage more power when Street League Skateboarding (SLS) was established in 2010 and later partnered with the ISF. Early successes included skateboarding making a debut in the 2014 Youth Olympic Games as an exhibition session, and in 2016 it was confirmed that skateboarding would make its official debut in the 2020 Tokyo Summer Olympic Games.

There were many dedicated people at the elite athlete, training, and managerial level in skateboarding who supported its incorporation into the Olympics. However, more broadly across the skate community, there was also strong resistance to the "sportification" of something many saw as a lifestyle and subculture that should not be quantified in official sporting realms (Nowicki 2018). Key points of protest, as observed by Holly Thorpe and Belinda Wheaton (2011: 831), include that the alternative cultural values with which many "core" skateboarders, in particular, felt strongly aligned are "incompatible with the disciplinary, hierarchical, nationalistic *Olympic* regime." The dissent and pushback were significant, with many of the oppositional viewpoints and groups who were opposed to its inclusion mapped out in Mikhail Batuev and Leigh Robinson's (2017) report titled *How Skateboarding Made It to the Olympics: An Institutional Perspective*. Other studies also highlight protests against skateboarding being in the Olympics such as through an online petition in 2015 with over 5000 signatories (the full petition is posted at Butler 2015, and also see Schwier and Kilberth 2020).

At the same time, skateboarding researchers point to a more complex picture of attitudes that skateboarders at the elite level can have on certain strategic benefits emerging from the Olympics, especially from women and a range of marginalized skateboarders who lack opportunities in "core" skateboarding (Schwier and Kilberth 2020; Thorpe and Wheaton 2011; Williams 2021, 2022). We can also observe that while some skaters may agree to be a part of the Games, they end up struggling to feel like they belong due to Skateboarding USA and the Olympic Games upholding a gender binary of men's and women's divisions only governed by ambiguous rules that can pressure, compromise, and exclude transgender and non-binary skateboarders (Pape 2019; Willing and Barbier 2020).

We aim to shed more light on such intricacies and tensions in Chap. 5 when exploring what meanings change-makers attach to competitions and the Olympics. What is important to note here is that it is not always a clear case of skateboarders versus the Olympics, with the existence of alternative viewpoints about its incorporation, particularly from women and others for whom large-scale exposure may help equalize their status. Yet it is also the case that within the formalities and rules of how events like the Olympics are structured, people such as transgender and non-binary skaters who are willing to compete can be restricted by having to conform in ways that deny their authentic selves and impact on their human rights. We shall discuss more of the complexities of the Olympics in future chapters.

There are many other examples of how queer and LGBTQIA+ skaters have pushed to make space for themselves or removed their participation in the history of skateboarding. We highlight some of the intense barriers of discrimination these populations faced and some of their break-throughs in the period from the 1990s to just before the present day. This includes the lack of support Tim Von Werne experienced as a gay man in the 1990s to highlight how entrenched homophobic attitudes in the "core" skate industry gatekeepers could be. Our attention then turns to the impact of former professional skateboarder Brian Anderson publicly identifying as a gay man in 2016.

In the 1990s power brokers such as brand managers, skate editors, sponsored skaters, and others with influence over what was still a men's dominated skateboarding industry were still reluctant to advocate or sup-port LGBTQIA+ skaters publicly. For all its "countercultural cool," skate-boarding was still party to the same kinds of homophobia found in other male-dominated institutions (Dubler 2016). In private, many skate-boarders were "out" about their sexuality and with the knowledge of fel-low team members, friends, and connections in the skate industry (Fitch 2017). In a sense, there was a culture of tolerating yet not amplifying queer skaters that echoed the US military's former "Don't Ask, Don't Tell" federal policy in 1994 toward LGBTQIA+ rights (Fitch 2017).

Until fairly recently, many skateparks had a certain locker-room feel, with gay slurs and insensitive jokes. There is even a 1980s-era trick called the "gay twist," a homophobic reference to it being "the gay way" of per-forming a particular kind of aerial. Such casual homophobia joins other gay slurs such as "f*g," seen being used as a taunting device and hierarchi-cal form of banter in skateparks, skate videos, and skate interviews (Dubler 2016). Notable historical examples of professional skateboarders that have been overtly anti-gay in the press also include Jason Jessee (such as discussed in Beachy 2018, 2021). While not always said to intention-ally harm gay people, it does that very work through forms of symbolic violence (Bourdieu 2002) that normalize heterosexuality and position other types of sexuality as something inferior and undesirable. The impacts and dangers are serious (Dubler 2016). Violent crimes toward gay men are detailed in an article by Nathan Fitch (2017) in *The New Yorker* with the case of Jay Adams, who served prison time for fight-ing with and provoking a group assault of Dan Bradbury in 1982 that led to his death, and that of skateboarder Josh Swindell who went to prison for the murder of Keith Ogden (also see Hamm 2004; Smith 2014).

For former sponsored skater Tim Von Werne, the industry's intolerance toward him being gay curtailed his career in 1998 when an interview scheduled to run in the *Skateboarder* magazine was pulled by business managers at his sponsoring company Birdhouse when it was revealed that it discussed his sexuality. As he told *Huck Magazine* in 2012:

> It became pretty clear straight away that, if they weren't willing to print the article, if I wanted to be a professional skateboarder, I may have to think about going into the closet, which I wouldn't feel comfortable doing. I've never been ashamed of being gay and I wouldn't want to have to start feeling that I needed to be. (quoted in Welch 2012)

Patrick Welch's (2012) article illustrates how constrained the skateboarding industry made life for LGBTQIA+ skaters, with interviews of various figureheads suggesting numerous professional skaters and creatives like photographers were "in the closet" for fear of how it would affect their careers. Von Werne cited his retirement from professional skateboarding as being from an ankle injury but that the lack of support for his article was also a turning point for him with Birdhouse, which was co-founded by Tony Hawk and Per Welinder in 1992. Von Werne has not claimed that Hawk opposed the story (Welch 2012). In 2022 Hawk posted an Instagram story about him visiting Von Werne in the UK, and Hawk has recently also spoken in broader terms about how the industry made mistakes in the past and needed the support of LGBTQIA+ skateboarders in the documentary *Humanity Stoked* (Cohen 2022).

One of the biggest turning points for creating a space and normalizing LGBTQIA+ skaters and challenging stereotypes in skating happened in 2016 when Brian Anderson (also known as B.A.), a high profile and well-respected professional skateboarder, came out in a documentary for *Vice Sports* directed by Giovanni Reda (2016). In an iconic moment, Anderson states directly to the camera, "My name is Brian Anderson, I'm a professional skateboarder, and we are here to talk about the fact that I am gay." With those words, Anderson, who now lives in Queens, New York, became skateboarding's most prominent professional star to come out as a gay man.

Throughout *Vice*'s half-hour video, several fellow professional skaters in interviews state they were excited about the prospect of him coming out because of his status, which included being a former *Thrasher* Skateboarder of the Year (in 1999), and made him an ideal subject to make "core" skate fans and business alike rethink their bigotry. Ed Templeton, who founded the company Toy Machine which was Anderson's board sponsor and was also a professional skateboarder from the 1990s, stated, "All the kids who were sitting there at home thinking, like, 'Wait, my favorite skater is gay?' would be forced to decide: What does that matter?" (13.57 minute mark, quoted in Reda 2016). Shortly after the video was posted, social media blew up with affirmations and support. The outpouring of "hearts and hashtags" came from a range of sources, such as fellow pro skaters and sponsors like Nike, but also broader popular culture. Andy Cohen (2016), the host of the Bravo network's *Watch What Happens Live*, tweeted, "major skateboarder came out today and the community saluted him. Amazing story and BRAVO, Brian Anderson!!!"

In the immediate years after Anderson's coming out, several other professional men skaters such as Hopps team member Steve Brandi and Forrest Kirby from the Zoo York team publicly announced their sexuality. Several people and brands in the skateboarding industry were also willing to shift into being openly supportive, such as Anti-Hero Skateboards commissioning artist Todd Francis' graphic celebrating same-sex or "gay marriage," and magazines such as *Jenkem Magazine* (Dubler 2016) exploring why so few men professional skateboarders had come out. Anderson's and Von Werne's experiences are an interesting example of how polarized responses can be and perhaps also the extra fame and gravitas men need to find wider acceptance, with the former able to maintain his icon status and be influential in the culture, and the other still without any amplified recognition and regret over how he was silenced. It also speaks to the complexity of gender within skateboarding, as the women in skateboarding have been historically more open and vocal about their sexuality and gender.

The stories of LGBTQIA+ skateboarders are yet to be given and take up the space they long deserved, but there have been other efforts and some with more exposure than others. In 2011 Hilary Thompson started to speak openly about her experiences as a transgender woman skateboarder receiving a sometimes awkward yet overall supportive reception in skate media (Nieratko 2011; Maguire 2013). Other notable projects and productions in the US in the 2000s include *Mixed Rice Zine* launched in 2015 by J Wu which is dedicated to queer PoC skaters (https://www.mixedricezines.com). In 2016 the Pave the Way Skateboards company was launched, which we discussed in an earlier section of this chapter, and in 2020 Annie Dean Ganek's *Carving Space* documentary about queer skaters was launched. These are just some of the predecessors of queer-focused skateboard brands and documentaries that would emerge in 2020 and the years after, an era that we explore in the following chapters.

Although a utopian vision of skateboarding would consist of a journey of like-minded individuals all progressing together, it is important to remember that skateboarding's commonality is the activity, not the lifestyle. Skateboarding culture also does not fit into a neat and linear historical narrative of going from discriminatory to a wholesale embrace of equity and diversity. There remain a range of outlooks and attitudes, with some at complete odds with each other. The presence of social media has also put these biases in the open and indicates there is still work to do to challenge the bigotry of the past (MacKay 2016). We now conclude our historical overview in this chapter to turn our attention toward skateboarders who are making changes in the current decade and contemporary times in the chapters ahead. Many barriers in skateboarding remain upheld or re-positioned, such as with emerging critical viewpoints in the competition space by some who lobby to exclude transgender women (Pappalardo 2022). And while things like pay parity or representation on teams may be evening out, there is also a more prominent critical awareness around the work left today, and this includes addressing issues of sexual harassment and sexual violence (Willing 2020b). There are other realms of the social world where power operates, such as race, ethnicity, class, gender, and sexuality, which also can shift and turn within the culture of skateboarding. We start our exploration in the next chapter by highlighting more recent key moments of change and an overview of the social change-makers we interviewed.

References

Abramovitch, S. (2022) Pain, Porn and a Wanna Be Clown: A Jackass Oral History, *The Hollywood Reporter*. Posted 27 January. Downloaded 18 August 2022: https://www.hollywoodreporter.com/feature/jackass-oral-history-johnny-knoxville-steve-o-interview-1235080408/

Abulhawa, D. (2021) *Skateboarding and femininity: gender, space-making and expressive movement*. London: Routledge.

Arts Selectronic Staff (2020) Hidden in Plain Sight, *Arts Selectronic*. Posted 19 September. Downloaded 16 August 2020: https://artselectronic.wordpress.com/2020/09/19/hidden-in-plain-sight-skateboardings-legendary-spots/

Atencio, M., Beal, B and Yochim, E. C (2013) "It Ain't Just Black Kids and White Kids": The Representation and Reproduction of Authentic "Skurban" Masculinities. *Sociology of Sport Journal*, 30(2), 153–172.

Atencio, M, Beal, B., McClain, Z., and Wright, M (2016) No One Wants to Mess with an Angry Mom: Females' Negotiation of Power Technologies Within a Local Skateboarding Culture. (eds) Thorpe, H, and Olive, R. *Women in Action Sport Cultures*. London: Palgrave Macmillan. pp. 175–191.

Atencio, M., Beal, B., Wright, M. E., and ZáNean, M (2018) *Moving Boarders: Skateboarding and the Changing Landscape of Urban Youth Sports*. Fayetteville, AR: University of Arkansas Press.

Barbier, E (2020) Blazing the Trail in the 1970s, *Skateism*. Posted 4 July. Downloaded 29 August 2022: https://www.skateism.com/blazing-the-trail-in-the-70s/

Batuev, M and Robison, L (2017) How Skateboarding Made it to the Olympics: An Institutional Perspective, *International Journal of Sports Management and Marketing*, 17: 4–6.

Beachy, K (2018) Primitive Progressivism, *Free Skate Magazine*, posted 5 June. Downloaded 8 July 2022: https://www.freeskatemag.com/2018/06/05/primitive-progressivism-by-kyle-beachy/

Beachy, K (2021) *The Most Fun Thing: Dispatches from a Skateboard Life*. Grand Central Publishing.

Beal, B (1995) Disqualifying the official: An exploration of social resistance through the subculture of skateboarding. *Sociology of Sport Journal, 12*(3), 252–267. https://doi.org/10.1123/ssj.12.3.252

Beal, B and Wilson, C. (2004). "Chicks dig scars": Commercialisation and the transformations of skateboarders' identities. In B. Wheaton (Ed.), *Understanding Lifestyle Sports: Consumption, identity, and difference* (pp. 31–54). Routledge.

Bourdieu, P. (2002). *Masculine Domination.* Stanford, CA: Stanford University Press.

Borden, I (2019) *Skateboarding and the City: A Complete History.* Oxford: Berg

Borden, I (2001) *Skateboarding, Space and the City: Architecture, the Body and Performative Critique.* Oxford: Berg, 2001.

Briggs, K (2018) Ramp it Up Tells the Story of Native Vibrant Skate Subculture, *Indian Country Today.* Posted 13 September, Downloaded 29 August 2022: https://indiancountrytoday.com/archive/ramp-it-up-tells-story-of-native-americas-vibrant-skateboard-subculture

Brodka, A (2013) *Under-Exposed: A Women's Skateboarding Documentary.* USA: Exposure Skate.

Brown, A (2022) Honouring the Lineage of Black Skateboarders, *Nosesliders,* Posted 15 February. Downloaded 18 July 2022: https://nosesliders.substack.com/p/honoring-the-lineage-of-black-skateboarders?r=z8hv9

Browning, I (2020) How a Group of Women Fought for Equal Pay in Contest Skating, *Jenkem Magazine.* Posted 8 January. Downloaded 20 August 2022: https://www.jenkemmag.com/home/2020/01/08/group-women-fought-equal-pay-contest-skating/

Butler, N (2015) Petition Unveiled Campaigning Against Skateboarding Being Added to the Olympics. *Insider the Games.* Posted 12 October. Downloaded 17 August 2022: https://www.insidethegames.biz/articles/1030894/petition-unveiled-campaigning-against-skateboarding-being-added-to-olympic-programme

Carayol, S. (2014). *Agent provocateurs: 100 subversive skateboard graphics.* Gingko Press.

Cleophas (2021) How colonial history shaped bodies and sports at the end of the empire, *The Conversation.* Posted 25 August. Downloaded 24 May 22: https://theconversation.com/how-colonial-history-shaped-bodies-and-sport-at-the-edges-of-empire-166192

Clifford, G (1989) *Gleaming the Cube,* USA: 20th Century Studios

Cohen, A (2016) Tweet posted 28 September, *Twitter:* https://twitter.com/Andy/status/780900959144779776

Cohen, Michael (2022) *Humanity Stoked,* USA. https://humanitystoked.com/

Delardi, C (2021) *Pushing Boarders, Creating Alternative Futures: Resistance and Radical Inclusion in the Production of Non-Traditional Skateboarding Culture,* MA Thesis, Gallatin School of Independent Study, New York University.

Dinces, S (2011) Flexible Opposition: Skateboarding Subcultures under the Rubric of Late Capitalism, *International Journal of the History of Sport*, 28 (11): 1512–1535.

Dobija-Nootens, S (2017) Revisiting the Hanging Klansman Board, *Jenkem Mag*, Posted 14 August. Downloaded 5 July: https://www.jenkemmag.com/home/2017/08/14/revisiting-hanging-klansman-board/

Dubler, M (2016) A Brief Look at Skateboarding's Gay Past, *Jenkem Magazine*. Posted. Downloaded 18 August 2020: https://www.jenkemmag.com/home/2016/09/29/a-brief-look-at-skateboardings-gay-past/

Drake, J (1984) *Police Academy 4*. USA: Warner Bros.

Fitch, N (2017) The Skateboarding Legend Brian Anderson Comes Out, *The New Yorker*. Posted Downloaded 18 August: https://www.newyorker.com/sports/sporting-scene/the-skateboarding-legend-brian-anderson-comes-out

Florêncio, J (2018) AIDS: Homophobic and Moralistic Images of 1980s still Haunt our View of HIV—That Must Change, *The Conversation*, Posted 18 November, Downloaded 28 August 2022: https://theconversation.com/aids-homophobic-and-moralistic-images-of-1980s-still-haunt-our-view-of-hiv-that-must-change-106580

Foucault, M (1978) *The History of Sexuality*. New York: Pantheon Books

Foucault, M (1979) *Discipline and Punish*. New York: Vintage Books

Foucault, M (1982). The Subject and Power, *Critical Inquiry*, 8(4): 777–795.

Gabert-Doyon, J (2016) A Post-Mortem on Big Brother, One of Skateboarding's Most Influential Magazines, David Carnie and Sean Cliver and in Paris, *Huck Magazine*. Posted 18 April. Downloaded 18 August 2022: https://www.huckmag.com/art-and-culture/post-mortem-big-brother-one-skateboardings-influential-magazines/

Gazeres, R. (2022). Challenging Neoliberal Sport: Skateboarding as a Resilient Cultural Practice. *Geography Compass*, Preview: e12671. https://doi.org/10.1111/gec3.12671

Geckle, B and Shaw, S (2020) Failure and Futurity: The Transformative Potential of Queer Skateboarding, *Young*, First preview online, 1–17: https://doi.org/10.1177/1103308820945100

Gordon, B, Rogers, J, Mullen, R and Hawk, T (2022) *Four Wheels and a Board: The Smithsonian History of Skateboarding*, USA: Smithsonian Books.

Grimes, M, Brown, E and Chilli, C (2011) *The Spades: History of Black Skateboarding*, Holding Company Media. Posted on YouTube 2011: https://www.youtube.com/watch?v=NBfSfHYGSGs   Website: https://www.thespadesmovie.com

Grosso, J (2020) Love Letter To LGBTQ+ | Jeff Grosso's Loveletters to Skateboarding, VANS, Posted 12 June: https://www.youtube.com/watch?v=kqD4xfNwd6k

Smith, J (2014) Maybe We Shouldn't Be So Sentimental about a Gay Bashing Skateboarder, *Vice*. Posted 20 August. Downloaded 19 August 2022: https://www.vice.com/en/article/jmbbk3/maybe-we-shouldnt-be-so-sentimental-about-a-gay-bashing-skateboarder-658

Hamm, K (2004) *Scarred for Life: Eleven Stories about Skateboarders*, USA: Chronicle Books.

Hardwicke, C (2005) *Lords of Dogtown*, CA, USA, Columbia Pictures and TriStar Pictures.

Harrison-Cadwell, M (2019) Core: On Authenticity in Skate Culture, *Skateism*, Posted 31 May. Downloaded 20 August 2022: https://www.skateism.com/lets-put-this-shit-to-bed/

Ho, S (2021) Olympic surfer exposes whitewashed Hawaiian roots, *AP News*. 14 August. Downloaded 24 May 22: https://apnews.com/article/2020-tokyo-olympics-games-racial-injustice-hawaii-surfing-5048591ab4620f8796a08ff54331fec0

Jenkem Staff (2014) A collection of some of the most offensive board graphics. *Jenkem Mag*. Posted 10 October, Downloaded 4 August 2022: http://www.jenkemmag.com/home/2014/10/10/a-collection-of-some-of-the-most-offensive-skateboard-graphics/

Kerr, C (2019) Editors' Notes: Brutally Honest Skate Journalism, *Pushing Boarders* Conference website: https://www.pushingboarders.com/talks-2019-watch

Lombard, K.J. (2010). Skate and create/skate and destroy: The commercial and governmental incorporation of skateboarding. *Continuum: Journal of Media & Cultural Studies, 24*(4), 475–488. https://doi.org/10.1080/10304310903294713

Mackay, S, Dallaire, C. (2013). Skirtboarders.com: skateboarding women and self-formation as ethical subjects. *Sociology of Sport Journal, 30*(2), 173–196.

MacKay, S (2016) Carving from Out of Space in the Action Sports Media Landscape: The 'Skirboarders' Blog as a 'Skate Feminist' Project, (eds) Thorpe, H. and Olive, R. *Women in Action Sport Cultures*. London: Palgrave Macmillan. pp. 301–308.

McDuie-Ra, D (2021) *Skateboard Video: Archiving the City from Below*. Palgrave Pivot.

Maguire, S (2013) Is Skateboarding Ready to Openly Embrace a Transgender Skater, *Jenkem Mag*, Posted 18 March. Downloaded 18 August 2022: https://www.jenkemmag.com/home/2013/03/18/is-skateboarding-ready-to-openly-embrace-a-transgender-skater/

Marcus, B (2011) *The Good, The Rad, and the Gnarly: An Illustrated History*, MVP Books.

Nieratko, C (2011) Meet the Nieratkos: The First Transsexual Skateboarder, *Vice*. Posted 10 June. Downloaded 18 August 2022: https://www.vice.com/en/article/av883b/meet-the-nieratkos-the-first-transsexual-skateboarder

Nowicki, C (2018) Why Skateboarding Should Not be an Olympic Sport. *Vice*. Posted 29 May. Downloaded 24 August 2022: https://www.vice.com/en/article/evkpvw/why-skateboarding-should-not-be-an-olympic-sport

O'Connor, P (2017) Beyond the youth culture: Understanding Middle-aged Skateboarders through Temporal Capital, *International Review for the Sociology of Sport*, Preview Copy. 1-20

O'Sullivan, S (2021) The Colonial Project of Gender (and Everything Else), *Genealogy*, 5(67): 1-9 https://doi.org/10.3390/genealogy5030067

Pappalardo, A (2019) Skateboarding is Not Progressive. *Artless Industria*. Posted 17 December. Downloaded 17 July 2022: https://anthonypappalardo.substack.com/p/skateboarding-is-not-progressive

Pappalardo, A (2022) Trans Women Don't Have an Advantage in Skateboarding, *Artless Industria*. Posted 4 June. Downloaded: https://anthonypappalardo.substack.com/p/do-trans-women-have-an-advantage

Pape, M (2019) Expertise and Non-binary Bodies: Sex, Gender and the Case of Dutee Chand. *Body & Society*, 25(4), 3–28. https://doi.org/10.1177/1357034X19865940

Peralta, S (2001) *Dogtown, and Z-Boys*. Santa Monica, CA, USA, Sony Pictures Classic.

Peralta, S (2012) *The Bones Brigade*. Santa Monica, CA: NonFiction Unlimited Productions.

Reda, G (2016) Brian Anderson on Being a Gay Professional Skateboarder. *Vice Sports*. Posted: https://video.vice.com/en_us/video/Brian-Anderson-on-Being-a-Gay-Professional-Skateboarder/57e2990ec6e3592ab7a6073b

Roechoudt, J and Quell Skateboarding (2021) How Rookie Skateboards Shaped Women's Skateboarding, Jenkem Magazine. Posted 21 July. Downloaded 5 August 2022: https://www.jenkemmag.com/home/2021/07/02/rookie-skateboards-shaped-womens-skateboarding/

Savage, E (2017) In the 1980s This All Girl Skate Gang Took Over the Streets of LA, *Bust Magazine*. 17 January. Downloaded 29/11/22: https://bust.com/living/18944-hell-on-wheels.html

Schwier, J, Kilberth, V eds (2020) *Skateboarding Between Subculture and the Olympics: A Youth Culture under Pressure from Commercialization and Sportification*. Columbia University Press.

Snyder, G. J. (2012). The city and the subculture career: professional street skateboarding in LA. *Ethnography, 13*(3), 306–329.

Snyder, G. J. (2017). *Skateboarding LA: Inside professional street skateboarding*. New York University Press

Stecyck, C, Friedman, G (2000). *Dogtown—The Legend of the Z-boys*, Burning Flags Press

Stevenson, J (1964) *The Quarterly Skateboarder*. 1. USA

Thorpe, H (2007) Extreme Media, in *Berkshire Encyclopedia of Extreme Sports*, Berkshire Publishing Group. 1–6

Thorpe, H, and Olive, R. Eds. (2016) *Women in Action Sport Cultures: Identity, Politics and Experience*, London: Palgrave Macmillan.

Thorpe, H, and Wheaton, B (2011). 'Generation X Games', Action Sports and the Olympic Movement: Understanding the Cultural Politics of Incorporation. *Sociology, 45*(5), 830–847

Thrasher Staff (2020) The Pioneers, Firsts in Black Skateboarding, *Thrasher.* Posted 9 September. Downloaded 30 May 22: https://www.thrashermagazine.com/articles/the-pioneers-firsts-in-black-skateboarding/

Welch, P (2012) The Last Taboo: Why are there so Few Gay Skaters? *Huck Magazine*. Posted 9 August. Downloaded 18 August 2022: https://www.huckmag.com/perspectives/reportage-2/gay-skaters/

Wheaton, B, Beal, B (2003). 'Keeping it Real': Subcultural Media and the Discourses of Authenticity in Alternative sport. *International Review for the Sociology of Sport, 38*(2), 155–176. https://doi.org/10.1177/1012690203038002002

Williams, N (2021) Understanding Race in Skateboarding: A Retrospection and Agenda for the Importance of Being Seen, Dupont, T and Beal, B (eds), *Lifestyle Sports and Identities: Subcultural Careers Throughout the Life Course*, London: Routledge, pp. 284–296.

Williams, N (2022) Before the Gold: Connecting Aspirations, Activism, and BIPOC Excellence Through Olympic Skateboarding, *Journal of Olympic Studies*, 3 (1): 4–27. https://doi.org/10.5406/26396025.3.1.02

Willing, I (2014) Interview with Kim Woozy, founder of MAHFIA Web TV, *Asian Australian Film Forum and Network Interview Series*, Posted March. Downloaded 31 July 2022: https://asianaustralianfilmforum.wordpress.com/2014/03/03/aaffn_interview2014_with_kim_woozy/

Willing, I (2019) The Evolution of Skateboarding and Why Pushing Boarders is a Sign of the Times, *Yeah Girl*. Posted 10 October. Downloaded 6 August 2022: https://yeahgirlmedia.com/the-evolution-of-skateboarding-and-why-pushing-boarders-is-a-sign-of-the-times/

Willing, I (2020a). 'Skate and Regenerate: How Skateboarders are Making a Difference to the Environment. *Yeah Girl*. Posted 1 December. Downloaded from URL: https://yeahgirlmedia.com/skate-and-re-generate-skateboarders-making-a-difference-to-the-environment/

Willing, I (2020b) 'The Film Kids 25 Years On: A Qualitative Study of Rape Culture and Representations of Sexual Violence in Skateboarding'. *Young*, Special Issue on Skateboarding. Accepted 20 July 2020. First published 6 November: https://journals.sagepub.com/doi/10.1177/1103308820966457

Willing, I and Barbier, E (2020), Beyond the Gender Binary: Skateboarding and the Olympics, *Skateboard, de la rue à l'olympisme Conference*, Rouen University, 29 October. Talk posted 2 November 2020: https://webtv.univ-rouen.fr/videos/skateboarders-the-olympic-games-and-re-thinking-and-resisting-the-gender-binary-indigo-willing-et-emanuele-barbier/

Willing, I, Green, B and Pavlidis, P (2020), The 'Boy Scouts' and 'Bad Boys' of Skateboarding: A Thematic Analysis of *The Bones Brigade*. *Sport in Society*, 23(5), 832-846. https://doi.org/10.1080/17430437.2019.1580265

Willing, I and Shearer, S (2016) Skateboarding Activism: Exploring Diverse Voices and Community Support, Lombard, KJ (ed) *Skateboarding: Subcultures, Sites and Shifts*, London: Routledge. pp. 44–58.

Winters, D (1986) *Thrashin'*. USA: Winters Entertainment Group.

Wheaton, B (2013). *The Cultural Politics of Lifestyle Sports*. Routledge. https://doi.org/10.4324/9780203888179

Wheaton, B, and Thorpe, T (2019) Action Sports Media Consumption Trends across Generations: Exploring the Olympic Audience and the Impact of Action Sports Inclusion, *Communication, and Sport* 7(4): 415–45, https://doi.org/10.1177/2167479518780410

Wheaton, B, and Thorpe, H (2021). *Action Sports and the Olympic Games: Past, Present, Future*, Routledge.

Yochim, E (2010) *Skate Life: Re-imagining White Masculinity*. San Francisco: University of Michigan Press.

Zemeckis, R (1985) *Back to the Future*, USA: Universal Pictures.

3

Change-Makers in Skateboarding

Introduction

Various figures are change-makers throughout the history of sport, some famous and many others whose acts are not always in the spotlight, but whose impacts can still be ground-breaking and revolutionary such as opening up participation, bringing pay parity and better representation for athletes who were excluded (Armstrong and Butryn 2022; Brown and Foxx 2022; Lee and Cunningham 2019; Magrath 2022; Schmidt 2022). Athletes who use their public profiles, charisma, connections, and platforms to address issues affecting their immediate and wider social worlds dispel the idea that sport is apolitical (Armstrong and Butryn 2022; Brown and Foxx 2022; Schmidt 2022). Forms of activism and calls for change may be dedicated to local issues or a particular sport and discipline, or macro issues on the domestic or international stage. Individuals may also be pushed or compelled to react to specific circumstances of oppression and inequity and only call for change temporarily, while others can dedicate their lives to fighting for forms of social justice.

In this chapter, we introduce the people we interviewed for this book due to their contributions to social change within, and sometimes beyond skateboarding. Our discussion begins by highlighting exemplary icons in

I. Willing, A. Pappalardo, *Skateboarding, Power and Change*,
https://doi.org/10.1007/978-981-99-1234-6_3

mainstream sports. We then introduce some figures who constitute skateboarding counterparts to these mainstream sports figures due to their taking a stance and the significant sacrifices and commitments they make to bring about social change.

We then move our attention beyond just high-profile examples of "change-makers" to introduce the individuals involved with our exploration, some who are famous and veterans of skateboarding, and some whose skateboarding journey is recent, and grounded in the grassroots and DIY side of the culture. An overview of our process of interviewing and the backgrounds of interviewees is also presented. Our discussion is presented through the following themes: (1) Icons for Change in Sport and Counterparts in Skateboarding, (2) Change-Makers as Cultural Guides, (3) Icons, Iconoclasts, and Breakthrough Figures, (4) Strategists and Community Builders, and (5) Storytellers, Creatives, and Provocateurs. We use various typologies as heuristic devices, rather than proposing they are static or mutually exclusive, as many skateboarders we interviewed fit within and across these categories. We propose that there is no singular personality type but rather a range of people, from different backgrounds, demographics, and experiences, who can challenge power and bring about social change.

Icons of Change in Sport and Counterparts in Skateboarding

In mainstream sport we can find many powerful examples of people taking a stance, levering their power, connections, and fame to lift, shine a light on and help various social movements, and cease forms of social injustice. Spectacular examples include Muhammad Ali who refused to serve in the military when drafted to go to the Vietnam War in 1967 at the risk of jail and with his career in boxing stalled for many years (Brown and Foxx 2022). Kathrine Switzer is another example who also made headlines. In 1967 she ran the Boston Marathon at a time women were not allowed and was pushed by one of the officials. There is also the famous act of defiance that took center stage on the *Olympic* podium in

Munich in 1971 by Wayne Collett and Vincent Matthews. Both men were African American athletes who raised their fists in a stance used by the *Black Power* movement, which led to their ban from competing in the Games thereafter.

Moving into our current era with the COVID-19 pandemic arriving in 2020, we can observe the example of Naomi Osaka who chose to wear seven face masks for the US Opens with the names of seven Black people killed by police or in hate crimes: Breonna Taylor, Elijah McClain, Ahmaud Arbery, Trayvon Martin, George Floyd, Philando Castile, and finally, Tamir Rice as a form of protest against police violence. Taking a stance in sport can also emerge from collective action, including athletes, sponsors, and large sports organizations boycotting competitions as seen in South Africa due to apartheid until its demise in 1994 (Magrath 2022).

In the world of mainstream sport, Colin Kapernick became one of the most recognizable activist athletes in the twenty-first century. Kapernick was a *National Football League (NFL)* quarterback in the *San Francisco 49ers*, who have both Black and White parentage and who famously "took a knee" in 2016 alongside his fellow teammate Eric Reid. Their choice to kneel instead of standing for the National Anthem was to protest police brutality and racial inequality toward Black people, and Kapernick continued to kneel throughout the season.

In 2017, then President Donald Trump put pressure on Kapernick to be fired, and Kapernick has remained unsigned to any team in the NFL to this day even though "taking a knee" was also adopted by athletes and non-athletes, within and outside of football, and with renewed support following the murder of George Flloyd in 2020. The enormous impact that taking a stance has had on Kapernick's own life is one of surrendering his place in competitive football and intense criticism and even violent threats from conservatives. But his integrity has also attracted supporters from powerful places. This includes *Nike*, an American corporate brand worth hundreds of billions of dollars, which also has a *Nike SB* division marketing to skateboarders.

In 2018 Nike (2018) released the *Dream Crazy #JustDoIt* video, narrated by Kapernick and with a strong social justice message woven into a traditional advertising campaign. The video features various people in sports who are marginalized, including athletes who are Black, Muslim, and para-athletes. All are represented in defiant poses, or doing something highly physical or looking strongly into the camera, and with motivational words spoken by Kapernick about overcoming insults of being "crazy" to want to do a sport as outsiders, and see being called "crazy" as a compliment and invitation to be "the best they've ever seen."

Within the halfway mark (0.57 mark) skateboarder Leo Baker appears. Baker is the first skateboarder who is "openly" transgender (noting historical and societally oppressive reasons other skaters may also be trans but not publicly identify) to be endorsed by *Nike SB*. Baker has been highly involved with product design for Nike SB and has appeared in several campaigns for both *Nike SB* and *Nike*. In the *Dream Crazy #JustDoIt* video when Baker's footage is shown, Kapernick states in his voice over "don't believe you have to be like anybody. To be somebody." In these scenes, Baker is skating down a street and then featured in a midlength shot standing in a skatepark, turning his face to face the camera to look directly into it peacefully yet powerfully.

At the end of the short video (1.51 mark), Kapernick finally appears, walking with a proud stride down a dark street looking purposeful. He looks to the camera to say his final line, "so don't ask if you're crazy, ask if you're crazy enough," and then, as he walks off camera, the video shows a building behind him which has a video projection of Leo Baker at the skatepark, before fading into a montage of all the athletes featured. Baker's inclusion here is an indication of his rising iconic status. Yet in a documentary, it is revealed his impact on the skate industry and incorporated institutions like *USA Skateboarding* would sometimes take a personal toll on him and provides insightful lessons on the hegemonic ways people are forced to conform to a version of themselves and skateboarding that becomes alienating and harmful.

In 2018, Baker had not yet transitioned to publicly affirming their identity as a transgender man due to fear of negative repercussions from the skate industry, sponsors, and fans. But media articles and other platforms map how he was eager to challenge gender binaries and gender roles and was frustrated with how the industry wanted to corner and label what he and his skateboarding were about due to how others perceived his gender. In an interview, he stated his wish was "to be unapologetic about my image and who I am and then to have people acknowledge how important that is in the skate industry … I can't even describe how that feels" (Pappalardo 2018).

From 2019 to 2020 Baker started to openly use he/him pronouns and speak freely about his identity, drawing strength from a supportive network that included Sam McGuire, Elissa Steamer, Alexis Sablone, Vanessa Torres, Kristin Ebling, Jeff Cheung, Cher Strauberrry, Steven Ostrowski, and others in addition to his partner who also encouraged him to be his authentic self (March and Reda 2022). Baker was also supported by Tony Hawk who included him as a character in *Tony Hawk's Pro Skater 1+2* new release in 2020. Baker's story is explored in more depth in the documentary *Stay on Board: The Leo Baker Story* (March and Reda 2022). This includes interviews with Baker revealing the turmoil he faced with his original inclusion in *USA Skateboarding's* women's team to get ready for the 2020 *Olympic Games* and the joy he felt after he decided to quit competitive skating to create a space for queer and transgender skaters through his skate company *Glue*.

It is important to state that Baker is more than just his gender, and he makes a point about his struggles from being labeled and only seen through that lens of identity. Baker's story is important on its own. At the same time, stories about him where he talks about the barriers he faces from being transgender have, for many people who are cisgender, become "a gateway into learning, opening up, and understanding" (Pappalardo 2022). Baker's story is also a sharp indication of how the industry structure of skateboarding can suppress individuality and lead to mental health struggles. For Baker, the weight of giving up the identity the industry had put upon him to be misgendered as a competitive skateboarder meant not only having to go through his gender affirmation in the public eye but under the pressure of feeling it had negative, rather than only revolutionary and positive repercussions. Attention to the rights of all transgender skaters to be their authentic selves also has an urgency in light of the rise of some women skateboarders who are joining trans-exclusionary movements that attempt to ban transgender athletes from sporting competitions, and who perpetuate transphobic beliefs of unfairness that are void of scientific evidence (Pappalardo 2022).

As we highlighted in the last chapter, skateboarding has other icons who have taken a stance and in a sense, become iconoclastic of its image and break new ground for others to participate and be treated equally. In the US context, this includes skateboarders such as Cara-Beth Burnside and Mimi Knoop, whose interventions and boycotts to progress opportunities, status, and pay for women in the X Games were met with success. On 7 August in 2022 Knoop would again make a pivotal move in her role as the High-Performance director of *USA Skateboarding* when she and the entire High-Performance team quit, announcing their resignation in a synchronized series of posts on social media, which we discuss in the next chapter in a section on competitions.

Oscar Loreto Jr., a filmmaker and sponsored skateboarder who advocates for adaptive skateboarding in elite competitions, also resigned from the High-Performance team at that time, but who continues his advocacy work today (Forbes 2021). He stated on Instagram from his perspective "I'm grateful and thankful for the opportunity to have been a part of USAS but sadly my time has come to an end … where organizations and corporations paraded adaptive skateboarding to benefit themselves and have the appearance of inclusion and not come through" (Loreto 2022).

On 11 August in 2022 the *US Olympic and Paralympic Committee (USOPC)* publicly announced it was initiating proceedings to decertify *USA Skateboarding* as the sport's national governing body (NGB). Issues raised included an alleged lack of respect for athletes and trainers, neglecting pledges to support calls for the inclusion of adaptive skating and WCMX to be part of the *Olympics* and *Paralympics*, and failure to meet with *Safe Sports* which compromises the safety of athletes, especially those who are minors. While some of the specific reasons are different from why Baker withdrew, these skateboarders were again harnessing their power to resist a version of skateboarding that was failing to ensure equity and respect.

There are many other moments where skateboarders will move boldly into step into situations that are unforeseen, unplanned, and heroic. Some involve sacrifices that end in tragedy. This includes 26-year-old Anthony Huber who on 25 August 2020 was shot and killed trying to disarm 17-year-old active shooter Kyle Rittenhouse who was threatening *Black Lives Matter* supporters with a gun at a protest in Kenosha, Wisconsin. His death was rare but his commitment to protest is not, with many skateboarders participating in similar marches, some of who we interviewed for our book allowing us to have a more in-depth understanding of what motivated them and the meanings they attached to their experiences.

Importantly, not everyone in skateboarding who are change-makers will be famous or known outside skateboarding, nor will the activities they engage in be picked up by the media or able to reach huge audiences. Transformations in sports and society, including through skateboarding, can also take place in ways that are very much behind the scenes and maybe incremental, with multiple approaches and levels of resources to problem-solving. We argue there is a need to include and understand all kinds of change-makers in sports to understand how power operates and can be redistributed to effect social change within and beyond their fields.

Skateboarding consists of an array of individuals who are involved in activism, advocacy, lobbying, and other efforts for social change (Ahmad and Thorpe 2020; Chiu and Giamarino 2019; Foley 2020, 2022; Glover et al. 2021; Warin 2020; Williams 2022; Willing and Shearer 2016). While skateboarders are typically seen as just members of youth and subcultures or increasingly as elite athletes, we argue that they are also taking a stance and contributing to social change like their mainstream sports counterparts. In our case study of skateboarders who are change-makers, we identified and developed several main typologies: "icons," "iconoclasts" and "breakthrough figures," "strategists" and "community builders," "storytellers," "creatives," and "provocateurs." These categories of skateboarders are not mutually exclusive and can overlap. What unites all these types is how their work acts to tackle social problems within skateboarding or broader pressing issues of our time. Many are also able to disrupt narrow notions of skateboarding as an imagined playground exclusive to White, heterosexual, and cisgender men.

We chose to use the term "change-makers" to describe the people that were interviewed, shaped by what people had to say to us, and from the emerging themes in our conversations. Drawing insights for studies of disability rights (Haslett and Smith 2022) we need to pay heed to not labeling people as "activists," "advocates," or "lobbyists" even if those categories might align with some or many of their actions. Activism can be singularly focused and purpose-driven, or a lifelong identity and commitment, or something temporal, sparked in reaction to a remarkable moment or circumstance (Magrath 2022). But as a label, activists can also be stigmatized and not fit how skaters see themselves, particularly those sitting on more moderate than radical vectors of the political spectrum. Advocates and lobbyists on the other hand can seem too affiliated with a formalized approach that abides by or just wishes to modestly reform rules or terms rather than breaking away and being revolutionizing. We feel the description of change-makers suitably captures the intent and impact of the people in skateboarding we interviewed while allowing for their different approaches and stances.

As discussed in the last chapter, diversity has always been a part of the history of skating but is not always held up or recognized. But as we shall reveal, there are many figures, some who are well known and others not in the spotlight who are "changing things up." The changes they make may be sparked and rolled out in symbolically or significantly structural ways. Sometimes their power to change things starts with their presence alone, for example, as an act of representation that defies homogenizing and monolithic images and narratives. In the chapter ahead we will further elaborate on the typologies we used to understand key characteristics and strengths that people can bring to skating. In doing so, we can better understand how forms of power can be taken in and shared by all kinds of change-makers, and how the diversity they bring to skateboarding is a strength for its progress and longevity.

Change-Makers as Cultural Beacons and Guides

The types of individuals we were able to interview include a collection of individuals who are "insiders" in skateboarding meaning they belong to the community and are recognized as such. We view the change-makers we spoke to as "cultural beacons and guides" who, through our conversations, provide fresh and important insights into the culture of skateboarding. We include a range of individuals who work as professionals or volunteers for programs, networks, non-profits, brands, media, or industry areas that work toward some form of social change. Such parameters may prompt questioning over issues of "sample bias," and whether our conversations became "an echo chamber." However, we intentionally employed what is known as a purposive sample made up of "experts" (Lincoln and Guba 1985) to keep the focus on populations most relevant to the aims of this inquiry. In short, the expertise we sought were insights from individuals who are social change leaders and have experienced "championing" social projects in skateboarding or issues that affect society more broadly but still utilize skateboarding as a platform to do so.

The demographic backgrounds of the individuals we spoke to are not homogenous. At the same time, we openly acknowledge how there is ample room for more diverse voices not extensively covered here. In our efforts to include a range of people we also faced very human and humbling challenges on top of spectacular national and global events, such as both of us having "day" jobs and "life stuff" to juggle. By the time some people reached out to us to be involved, we needed to decline as we were already well into the research and needed to concentrate on analyzing existing interviews and writing the book to a deadline. As such, there is room in future research to expand the conversations to more individuals from "non-traditional" and marginalized populations in skating or those who are allies and leveraging their comparatively greater access to power. This is especially the case with change-makers at the frontline addressing issues such as trans-exclusionary attitudes and policies, forms of ableism, religious discrimination such as Islamophobia and anti-Semitism, class discrimination, ageism, and linguistic and further cultural barriers. We recommend future works or collaborations with people with such lived experiences and expertise be fully supported.

Our exploration also does not aim to be representative in a statistical sense. Rather, we aimed to achieve what is known in the qualitative research approach as "depth over breadth" with the goal of quality over quantity of insights (Lincoln and Guba 1985). In the early stages of research we put out an open call and a recruitment notice was also distributed through contacts we met at *Pushing Boarders*. Our main research criteria were people 18 years old or over, whose work had a focus on social change and whose work had influence in the US. We made an effort to be flexible around how individuals fit the category of change-makers (such as from grassroots activism to industry). We concluded interviews once the insights and themes arising from the interviews for thematic analysis (Braun and Clarke 2003) were predictably consistent and reached what is known as "theoretically saturation" (Glaser and Strauss 1967) meaning themes in the interviews started being repeated and covering similar ground.

For purposes of validity and safety, we chose groups who are well-known, have good relations with other skateboarders we know, and people we feel have a certain degree of recognition in skateboarding. This was particularly important due to the level of cyber-harassment and aggression that the *Consent is Rad* campaign receives. Throughout the writing of this book, the consent campaign had to navigate harassment toward its volunteer staff members and is currently working on strategies to share with their team and more widely with others doing similar work.

Overall, our participants include many individuals who are "non-traditional" so far as experiencing some form of disadvantage, or discrimination, such as from being women and/or from gender diverse and LGBTQIA+ communities Indigenous, Black, Latino, Hispanic, Asian, or of "mixed" ancestry and non-English speaking backgrounds, disability and migration. Other individuals who were included are White, cisgender, and heterosexual men, which positions them as more socially privileged across socially constructed lines of race, gender, and sexuality. Their inclusion remains valuable, especially in recognition of how such men can be valuable peers and allies, and have insight into how they can leverage their own power in efforts to be supportive of "non-traditional" skaters. This population is also not monolithic and can face challenges such as class, mental health struggles, and many other barriers of discrimination.

The sections ahead provide a window on how versatile and varied change-makers can be, and who can offer knowledge on micro and small-scale changes to structural and macro changes. This includes insights from people creating zines and local skate meet-ups to large-scale skate facilities, education programs, scholarships, industry overhauls, and environmental strategies. Others we introduce ahead use their skills to write about film, and photograph skating, while also offering forms of critique, analysis, and even satire. Above all, we see the individuals ahead as people as valuable cultural guides offering specialized and relevant knowledge, advice, and recommendations on the themes of skateboarding, power, and change.

Icons, Iconoclasts, and Breakthrough Figures

"I feel like there's a lot of people in skating that have been around for a long time who are like, 'Oh, shit, we need to do better. And they're leveraging their power"—Kristin Ebeling, sponsored skateboarder, Founder of *The Skate Witches,* and Executive Director of *Skate Like a Girl.* (Quoted by Alex White 2021)

Throughout the history of skateboarding are various "icons," "iconoclasts," and "breakthrough figures" who have brought "non-traditional" skaters' stories, skills, and communities to light, via their example or through elevating others. An iconoclast is someone who strongly disrupts, critiques, and opposes "how things are" in terms of accepted beliefs and traditions. Breakthrough figures are people who instigate, facilitate, and generally bring about dynamic and dramatic changes, offering fresh ways to think and pathways for moving forward. Both typologies have the power to turn things around, not just through hard work, will, and determination, but also through things like wisdom from lived experience, perhaps star power from being famous or infamous, and intangible qualities like excluding authenticity, charisma, and confidence that can produce loyal followers or backers (Magrath 2022; Thorpe et al. 2017).

In the history of skateboarding, there are many icons, iconoclasts, and breakthrough figures that come to mind. Our main focus is on an emerging and new generation. However, many skaters from older generations still actively contribute to the community today. In acknowledgment of this, we spoke to three *Skateboarding Hall of Fame (SHoF)* inductees who have broken various stereotypes and "glass ceilings" in skateboarding. Created by skateboarders, the SHoF (https://skateboardinghalloffame. org) began in 2009 in California and 2016 was formalized by a committee that includes Lance Mountain, Jim Muir, Laura Thornhill-Caswell, Steve Olson, Dave Hackett, Todd Huber, Glen E Friedman, and Thomas Barker. They oversee and select inductees from a Nominations Committee made up of 68 people from the skateboarding community. While the majority of inductees are White, cisgender men, we spoke to people awarded the honor who reflect more diversity.

Firstly, born in San Francisco, Tommy Guerrero joined the skate company *Powell Peralta* in 1984 and became one of the original members of the legendary *Bones Brigade* team. Guerrero has been playing music since the late 1970s with his brother Tony, who was both raised on a "steady diet of DIY punk music/ethos and skateboarding," which informed and shaped the person he is today. Since then, Guerrero has become an accomplished bassist and guitarist who consistently tours and releases music. Guerrero also co-founded *Real Skateboards* with Jim Thiebaud in 1991 through *Deluxe Distribution (DLX)* with Fausto Vitello. He currently assists with *Real* as well as the *Krooked* brand, also distributed through *DLX*.

Secondly, Peggy Oki was a champion women's skater from the iconic *Dogtown* crew in the 1970s as part of the "Z-Boys" *Zephyr* team. She is also an artist, surfer, and rock climber. In the 1970s, Peggy broke barriers in the world of skateboarding as the only female member of the *Zephyr Skateboard* team and was featured in the film *Dogtown & Z Boys*. In 2012, she was inducted into the *Skateboarding Hall of Fame*. She is now an environmental activist for ocean life and founder of the *Origami Whale Project* cetacean rights through her *Origami Whales Project*, and "Let's Face It" Visual Petition campaign.

And thirdly, Cindy Whitehead who was at the forefront of skating in the 1970s and 1980s as a women's vert and pool skating champion and is the founder of *Girl is Not a 4 Letter Word* launched in 2013, and author of the first hardback book for young girls and women called *It's Not About Pretty: A Book About Radical Female Skaters*. Her skateboard history sits in the Smithsonian's National Museum of American History's sports collections. Whitehead has spoken about equity and inclusion in a TEDx talk, at the Smithsonian Museum in Washington D.C., *Snapchat* HQ, and the 2019 ESPNW Summit where she gave a "power talk" to leaders in the sports industry.

From an older generation, we also spoke with Lynn Kramer, who is a 15-time world champion slalom winner and ran the *Women's Skateboard Network* from 1988 to 1990, publishing four zines and writing articles for magazines like *Thrasher*. She started skating in 1985 at UCSD and has been involved with the industry since then. She was in the UCSD "Ready to Shred" skateboard club, building ramps on campus and writing about it for *Thrasher Magazine*. As a mechanical engineer, she helped develop the "Turner Hybrid Skateboard," a composite slalom racing deck built with CNC technology. Currently, Kramer is the head coach of the non-profit La Costa Racing Team in San Diego County, while working as a support engineer to manufacturers of skateboards and surfboards.

In their current lives, all still contribute to skateboarding as well as having other roles and interests, such as music, fashion, and art. Insights they offer cover formative experiences such as being seen as outsiders when they were younger skaters. For Guerrero and Oki, this also included receiving discrimination due to their racial or ethnic backgrounds. And for Oki, Whitehead, and Kramer, forms of gender bias and exclusion also needed to be overcome. These icons and veterans of skating also offer wisdom and insights about what it was like to take risks, stand out and have a stance on social issues like racism, sexism, and the environment as younger skaters to now middle-aged and older skaters who are running their brands, businesses, and organizations.

Our book also includes a mix of generations. We interviewed an iconoclastic senior figure and a new generation breakthrough figure in Native skateboarding, who are also a father and son and come from the Apache Nation and San Carlos Reservation. Douglas Miles Senior has been involved in celebrating and uplifting Native skateboarding for over twenty years, as well as challenging colonialism and racism in skateboarding. His creative output is prolific and includes fine art, street murals, photography, videos, social media platforms, and activities with *Apache Skateboards* (http://apacheskateboards.com), the skateboard company he founded in 2002. His work has been exhibited across the US and he has held several art residencies as well as numerous speaking engagements. He is also the co-writer of the documentary *The Mystery of Now* (Buchanan 2019) which was showcased by National Geographic and in which he states "when you realize the land is forever, you realize you're forever. We are forever." In his artist's statement on his website, Miles states that he "has been capturing Native American reality. Not romanticism. Triumph. Not tragedy" (Miles 2022).

Douglas Miles Junior is the founder of the skate company *Indellica* (https://indellica.com) and has overseen projects such as the *Apache Passion Project* which raised funds for a skatepark in Whiteriver Reservation in Arizona where he now also lives. He is now combining his team's efforts with additional support from *The Skatepark Project* to build a skatepark there, following the successful build of a new one in San Carlos Reservation, and has been featured in numerous skate parts and videos such as in *The Mystery of Now* documentary, a *Red Bull* special by Madars Apse (2022) and the *Etnies Visits Apache Nation* (2022) video and also on television shows like *NBC Today* (also in 2022). His son Miles Sr. states "Doug Jnr is the pro skateboarder of the future … as more and more skate companies look to sponsor impactful skaters, it's people like Doug who stand for something greater and who represent a community within skateboarding that's greater to contribute" (quoted in Foley 2022).

Others who spoke to us are often comparatively new to skateboarding but their presence and work to address themes of racism and representation have been remarkable. Such themes are observed to often be averted or downplayed by industry and skate media (Williams 2021). In our exploration of change-makers, we also turn the spotlight to Black skaters from a new generation. Our conversations include President and Founder Karlie Thornton and Vice President L Brew from *froSkate* (@froSkate). More than just a skate network, the *froSkate* website (https://www. froskate.com) explains they are "Black women found and Queer led … Chicago's first collective for the non-traditional skate community" (froSkate 2022). In their role, Thornton and L Brew have overseen numerous skate meet-ups and skate workshops for Black, PoC, and queer skaters, as well as providing community learning guides, doing public speaking, and producing apparel with some displaying Black empowerment and social justice messages such as Black Skaters Matter. The froSkate crew are also the first Black women and non-binary skaters to design a shoe with *Nike*, released in August 2022, in a campaign photographed by Norma Ibarra who we also interviewed.

We also spoke with Latosha Stone, who is the founder of *Proper Gnar*, the first Black woman-owned skate company that was launched in 2012. The *Proper Gnar* (2022) website (https://propergnar.com) states that the "brand has disrupted the skateboarding landscape - from a sport primarily viewed as young and male-oriented … to banish the stereotypes and orchestrate the beginning of a new dawning. Her brand empowers, uplifts, and showcases women, especially women of color, to jump on board and skate." The website also emphasizes things such as sisterhood and creativity and sells decks and fashion apparel, as well as a blog with articles and interviews with Black and non-Black skaters from around the world on themes such as art, lifestyle, and skate culture.

We also interviewed Atiba Jefferson, who is a skateboarder and regarded as an iconic photographer and director who has worked with high-profile magazines such as *Thrasher, Slap Magazine,* and *Transworld,* as well as magazines outside of the skateboarding space. He is also featured in the *Tony Hawk Pro Skater 4* video game. His professional background also includes basketball photography and music, with him photographing people such as Drake, Lil Yachty, Steph Curry, A$AP Rocky, Flea, Lebron James, Shaquille O'Neal, Kobe Bryant, and Pharrell Williams. He also photographed the cover of *Thrasher's* Black Lives Matter issue.

Gender equality and discrimination toward skateboarders' sexuality are also key issues in skateboarding in terms of understanding the uneven access to power, and the change-makers who challenge that. Some of the iconoclastic and breakthrough figures challenging stereotypes and removing barriers around gender and sexuality that we interviewed are Alex White and Kristin Ebeling, whose experiences and work bridge various intersectional aspects of skateboarding.

Alex White is the brand manager for *Krux* and her influence in skateboarding extends to elite competition work as an announcer, industry brand management, filmmaker, skate writer, podcaster with *Vent City,* and work for community programs. As a university student, she made the short film "Can you Kickflip?" documenting the challenges women and non-binary skaters can face. White also features in an iconic moment symbolizing how heavy-handed hegemonic masculinity in skateboarding can be in the 2005 *Getting Nowhere Faster* video. The video includes a highly physical exchange White has, as a young woman, with a hostile male security guard who pins her to the ground and sits on her in a physically inappropriate way to assert dominance and control. The scene has since been created into many memes, a format very much embraced by

White, and even a pin used to fundraise for charity at https://www.pokeypin.com/product/alex-white.

Kristin Ebeling at the time of writing this book is the Executive Director of *Skate Like a Girl*, which is one of the largest non-profit organizations of its kind in the US with branches in Seattle, Portland, and the San Francisco Bay Area. She is also a professional skateboarder for *Meow Skateboards* and holds many sponsorships. Her professional roles and her commitment to issues of equity and access in skateboarding extend to activities such as mentoring youth, community development, and activism, and she is also a skate writer, podcaster, and public speaker. Ebeling founded the annual *Wheels of Fortune* event, co-founded *The Skate Witches* and *Mess Magazine*, and she is a co-host of the *Vent City* podcast. Ebeling could easily be described as someone who is what Kim Woozy calls a "possibility model" (Willing 2014). Keen to "share the mic" rather than guard it, Ebeling is also a powerful figure behind the scenes and has significantly advanced the presence and participation of women, non-binary, and gender-diverse skaters using her power within the industry as well, such as with *Krux Trucks*.

We also spoke with Amelia Brodka, who is based in the US, and an *Olympian* who represented Poland in the Tokyo Games. Brodka has placed in the top three in several world transition championships (3rd in one world vert championship but 1st in European Park Championships 2 years in a row). In 2012, Brodka directed *Underexposed: A Women's Skateboarding Documentary* focused on the challenges women skaters face. After the *X-Games* canceled the women's vert event, Amelia co-founded *Exposure Skate* through a partnership with Lesli Cohen. Today she is the president of *Exposure Skate*, a non-profit organization that empowers women, trans, and non-binary individuals through skateboarding. The annual event raises money and awareness for survivors of domestic violence and each of *Exposure's* programs has an element of giving back to at-risk communities and an annual event that also raises donations for services to support survivors of domestic violence. *Exposure Skate* has also partnered with Calli Kelsay in the *Skate Rising* program which provides empowerment through skateboarding and compassion through service to girls aged 4–18 and promotes youth engagement to support vulnerable and under-served communities. In 2021 they also added a college scholarship program in partnership with *College Skateboarding Education Foundation (CSEF)* as well as *Sesh(E)*, inclusive sessions for women, trans, and non-binary individuals.

Representing men who are allies and are also part of a younger generation, we interviewed Ryan Lay, a professional skateboarder who represents an "alternative masculinity" (Beal 1995; Willing et al. 2020) that has foundations in ethically reflecting on how he interacts and making an effort in being community-oriented rather than hyper dominant and individualistic. Lay does not shy away from contemporary activism, and his activities are supportive of social justice issues ranging from Palestine in his role as an Ambassador for *Skate Pal*, raising bail funds for people arrested during *Black Lives Matter* protests and through the podcast *Vent City* which he co-hosts with Kristin Ebeling, Alex White, Kyle Beachy, Ted Barrow, and Ted Schmitz.

The skateboarders we have so far discussed can also belong to the following other categories we shall now introduce, as none of these typologies are mutually exclusive. Rather, we use these various categories of change-makers simply as a heuristic device to pinpoint some of the dynamic impacts, personalities, leadership styles, and experiences we identified in the people we interviewed. We also felt they warranted more specific ways to address their presence and impact beyond often homogenizing and traditional labels such as activists and advocates.

Strategists and Community Builders

In this section, we provide a summary of a range of skateboarders who we saw as "strategists" and "community builders." Strategists are observed to have strong organizational abilities, may draw on formal qualifications and business training, and value things such as having a well-planned if not budgeted "game plan" to deliver outcomes. A large majority of their work is also done behind the scenes. Community builders can share these skills and attributes but may also work from a more upfront and visible, spontaneous, low or no budget and grassroots status, and have a style of engagement that does not rely upon or desire a high level of formality, administration, or planning. Both categories can overlap, and people from both groups tend to be skilled networkers and orientated toward tangible outcomes. Having the characteristics of being strategic or community development also does not exclude skaters from the other typologies of change-makers we discuss throughout this chapter.

We propose that the more visible figures we introduced in the last section can also share many of the characteristics of strategists and community builders, although their public profiles and ability to "influence" via a certain gravitas are also key to how they can bring about change. But to also gain more insight into all kinds of strategists and community builders for our exploration we also spoke to a mixture of people who may have skate sponsors and/or be public speakers and have community recognition, but whose work in the area of social change is more behind the scenes.

The strategists and community builders of this nature we interviewed include Kim Woozy, whose work focuses on women and non-binary skaters, and whose professional experiences cover industry, creative production, and community. Woozy previously worked as the Girls Marketing Manager for *Osiris* shoe company (2006–2009), before leaving to launch *Mahfia TV* (2010 to 2018), a media platform that showcased women in action sports. Other activities that Woozy has been a part of that are pivotal to advancing gender equity include in 2019 when she advocated for California State Bill AB467 (Equal Pay for Equal Play) which was signed into law in 2020. She is currently the Director of Marketing & Partnerships at *Skate Like a Girl*. In this role she provides rare insights into how the relationship between community and industry is not always antagonistic, and that the former can assist the latter to be more inclusive and supportive.

Ashley Masters is also from *Skate Like a Girl*, with a role as the Director of *Skate Like a Girl SF Bay Area*, and part of the *Squeezing the Juice* podcast. Masters has been a competitive skateboarder and is also now a health coach and fitness trainer for elite athletes as well as community members who don't always feel there's space for them in fitness and movement. One of her roles is also to co-develop and co-run the "Allysk8" program through *Skate Like a Girl* which is run for the community, skaters, skate company employees, people running skate teaching programs, and other industry figures.

While *Skate Like a Girl* is carving out what is possible for larger non-profit skate organizations, we also spoke with representatives from smaller grassroots networks. Kaily "Bayr" Blackburn is the co-founder of *Cornerstone Skate Foundation* (https://www.cornerstoneskatefdn.org) in the Colorado area. As a small informal network, they offer skateboard lessons and meet-ups, which include "ShredTalks" which focuses on mental health and self-care.

Other strategists we spoke to include Timothy Ward who is the Program Director of *Skate After School* in Phoenix, Arizona, in which Ryan Lay is also involved as an Executive Director. Ward was also a Skate Program Director at *Woodward West* skate training facility. The main aim of *Skate After School's* work is to provide mentorship opportunities for school-aged children from disadvantaged and underserved schools, as well as give away boards and scholarships to visit Woodward West. Ward also is behind several team-run satirical social media accounts about skateboarding such as *The Nut Daily News*.

In the area of skating, college-level education, and social change, we interviewed representatives from the *College Skateboarding Education Foundation (CSEF)* which provides scholarships for skateboarders to help them during their degrees. Thomas Barker is the Co-Chairman of *CSEF* but also guided us through various insights on industry and advocacy work too. He is a lifelong skater who is based in LA. In his youth, he grew up in the semi-rural area of Elfin Forest and first gained industry experience within the outdoor recreation brands and skate marketing world including at *Blackbox*. His main role now is as Director of Partnerships for *Jenkem Magazine* and he has twenty years of experience as an industry expert, including time in industry associations and as a business analyst. He also has non-profit experience with *Rolling from the Heart*, skatepark advocacy such as *Poods Park* (Encinitas Skate Plaza), and also works for the *Skateboarding Hall of Fame* awards.

Keegan Guizard is the executive director of *CSEF* and describes himself as a skateboarder, entrepreneur, writer, and traveler living in LA who was born in New York and grew up in coastal North Carolina. His knowledge and experience around social change in skating include how he approaches his work in the skating non-profit field drawing on his degree in business administration and marketing and content management experience, as a board member of *Make Life, Skate Life,* and *Salad Days of Skateboarding,* and as the founder of *Collegiate Skate Tour.*

We also interviewed Chris Giamarino who is one of *CSEF's* scholarship recipients and who is doing his PhD in Urban Planning at UCLA. Giamarino provided insights into how studies and activism can overlap. At 30 years, he represents a younger generation of skateboarding academics that follows breakthrough figures in the field of skateboarding research such as Professor Ocean Howell in the US and Professor Iain Borden in the UK. Giamarino's research looks at skateboarding and public space, issues of hostile architecture, and policies that inhibit skateboarding in the streets. As an activist, he has been involved in campaigns addressing issues of homelessness in LA, and also efforts to remove policing at university campuses.

Expanding the focus on the relationship skateboarders have with space and their need to negotiate with a range of others outside their scene to have skateparks built, we also spoke to Alec Beck. A former competitive and professional skater, Beck is the manager of Public Education from *The Skatepark Project* (formerly *The Tony Hawk Foundation*). His work has also involved advocating for numerous communities to have skateparks built including Stoner Park, and also for the preservation of famous skate spots such as the LA Courthouse. We also spoke with Paul Forsline who is president of *City of Skate*, which advocates for skateparks in the Twin Cities of Minneapolis and St Paul Minnesota. The *City of Skate* project at the time of writing this book were advocating for $15 million to fund a comprehensive skatepark funding program.

In terms of activism that specifically emerged in response to the *Black Lives Matter* movement, we spoke with Patrick Kigongo who is a skateboarder, chair of the board for the Harold Hunter Foundation, a Digital Product Manager, and the creator of *The Black List*, which was created in June 2020 to highlight Black-owned skate businesses such as brands and skate shops. *The Black List* was featured in Thrasher (2020). Kigongo is also a podcaster with *Mostly Skateboarding* with Templeton Elliott, Mike Munzenrider, and Jason Berelovitz which covers a range of topics on skating. A street skater since 1994, Kigongo states that he is influenced by punk and alternative music scenes and growing up in New York among African migrants and diverse populations from around the world.

On the theme of talking to White people who, as allies, are involved in efforts to address racism in skateboarding sparked by *Black Lives Matter* we also spoke with Kevin Pacella, who is a White cisgender man who co-organized a protest skate in collaboration with Ben Jones from *Kinetic Skateshop* in Wilmington, Delaware, in 2020. *Kinetic Skateshop* represents one of the many skate shops that became active in *Black Lives Matter* protests in 2020 (Pappalardo 2020). We also spoke to Rhianon Bader from the *Goodpush Alliance* who was a key co-creator of the *Pushing Against Racism* campaign (https://www.goodpush.org/blog/pushing-against-racism) alongside Sandy Alibo, a Black woman, from *Surf Ghana*. The campaign has a working group committee made up of over 20 representatives from skate networks and the industry. The Goodpush Alliance is a knowledge-sharing network created by Skateistan, which is a non-profit that combines skateboarding with creative, arts-based education and has built state of the art Skate Schools in Afghanistan, Cambodia, and South Africa.

The *Pushing Against Racism* campaign was launched on May 25th, 2021, on the anniversary of George Floyd's murder. The campaign called for signatories to sign a commitment to challenge racism and anti-Blackness in skateboarding, and hosts webinars for the social skate sector on themes of anti-racist policies, practices, and attitudes. In May 2022 it also launched a funding program that awards small grants to skate organizations to run projects addressing racism. Sixteen organizations from around the world received small grants in its first round. Although regionally awarded, there is strong sense of community and familiarity in the non-profit and social projects sector, and to address any familiarity or cross over roles, some individuals were evaluated by assessors outside their region for fairness. Additionally, rather than being about "winning" and gatekeeping, some grantees reached out to partner with the applicants who were not successful to conduct their proposed anti-racism project.

Storytellers, Creatives, and Provocateurs

Skateboarding has many types of people who can effect change and including those who are high-profile professionals, charismatic public figures, and strategic thinkers behind the scenes who have administrative and community work experience. There are also people we spoke to who we call the "storytellers," "creatives," and "provocateurs." Like skaters from previous generations, these individuals make use of writing, videos, photography, satire, and artistic expressions to both celebrate and critique skating. Again, these categories are not mutually exclusive and individuals in the above sections can share such attributes and activities. Our aim in the following is to just further highlight an expansive range of skills and strengths that change-makers bring to skateboarding and expand notions of who is making change happen and how.

Skate media was once predominantly ruled by the print magazine and zine formats but in its evolution also consists of things such as online platforms like social media, video channels, podcasts, and blogs. The types of skate media we were interested in for our exploration target particular audiences, with a focus on women and non-traditional skaters (such as *Yeah Girl, Quell,* and *Skateism*) and men with an alternative take that includes satire and socially overlooked skate scenes (*Jenkem Magazine,* the *Manramp* project and *The Nut Daily News*).

The storytellers from media platforms and magazines include Sarah Huston, a graphic designer and skateboarder who is the founder of *Yeah Girl;* Adrian Koenigsberg, who also works as designer in advertising and is skateboarder who is the co-founder of *Quell Magazine* (which ran until 2021); Denia Kopita, a skateboarder and volunteer with *Free Skate Movement* who at the time of writing this book was the editor of *Skateism;* and Lynn Kramer who published the zines *Girls Who Grind,* which later became *Equal Time.* We also spoke with Shari White, a filmer and co-founder of *The Skate Witches* and *Mess Magazine,* Izzi Cooper who created a DIY zine *Heal Flip,* and Christian Kerr who is a writer and social researcher from *Jenkem Magazine.*

Skate project work can span multiple roles, and it is worth noting that people like Kim Woozy also have experience in skate media via her work in *Mahfia*, Kristin Ebeling in *The Skate Witches* and *Mess Magazine*, and others who occasionally write or make content for various skate platforms. We also spoke with several skateboarders who are involved with podcasts including Kim Woozy and Ashley Masters on *Squeezing the Juice*, Patrick Kigongo on *Mostly Skateboarding*, and Ted Schmitz who is part of the *Vent City* team alongside Ryan Lay, Kyle Beachy, Kristin Ebeling, Alex White, and Ted Barrow. Schmitz also works for *Thrasher* and is also behind the satirical skate account *The Nut Daily News* with Timothy Ward and others.

We also spoke to skateboarders who have an academic background, with our focus not just on their scholarly works but also on the types of social issues and skate projects they may engage in. Professor Kyle Beachy is a literary author whose works include his skate-themed memoir *The Most Fun Thing* (2021). He also authored a critical essay titled *Primitive Progressivism* (in Free Skate Magazine, Beachy 2018) about skateboarder Jason Jessee, whose problematic history includes sharing racist and homophobic views and was followed with an apology. Beachy is also part of the *Vent City* podcast team.

Other researchers we spoke with include Professor Brian Glenney, an author of two books on philosophy (Glenney and Silva 2019; Ferretti and Glenney 2021) who is also a recognized artist in the graffiti world. He is also known for community-driven projects like co-founding the *Accessible Icon Project* which was an artistic statement that challenges stereotypes about disability and wheelchair users that feature in major museums and is also taken as an official symbol in some American cities. Glenney is also a co-creator of humorous skate projects such as *Manramp* and features in videos by *The Worble* crew.

With an interest in non-traditional skateboarders, gender, and sexuality we talked with Dr. Bethany Geckle about her thesis (2021) and other research in the area of cultural and queer studies, sport, and skateboarding (including Geckle and Shaw 2022) where she highlights the positive social impact on skateboarding cultures in general by openly gay skateboarders such as Brian Anderson, trans women skaters such as Cher Strauberry and Peach Sørenson, as well as queer skate companies such as *Unity Skateboards*. Dr. Dani Abulhawa was another academic in our exploration. Abulhawa is the author of *Skateboarding and Femininity*

(Abulhawa 2021), which looks at the social construction and performance of gender and femininity as well as women's contributions across the history of skateboarding. She is also an ambassador of *SkatePal* and her research and community work also reflect on the role of skate charities and issues of intersectionality and colonialism.

Beyond written forms of expression, we were also interested in skateboarders involved in photography, fashion, art, and new areas of innovation. Norma Ibarra is one of these creatives who provided insights into her experiences. She is a photographer whose work features in high-profile and independent skate media such as *The Skate Witches* and covers mega-events like the world skateboarding *Olympic* qualifiers to DIY community events for non-traditional skaters. She is also a Mexican-Canadian who grew up in Hermosillo, Sonora, and released a book called *Pari Ti* in 2021 which is a 100-page book exploring the Mexican skate scene including the *U Can Skate* crew. Ibarra has also worked with videographer and *The Skate Witches* co-founder Shari White documenting *Credits* and *Maximum Flow*, the *Nike #AllLoveNoHate* shoe advertisements for *froSkate*, and a special series for *VANS* shoes on the Canadian skateboarding scene.

Our exploration was also interested in skate fashion and streetwear brands focused on women and gender-diverse markets, and with a commitment to social causes. Along with brands like *Proper Gnar* and *froSkate* we gained insights from one of the co-founders of *Doyenne Skateboards* "Mara," who requested to use her first name only. Although based in Glasgow, Scotland, *Doyenne* has an international focus and a number of their team are from the US. Their range is gender neutral and they have raised awareness and funds for *Skatepal* and *Concrete Jungle Foundation* and an event with *Unity Skateboards*, plus campaigns that raise awareness about neurodiversity and disability. Also recently, they have raised awareness about consent as part of the #ASKManifesto campaign alongside *Consent for Breakfast*, *Hera Skate,* and *Consent is Rad.*

We also included the perspectives of skaters who use art to bring attention to issues and push for social change, speaking with Adam Abada, who has contributed illustrations for this book and the *Skaters Vote* campaign, along with supporting movements such as *Black Lives Matter* and *Stop Asian Hate.* He is also a writer, with his own blog *Stoke of the Week* (https://stokeoftheweek.wordpress.com), as well as for skate media including an article for *Quatersnacks* that captured skateboarders' oral histories and photos documenting the World Trade Center's Twin Towers (2019) prior to September 11. We also spoke with Lisa Berenson who is based in the UK but whose international work includes digital activism projects including an environmental campaign *Flood the Streets* and *Vote for Climate or Die*.

Lastly, with an interest in how skateboarding might harness evolving technology more in the future for social change projects, we talked to Brennan Hatton about the potential of Virtual Reality (VR) for building empathy in the skate community. Hatton is a skateboarder who is Australian, but transits between there and the US to work with a company he founded called *Equal Reality* (https://equalreality.com) which does diversity and inclusion training. In the next section, we begin to explore what it was like for these change-makers when they first stepped on a board and then started to embrace skateboarding into their lives and construct it as a central part of their identities. We will also begin to look at the outlooks and values they have developed that they bring into their work in skateboarding.

References

Abada, A (2019) Unforgettable—The Oral History of the Twin Towers in Skate Videos, *Quarter Snacks*, posted September 11. Downloaded 10 July 2022: https://quartersnacks.com/2019/09/unforgettable-the-oral-history-of-the-twin-towers-in-skate-photos/

Abulhawa, D (2021) *Skateboarding and Femininity: Gender, Space-making, and Expressive Movement*, Routledge.

Ahmad, N and Thorpe, H (2020) Muslim Sportswomen as Digital Space Invaders: Hashtag Politics and Everyday Visibilities, *Communication and Sport*, 1-20. DOI: https://doi.org/10.1177/2167479519898447

Armstrong, C, and Butryn, T (2022) Educated Activism: A Focus Group of High School Athletes Perceptions of Athlete Activism, In Magrath, R (Ed) *Athlete Activism: Contemporary Perspectives*. Taylor and Francis Group. Pp. 20–31.

Beal, B (1995). Disqualifying the official: An exploration of social resistance through the subculture of skateboarding. *Sociology of Sport Journal, 12*(3), 252–267. https://doi.org/10.1123/ssj.12.3.252

Beachy, K (2018) Primitive Progressivism, *Free Skate Magazine*, posted 5 June. Downloaded 8 July 2022: https://www.freeskatemag.com/2018/06/05/primitive-progressivism-by-kyle-beachy/

Beachy, K (2021) *The Most Fun Thing: Dispatches from a Skateboard Life*. Grand Central Publishing.

Braun, V, and Clarke, V (2003) Using Thematic Analysis in Psychology. *Qualitative Research in Psychology* 3(2): 77-101.

Brown, L, and Foxx, D (2022) The Changing Face of Black Athlete Activism: Pariah Today, Hero Tomorrow? In Magrath, R (Ed) *Athlete Activism: Contemporary Perspectives*. Taylor and Francis Group. pp. 55-64.

Buchanan, A (2019) *The Mystery of Now*. The Woods Production. USA https://www.themysteryofnow.com

Chiu, C and Giamarino, C (2019) Creativity, Conviviality, and Civil Society in Neoliberalizing Public Space: Changing Politics and Discourses in Skateboarder Activism From New York City to Los Angeles. *Journal of Sport and Social Issues*, 43(6), 462–492. https://doi.org/10.1177/0193723519842219

Etnies (2022) *Etnies Visits Apache Nation*. Posted 15 June: https://www.youtube.com/watch?v=kUw9i5y5xaQ

Foley, Z (2020) From BLM Protests to the Olympics: Are Skateboarders Capable of Creating Social Change, *Skateism*. Posted 1 October. Downloaded 20 July 2022: https://www.skateism.com/from-blm-protests-to-the-olympics-are-skateboarders-capable-of-creating-social-change

Foley, Z (2022) Skate Tales Goes Deeper: the Douglas Miles Junior Interview. *Red Bull*. Posted 24 May. Downloaded 17 June 2022: https://www.redbull.com/au-en/doug-miles-junior-interview

Forbes (2021) Paralympian Even Strong Spotlights First Ever Dew Tour Adaptive Skateboarding Competition, *Forbes*. Downloaded 16 June 2022. https://www.forbes.com/sites/michellebruton/2021/05/23/paralympian-evan-strong-spotlights-first-ever-dew-tour-adaptive-skateboarding-competition/?sh=53a167ff16cc

froSkate (2022), *froSkate* official website: https://www.froskate.com

Ferretti, G and Glenney, B (2021) *Molyneux's Question and the History of Philosophy*, Routledge.

Geckle, B and Shaw, S (2022) Failure and Futurity: The Transformative Potential of Queer Skateboarding. *Young Nordic Journal*. Preview Issue Downloaded 8 July 2022. https://doi.org/10.1177/1103308820945100

Geckle, B (2021) *Queer World Making: Destabilizing Heternormativity Through Skateboarding*. PhD Thesis submitted to the University of Otago. New Zealand. Downloaded 8 July 2022: https://ourarchive.otago.ac.nz/bitstream/handle/10523/12335/Gecklee%2C%20Bethany_PhD%20Thesis.pdf?sequence=1&isAllowed=y

Glaser, B, and Strauss, A (1967) *The Discovery of Grounded Theory: Strategies for Qualitative Research*. Chicago, IL: Aldine.

Glenney, B and Silva, J (2019) *The Senses and the History of Philosophy*, Routledge.

Glover, T, Munro, S, Men, I, Loates, W and Altman, I (2021) Skateboarding, gentle activism, and the animation of public space: CITE—A Celebration of Skateboard Arts and Culture at The Bentway, *Leisure Studies*, 40:1, 42–56, https://doi.org/10.1080/02614367.2019.1684980

Haslett, D and Smith, B (2022) Disability, Sport and Social Activism: Para Athlete Activism, In Magrath, R (Ed) *Athlete Activism: Contemporary Perspectives*. Taylor and Francis Group. pp 65-76.

Lee, W, and Cunningham, G. (2019). Moving Toward Understanding Social Justice in Sport Organizations: A Study of Engagement in Social Justice Advocacy in Sports organizations. *Journal of Sport and Social Issues*, *43*(3), 245–263.

Lincoln, Y, and Guba E (1985) *Naturalistic Inquiry*. London: Sage.

Loreto Jnr, O (2022) Social media post. *Instagram*, 7 August: https://www.instagram.com/p/Cg71UYbvShg/

Madars, A (2022) *Skate Tales: S2 E3 Apache Skateboards*, Red Bull. https://www.redbull.com/gb-en/skate-tales-season-2-apache-skateboards

Magrath, R (2022) *Athlete Activism: Contemporary Perspectives*. Taylor and Francis Group.

March, N and Reda, G (2022) *Stay on Board: The Leo Baker Story*, Netflix, USA.

Nike (2018) Dream Crazy #justdoit. *Nike*. Posted on YouTube: https://www.youtube.com/watch?v=WW2yKSt2C_A

Pappalardo, A (2018) Leo Baker is the Skate Hero We've All Been Waiting For: New York Skate of Mind *Huck Magazine*. Posted 18 September. Downloaded 15 August 2022: https://www.huckmag.com/outdoor/skate/lacey-baker-interview-skate-hero/

Pappalardo, A (2020) How Skate Shops are Supporting Black Lives Matter. *Parade*. Posted 5 August. Downloaded 8 July 2022: https://www.parade-world.com/uk/news/how-skate-shops-are-supporting-black-lives-matter/

Pappalardo, A (2022) Stay on Board: The Leo Baker Story, Takeaways from a Must See Documentary, *Artless Industria*. Posted 12 August Downloaded 15 August 2022: https://anthonypappalardo.substack.com/p/stay-on-board-the-leo-baker-story?fbclid=IwAR0__RVMnr8oVQn-6K6OVw-O8GxYISOVogc-ivHC4UDG9oCF9cvnvJCDH-A

Proper Gnar (2022), *Proper Gnar* official website: https://propergnar.com

Miles Senior, D (2022), *Douglas Miles* official website: https://www.douglasmiles.co/about/

Schmidt, S (2022) Financial Implications of Athlete Activism: The Cost of Taking a Stance, In Magrath, R (Ed) *Athlete Activism: Contemporary Perspectives*. Taylor and Francis Group. pp. 44–54.

Thrasher (2020) The Black List. Posted 8 June. Downloaded 8 July 2022: https://www.thrashermagazine.com/articles/trash/the-black-list/

Thorpe, H, Toffoletti, K, and Bruce, T (2017) Sportswomen and Social Media: Bringing Third-Wave Feminism, Postfeminism, and Neoliberal Feminism into Conversation, *Journal of Sport and Social Issues*, 41, 359–383. https://doi.org/10.1177/0193723517730808

Warin, R (2020) The Skateboarders Fighting for a Better Future. *Huck Magazine*. Posted 2020. Downloaded 20 July 2022: https://www.huckmag.com/shorthand_story/the-skateboarders-fighting-for-a-better-future/

White, A (2021) Kristin Ebeling on Going Pro and Dethroning the Bros, *Thrasher Magazine*. Posted 20 October. Downloaded 21 August 2022: https://www.thrashermagazine.com/articles/kristin-ebeling-on-going-pro-and-dethroning-the-bros/

Williams, N (2021) Understanding Race in Skateboarding: A Retrospection and Agenda for the Importance of Being Seen, Dupont, T and Beal, B (eds), *Lifestyle Sports and Identities: Subcultural Careers Throughout the Life Course*, London: Routledge, pp 284–296.

Williams, N (2022) Before the Gold: Connecting Aspirations, Activism, and BIPOC Excellence Through Olympic Skateboarding, *Journal of Olympic Studies*, 3 (1): 4–27. https://doi.org/10.5406/26396025.3.1.02

Willing, I (2014) Interview with Kim Woozy, founder of MAHFIA Web TV, *Asian Australian Film Forum and Network Interview Series*, Posted March. Downloaded 31 July 2022: https://asianaustralianfilmforum.wordpress.com/2014/03/03/aaffn_interview2014_with_kim_woozy/

Willing, I (2019) Strength, courage, resistance: an interview with Navajo Nation skater Di'orr Greenwood. *Yeah Girl*. Posted 26 August. Downloaded 17 June 2022: https://yeahgirlmedia.com/strength-courage-resilience-an-interview-with-navajo-nation-skater-diorr-greenwood/

Willing, I, Green, B and Pavlidis, P (2020), The 'Boy Scouts' and 'Bad Boys' of SKateboarding: A Thematic Analysis of *The Bones Brigade*. *Sport in Society*, 23(5), 832–846. https://doi.org/10.1080/17430437.2019.1580265

Willing, I and Shearer, S (2016) Skateboarding Activism: Exploring Diverse Voices and Community Support, Lombard, KJ (ed) *Skateboarding: Subcultures, Sites and Shifts*, London: Routledge. pp. 44–58.

4

Formative Experiences, Values, and Outlooks

I. Willing, A. Pappalardo, *Skateboarding, Power and Change*,
https://doi.org/10.1007/978-981-99-1234-6_4

Chapter 4 Illustration by Adam Abada

Introduction

When people meet someone who skateboards, they will often be asked: why did you first get into skateboarding, and what was it like? Many social and internal factors can be a part of what is best described as the act of "becoming a skateboarder" rather than just simply being someone who may use a skateboard. Of course, it can simply be that it looked like a lot of fun. However, it may also include being drawn to aspects of the culture, such as clothing styles, people involved, and lifestyles. This can include classic elements of youth cultures, subcultures, or scenes that make it seem "cool" and attractive (Bennett 2011; Blackman 2005) such as an image of non-conformity and resistance (Beal and Weidman 2003; Dinces 2011). But this is just a part of the story.

In previous chapters, we have discussed why it is important to extend knowledge of skateboarding beyond just traditional theories of subcultures alone to fully understand its broader evolution, including from being a subculture to also an *Olympic* sport (Schwier, and Kilberth 2020; Wheaton and Thorpe 2021). There are already many studies that support the idea that skateboarding can be a central identity, a lifestyle, and one that can sometimes also endure across the life course of individuals (O'Connor 2017; Wheaton and Beal 2004; Willing et al. 2019). These insights are joined by a body of literature on traditional types of distinctions in skateboarding, based on things such as skill levels, insider knowledge, and notions of authenticity that can produce both a sense of belonging but also gatekeeping (Beal and Weidman 2003, Dupont 2014, 2020; Snow 2012; Snyder 2017). Moreover, studies have also demonstrated that anti-authoritarian and oppositional characteristics in skating can be "flexible" and mix alongside things such as mainstreaming, career building, and entrepreneurship (Dinces 2011; Snyder 2017).

In this chapter we direct our attention to the early experiences of the individuals we interviewed who represent more overlooked types of figures in skateboarding—the change-makers—whose significant rise and various typologies we outlined in the last chapter. The exploration here includes reflecting on how their journeys of embracing the identities of being a skateboarder reflect patterns found in existing literature, such as being attracted to skateboarding's subcultural elements and lifestyles.

However, our attention is also dedicated to how they make sense of any social barriers and issues they may have faced, which we will later discuss as opening a window onto a reflexive process in skateboarders that combines self-critiques as well as reflecting on external pressures by others they can face. As part of this discussion, we draw on conceptual and theoretical ideas such as symbolic violence (Bourdieu 1994, 2002), "emotional labor" (Hoschild 1979), and recent attention to "defiance labor" and "complicit reflexivity" (Sharp and Threadgold 2020).

Our exploration then moves to look more in-depth at what kinds of values and outlooks skaters hold. As part of this discussion, we continue to introduce various conceptual and theoretical frameworks that can further assist with identifying and understanding what standpoints shape and influence their roles as change-makers. We also look at the personal attachments skateboarders attribute to why they are dedicated to skateboarding, such as it providing them with a sense of gratitude due to skating offering them forms of salvation, tenacity from how skating requires commitment and resilience, and a sense of recognition of their how they want to express themselves which may not conform to dominant views and lifestyles. Finally, we consider some of the ethical and moral orientations they convey, which we link to ideas of "radical empathy" (Carroll and Cianciotto 2020; Tedam 2021) and "everyday" and "ordinary" cosmopolitanism (Lamont and Aksartova 2002; Plage et al. 2017).

Defiance Labor and Flexible Forms of Reflexivity

In this chapter, we soon illustrate how the individuals we spoke with recall and make sense of their personal journeys of going from "newcomers" to skating, to identifying as "skateboarders" as a significant part of their identity. Key insights from their stories reveal a gendered dimension within this transformation that creates a range of societal barriers. We also identify and illuminate a reflexive process that, while attentive to forms of exclusion, can also at times foster critical thinking, innovation, and a sense of agency that assists to empower them. For women and non-binary skaters this can include internalizing negative attitudes and a lack of external acceptance, but this also sometimes prompts them to construct their own cultural frameworks and sense of validity on their terms.

In contrast, the men in their stories of "becoming skateboarders" often display an awareness of various privileges and relationships to power that they could more strongly access because of their gender and comparative dominance. However, alongside gender hierarchies, people we interviewed of all genders, including men, also reflected on points of intersectionality (Crenshaw 1991) that can compound forms of disempowerment some skaters face, such as colonialism, racism, discrimination against sexuality, and disability.

The conversations ahead demonstrate examples of both "ethical reflexivity" (Plage et al. 2017), which we will also expand on a discussion of cosmopolitanism in a later section, and "complicit reflexivity" (Sharp and Threadgold 2020). The process of reflexivity typically refers to a self-evaluation process that can lead to ethical action, recognition, and accountability (Bourdieu and Wacquant 1992; Plage et al. 2017) whereas "complicit reflexivity" (Sharp and Threadgold 2020: 613) entails a process that rests upon and is resigned to "performative" levels of support that are superficial. This can include an evasive and "paternalistic passivity where some men can identify acts of symbolic violence which they then attribute to a performance of masculinity set apart from their own" (Sharp and Threadgold 2020: 613).

In instances of "complicit reflexivity," individuals are "reflexive about the gender-related problems in the scene, but did little to address or resolve them" (Sharp and Threadgold 2020: 613). Megan Sharp and Steven Threadgold (2020: 618) provide two useful examples to further illustrate the difference between complicit reflexivity that holds the belief, "it is what it is" and the more ethical action-focused orientation of, "it is not what it could be." The latter is perhaps best described as a form of "ethical reflexivity" that is both aware of things like injustice and action-orientated.

Ethical reflexivity is, we propose, a necessary process for being a change-maker in skateboarding. However, rather than place a hard line and propose people are either complicit or ethical, we feel reflexivity can be "flexible," drawing insights from other studies that observe participation in skate culture is rarely a binary experience, noting things such as how skaters are able to be both "core" to "consumer" (Dupont 2014) and enact "flexible opposition" (Dinces 2011).

We also propose that while "non-traditional" skaters may sometimes be complicit or internalize gendered expectations, they are also capable of developing and enacting forms of "defiance labor" (Sharp and Threadgold

2020) in their journeys as skateboarders, which builds on Hoschild's (1979) concept of "emotional labor." According to Sharp and Threadgold's (2020: 618) definition, defiance labor is:

> Situational confrontational moments where the complicity of symbolic violence is reflexively defied through reactions, responses, and actions, whether in situations of paid work or in general social situations. This distinction is important as 'work' in a DIY scene is often unpaid. Defiance labour differs from emotional labour as it is not about placating, educating, or managing discomfort, but creating discomfort to deliberately provoke offense and resist forms of gendered marginality from men.

Such labor is a way of navigating and challenging various forms of exclusion and "symbolic violence" (Bourdieu 1994, 2002). In punk music scenes women for example are observed to feel pressure to conform to emotional labor that entails a "type of expectation to perform femininity, to smile, be accommodating and look more like she is having fun" (Sharp and Threadgold 2020: 617). Symbolic violence in subcultures can include "microaggressions, dismissal and erasure" (609) that are embedded in "cultural logics of masculinity" (610) which privileges male knowledge, presence, and competence as superior. These ideas, we propose, are useful to the study of power and social change in skateboarding, including how "non-traditional" skateboarders can grapple with responding to people who are hostile toward their presence and sense of identity and place within the culture.

Becoming a "Skateboarder" and Early Social Barriers

An evocative saying in the world of skaters is, "Skateboarding doesn't make you a skateboarder. Not being able to stop skateboarding makes you a skateboarder" (attributed to Lance Mountain in Cutting Stone 2013). We have heard a range of similar sentiments and phrases across our time as skaters, including "skate every damn day," "skate and destroy," and "skate or die." The underlying principle behind such catch-cries often imbued with an unspoken alignment with masculinity is that to be a "skateboarder" one must be deeply immersed in that identity, and whose skateboarding habits are addictive, obsessive, and potentially destructive. Some of this indeed resonates if we think about the difficulties involved with mastering tricks, as many require persistent and regular practice through many kinds of injuries and frustrations. To be "good" at skateboarding requires commitment. Yet it is also important to emphasize that being "good" at skateboarding is not the only "criteria" for what makes someone a skateboarder.

The stories of becoming a skateboarder shared by the people we interviewed commonly involve themes of being an intriguing discovery, mostly through the encouragement of friends and relatives. After gaining access to their own skateboards, many also appeared to be "hooked" by (1) an ability to have fun and that the physical aspects of it make them feel good, despite how "good" they are at it, (2) felt inspired by the ability to progress and get tricks and hard work rewarded, and (3) that it was somehow a good fit with their sense of self, lifestyle, and outlooks.

However, certain barriers and forms of gatekeeping for some stood in the way of them feeling immediately recognized and accepted as a skateboarder including (1) gender stereotypes, (2) gendered expectations, (3) exclusion or token recognition only, and (4) not feeling actively welcomed due to being minorities and marginalized. These barriers were also not static and seemed to shift and alter across generations, and environments such as between cities with established skate scenes and smaller or more isolated locations. We now provide some examples ahead.

Men's Experiences of Becoming Skateboarders

Tommy Guerro, who is an innovator from an earlier generation of Californian street skaters, for instance, emphasizes that it was the sense of fun rather than wanting to belong to any scene that inspired him, explaining "I started skating in 75. In San Francisco. …A friend gave me a board with steel wheels. And I lived on a hill. It was super fun. .. And that's just where it really all began." Apart from skating with his brother, he recalls "It was very rare to see anyone else on the street with a skateboard."

Guerro is also an influential figure in street skateboarding as an original member of *The Bones Brigade*. But alongside introducing a style and tricks, he was also pushing against more hegemonic aspects of the culture and taking a stance against issues such as racism:

> In the 1989 skateboard video *Ban This*, Tommy Guerrero—of Chilean, Filipino, and Ohlone Native descent—rides through the streets of San Francisco on a board with "END RACISM" written on it. The image of Guerrero proudly displaying the board reemerged on social media amid the *Black Lives Matter* protests of 2020. (Gutierrez 2021)

Alec Beck's story of growing up skating in the 1990s in California belongs to an era after the first wave of vert and early street skating, and with the popularity of teams like *The Bones Brigade* firmly established. Through Beck's youthful eyes, skateboarding was an open-ended world of discovery for him when he first started. He states for instance, "I discovered a *Teenage Mutant Ninja Turtle* skateboard in my uncle's garage and started just kind of messing around. After a couple of hours, I realized that I could manipulate it the way I wanted to. It was doing what I wanted to do for the most part and that really got me hooked."

Feelings of independence were also attractive for skaters like Beck, which he describes as, "nobody was telling me what to do. And for whatever reason, it seemed like it was incredibly important to me to a little 10-year-old mind at the time." Later on, he found that "The purposefulness I felt with the skateboard was magnified…with a skateboard, you feel free, and like kind of an artist…because you're allowed to do whatever you want. It's all about freedom of expression." At the same time, he saw how precarious the activity sometimes could be if the spaces to skate were taken away. This includes the skatepark he went to at this time one day closing down, which influenced his activism later on with *The Skatepark Project*.

The journey of Adam Abada, who started in New Jersey in 1999 with a male friend who he still skates today, covers similar stages of joyful discovery and freedom, a taste of mastering tricks, and a desire for progression. He states, "I don't really remember how long it took, but once I was skating the curb outside pretty solidly and with conviction, I had a distinct epiphany where I was like, I can just go do this! I can just go skate." He adds "Honestly, it became kind of my identity pretty fast." Kevin Pacella, who started in 2003 in Wilmington, Delaware, also recalls he and a relative, "picked up these skateboards one day and just started fucking around on it. After riding around on them for a few days I knew I loved the feeling and wanted to progress and get better."

Despite skateboarding giving the men skateboarders we spoke with a sense of individual freedom, some describe that a social ladder and hierarchy could nevertheless exist among boys and men. Chicago-based Kyle Beachy explains, "I don't think it ever was utopian for us. I think from the get-go for me it was a place of great hierarchy and pressure…which is not to say that I felt in any way disempowered, or in any way subjugated. But I certainly never saw skateboarding at that age, as a sort of utopian escape from the otherwise kinds of social rigors in high school." Beachy adds that when his world expanded to skating with not just his friends, but others in his city, something that stood out was the:

> Unspoken sort of power dynamics…Now our crew has to slot into this city-wide hierarchy and we're way the fuck down here at the bottom, you know where the like suburban kids who have been all in skateboards and these guys have been going downtown and grinding and doing handrails, so like that it was always pretty clear to me, or it was always pretty much part of my experience of skateboarding that there was a real sort of pecking order.

The dominance of masculine hierarchies in skateboarding around the 1990s and first decade of the 2000s was something our interviewees often talked about being aware of and navigating, but not intentionally perpetuating. Only one of the men we interviewed, Brennan Hatton, felt fully resistant to the idea of becoming "a skateboarder" in his youth because of the aggressive masculine image and negative connotations it had for him. Hatton is from Australia but spent much of his young adulthood in "Silicon Valley" and Californian cities in the US where he works regularly with his VR business that designs empathy experiences. He recalls always having and riding on skateboards but, "I didn't consider myself a skateboarder, it was just a part of my life." He further explains,

"I think that was also very intentional to not think of myself as a skate-boarder…I saw it as intimidating."

Hatton describes that he originally felt, "like it's just not a welcoming culture. I did try to sort of like, be part of the skate culture but skate parks are a very intimidating place. I've never felt comfortable with a skate park." To this, he also adds, "I think there's a lot of, you know, internal and external thinking, where it's like, how much of that was just me ver-sus how much of that was the culture itself and I think those two things really go hand in hand."

Men who felt their earliest experiences of skateboarding were not intensely hindered by social pressures tended to have grown up outside of major cities in areas and away from large established skate scenes. Ryan Lay for instance grew up in Arizona and was introduced by a family member to skateboarding in the late 1990s. He states, "I think we weren't totally aware of the kind of cultural element of skating. We just kind of went and did it and then played roller hockey." Lay would soon become sponsored and thrown into the thick of a highly masculine skateboarding culture, going on skate tours with men who were professional skaters. However, he describes enjoying the lack of peer pressure in his earlier days where he was just able to enjoy the activity rather than question how he fitted in and states, "I think there was just the one [skatepark], maybe a 45-minute drive from me. so I didn't grow up skating skateparks." He explained, "I was a very naive and kind of suburban kid."

As Lay's skills increased he started skating in the city of Phoenix and was invited to go on tours, where he remembers "going on trips and skaters were smoking weed, and I was just not really into it." He explains that it was at times confronting and not alluring for him because "I didn't touch drugs or alcohol because I had some family members that had substance abuse issues." He adds, "I think with people who start to get in the sponsored path, and on trips, you see a lot of people who don't function well" but also that in a more positive sense, "it was an awakening. You know, you start to really encounter different things and people."

Lay as a young adult would later go on to become a professional skate-boarder with a range of sponsors and stood out for breaking stereotypical masculinity associated with "core" skating. For instance, he was openly critical of where the skate industry needed to do better in terms of fair pay, health insurance, and other things that are more regulated and come with more protections in other industries (Lay 2019). He also often talks about social issues like his brother's struggle with addiction, the need for skateboarders to humanize homeless and unhoused people and not exploit them as "exotic" characters in skate videos filmed where they are present, being a vegan, founding a non-profit *Skate After School* and doing work for overseas skate projects like *Skate Pal*. At the same time, he displays an effort to be aware of his privilege as a White male. In an interview with Nic Dobija-Nootens (2015) in *Jenkem Mag* for instance when asked about the broad range of individuals in skating he states:

> That's the thing I love about skateboarding. There are people in skateboarding whose views and backgrounds differ from mine, but I appreciate that they're a part of it because that's what keeps skating so diverse and not just some homogenized bullshit. More opinions, more girls, more homosexuality, more global representation. All different types of kids appreciate and love skating. The role models available to them, however, aren't incredibly diverse. And I realize the paradox, speaking as a skinny White guy.

Thomas Barker is also someone whose story includes going from a quiet town and being "airdropped" into the center of skate culture, and in this case, its industry. Barker started skating in a semi-regional town, his journey to becoming an insider was faster due to his father's industry involvement where "My family during that time period started this backpack company called *Clive*, which was a skateboarding backpack company. And so I started going to trade shows when I was 12." One of the results was "For the most part, you're thrust into the structure of skateboarding a lot earlier than a lot of people." His going to Encinitas YMCA California was also a formative experience where, "I went from thinking I was a kid from the middle of nowhere, to being in the heart of skateboarding overnight." For instance, his early memories for him include seeing Tony Hawk on his first day there.

Barker had a range of enviable opportunities as a young skateboarder, including the ability to give away free *Clive* backpacks, go to industry trade shows, and skate premiers, and having a budget to spend on skateboarding. He explains he had many friends who were well-known skaters and that he was also able to work with Blackbox which oversaw popular brands. He describes this period as:

> I was thrust into all that is possible. We left no stone unturned, we went to every premiere, took every opportunity, and lived that life. But this goes into what pushed me towards *CSEF* in the end. I basically stopped going to school as soon as I could drive because I was working full-time for a skateboard company. I was living the dream at the height of the boom of the late 90s, and early 2000s which did not last. I thought, 'Why would I ever need school for anything? I have this skateboarding life, I can live just like this'. (Barker from his interview)

Barker explains that a recession across the US then followed and the skateboarding industry was also affected. This was a pivotal moment for him, as he thought he was going to work for skate companies for the rest of his life but the money and jobs in the skate industry began to disappear. He reveals, "I never had a plan B or anything…within a few months most of the 'lifers' got let go because they can't afford any of us anymore." Faced with having to reinvent his career and with a concern for his community, he states, "So that's when my journey of nonprofits and giving back began. My lens had been so focused on skateboarding, but that's when the lens moved."

Douglas Miles Jr. is from the Apache Nation and grew up in San Carlos Reservation, Arizona, with his father Douglas Miles Sr. who started *Apache Skateboards* when his son wanted boards to skate and blank decks that were easier to access. Instead of copying existing styles, Miles Sr. decorated the board with his own art. Miles Jr. was raised with a specific outlook of innovation rather than replication, Indigenous culture, and influences from art, films, and music rather than pressure to conform to the "core" the skateboarding industry, which mostly ignored First Nations skaters.

Douglas Miles Jr. states his early skate experience were shaped by fun and joy, which contrasts with many skaters who were only exposed to White masculine culture normalized in "core" skate culture. He states that "I was always just having fun with it, with the homies, and anyone who was skating." He also was able to travel on tours growing up, but with a very different experience to Lay's. Miles Jr. traveled across the US with his father Douglas Miles Sr. who would combine his art tours with demonstrations by their *Apache Skateboards* team. He states, "the things that really influenced me were other artists, people who did art, or people who were creating things…we always admired people who were creating stuff that was cool."

Miles Jr. also emphasizes the progressive elements and innovative messages that were involved with going on tour with *Apache Skateboard*. He describes how his father Miles Sr. "would turn up to his art exhibitions and bring the skate crew with him, and people would freak out or the people would be very surprised, like 'why are you doing this?' And he would explain, 'because skateboarding is the art!'. Having those sorts of opportunities to meet a lot of artists. It's really cool."

Recalling his early experiences, Miles Jr. also outlines how these were not shaped by non-Native skateboarders but rather by fine artists, muralists, graffiti, and street artists at San Carlos and ones his family and team met on invited tours. He states, "I grew up in galleries all across the nation. I love skateboarding and I look up to a number of skateboarders too, but I really liked picking up on what the artists did." Miles Jr. explains, "People were looking at them at the art shows and they were revered for what they were doing and the reasons they were doing things." Moreover, he felt these artists "were doing something positive with their art, some of them had messages in their art. Then I started putting shit in my art—messages in mind, like being positive about skateboarding culture."

For the men we spoke to in urban and closer suburban areas on the East Coast, skateboarding was described as being easier to embrace into their overall identity and lifestyles due to them having access to other creative scenes and people they felt an affinity. Patrick Kigongo explains that as a Black skater, he has to navigate how racialized differences can make him experience skating in very different ways from his White peers. He nevertheless feels he has always found a place in skating. He started in his early teenage years and remembers, "I started playing electric guitar around the same time that I got my first skateboard. And because at the time skateboarding, punk rock and subcultures were still very, very intertwined. Especially in the suburbs, the two kind of went hand in hand. So yeah, that's when I actually started getting into street skating."

Patrick Kigongo explains that skating "does teach a certain amount of socialization and it definitely teaches you to become comfortable with approaching people and making new friends very quickly." At the same time, he throws light on barriers for some, explaining "the thing I've learned as I've gotten older, is that because skateboarding up until very recently—let's say 60-year history—was very much a heteronormative male-dominated space, the assumption of being able to go and approach people and say, 'Hey, what's up? Y'all trying to go session this curb?', there's a certain amount of privilege in being able to approach people like that without necessarily fearing for your safety."

Keegan Guizard spent his earlier years skating in North Carolina before moving to California and while he describes being able to embrace skateboarding as a central part of his lifestyle, he was also being reflexive about some of the privileges men skaters experience. When growing up skating he felt, "I don't remember ever being made fun of or put down or if I did, I just didn't give a fuck." Yet he also expresses a sense of awareness and reflection around how "I tried to fully acknowledge that privilege that I have. I think that privilege is part of the reason why I can be dismissive. Not everyone has that."

Timothy Ward, who grew up skating in Geneva, Illinois, and also works at *Skate After School* also expresses a similar sense of awareness of not everyone being able to embrace skateboarding with an equal level of social comfort. He now lives in Arizona but across his years of skating different scenes, he states, "I don't face many social hurdles to skateboarding other than some strange social media comments about my weight and size but those are usually expressed as compliments or at least they're intended to be compliments." In the next section, we will explore women and non-binary individuals' early and formative experiences of becoming skateboarders where we begin to get more insight into the various social hurdles they faced that the men above state they are aware of and critically reflect upon.

Women and Non-binary Individuals' Experiences of Becoming Skateboarders

For the women and non-binary people we interviewed the journey was a similar one of exciting discovery, often through a male friend or relative, and skateboarding having the main appeals of being fun, physically challenging, and rewarding in ways that could also be social and connected to a sense of identity. However, many described being in the minority in the skate scenes they started out in, and the younger generation more commonly described how they did not automatically feel they were able to build a strong sense of identity and belonging.

Typical issues included their being judged on their skills in comparison to men skaters, being sexually objectified, and some internalizing negative attitudes and feeling a sense of impersonator syndrome. At the same time, these frustrations and doubts co-exist and are challenged by their constructing their own sense of worth, authenticity, and interpretations of what it is to be a skateboarder on their own terms.

Interestingly, women from older generations tended to describe their journey into becoming skateboarders as one they could embrace without strong resistance by men skating alongside them in teams and competitions. For instance, Cindy Whitehead describes the skate culture for her, especially in California, as generally accepting. She states, "In the 70s to mid-70s when things were just really getting started, people were still just figuring it out. It was kind of like it is in other countries right now, right? Nobody knows what they're doing, everybody's learning, so nobody knows if it's a boys or girls sport or non-binary sport, or if you're straight, gay, or if you're queer." She also feels that in terms of girls and women, skate cultures where skateboarding is newly introduced, "It doesn't matter, everyone's figuring it out, and having fun, and that's how it was for us, that's the way I saw it."

However, in the past, it was not unusual for professional women to be lone figures among men in competition and demonstration spaces. Whitehead, who skated ramps, pools, and bowls, explains that "I'm very much one of those people who doesn't see a lot of negativity around me unless somebody says it directly to me and then I confront it. So, if there were slurs, if there were things said and I'm sure they were like I blocked a lot of it out. I'd wear headphones." She continues "I had ways of dealing with stuff but usually those comments were more sexual in nature…I wasn't hearing like you shouldn't be skating you're a girl. I was hearing, 'Oh nice ass' and those sorts of things." And the harassment was not typically from other skaters but onlookers who were men standing behind the barriers or watching her on the ramp in competitions. Whitehead explained she tried not to be "focusing on something that didn't need to be when I was focusing on skating. Like when you started going into vert and things got a little more gnarly, with pools and vert and everything, which is what I love to do."

Peggy Oki also became a skateboarder when what it meant as an identity and lifestyle was not exclusively attached to masculinity. She describes her attitude when she was younger as, "I was just doing what I wanted to do—the way I wanted to skate and skate stuff with the guys. We had found the banks that were skateable at the schools and we really loved that type of skating." She also describes her journey into becoming a skater as having a lot of freedom, "I didn't see myself trying to outdo anyone, I was trying to have fun rather than really trying to make any kind of impression on anybody. I was just being me."

Although Oki rode with a team dominated by men, she was able to compete with other women in flat ground freestyle competitions. However, she felt her unconventional style as a skater did make her different in the competition space. She pinpoints it to just a lack of imagination about what was possible for them, "I believe it because the girls at that time were still in that old paradigm of doing tricks but also wearing skirts and no shoes." Oki adds, "Being in more feminine girls roles versus me who was there with my Levi's jeans and my Vans shoes and team t-shirt and just like the rest of the guys on the team. They may have felt intimidated seeing me in that way." Her style was also seen as "nonfeminine." She adds "I was a really good skater at that time compared to what the other girls were doing." At the same time she states, "I don't recall directing any negativity towards the girls but you know, I was part of the team and we did have an attitude of like,' yeah, here we are. We're doing this different kind of style'… I was fine with that. I thought it was pretty cool."

Younger skateboarders from following generations who were not men and would go on to being sponsored and skating in elite competitions found attitudes from men skateboarders more of a challenge. Like their predecessors, these women and non-binary skaters are gifted athletes and dedicated to advancing their skills. However, for many from the 1990s onwards, it appears that forms of "hyper-" and "hegemonic" masculinity (Connell 1995) in skateboarding became more intensified, especially in how the industry and media promoted it. In contrast, women were rarely recognized, and many were pressured to be "conventionally attractive" through a heteronormative lens and male gaze that privileged "emphasized femininity" (Abulhawa 2020; Connell 1995) which is positioned as submissive and sexualized, while "hegemonic masculinity" is associated with strength, risk, and bravery.

For instance, Alex White first started skateboarding in 1994 when she asked her parents for a skateboard but they bought one that she did not like due to her wanting to do more tricks like street skaters she looked up to. She states, "My dad got me a board, got me a 'Dogtown' board and it had this big tattoo-looking graphic with a cross on it and I'm like, 'I don't want this,' so I took it back…for a Willy Santos board."

White's journey into becoming a skateboarder also fell at a pivotal time for street skating, where she "grew up in Los Angeles, skateboarding was getting into this kind of boom in the mid-'90s. I went to elementary school and middle school with Jonah Hill, and he later made a movie about our childhood basically." When we mentioned that the fictionalized film *Mid90s* by Hill (2018) which depicted the skateboarding culture he grew up with lacked girl skaters, White highlighted how it was still rare. At the same time, she states that it made her even more committed, replying "I immediately got really hooked on it, it was popular at my school, but none of the no girls were doing it so I liked it even more because, I don't know, I like to be weird."

The process of first stepping on a board and learning was for Alex White also a time of isolation rather than learning with a crew. She recalls, "I think in my preteen and prepubescent eras I didn't have any concept of like community around it, it was alone in my driveway or with my friend on the street…I didn't really find my tribe until I moved from Los Angeles to Monterey." It was then that she felt "skateboarding was then my entryway into friends and community at the high school level. I met up with this group of kids, they were all there was an indoor skate park here which is pretty rare now for California…I was just there all the time I had my group we were skating constantly. We got cameras and started filming and then like our whole life is just consumed with making videos."

White describes how they would also try and get sponsored from these videos, where "we all be down the VHS is and then like at 16 or 17 years old, we would go to ASR (Action Sports Retailer) trade show and like have 11 VHS tapes and hand them to our favorite brands and get ignored, I got ignored by everybody," she said while laughing. White further explains, "I kind of feel like in that era of skateboarding, it was the spectacle era, it was X Games and 'vert ramp men' doing 900s, and like girls can do this, but it was more the spectacle era." Moving to the present she feels that, "now we're getting into, like, the gender equity era and the community era but that past era was just like, you know, stupid, big time."

Despite White being comfortable calling herself a skateboarder, and joined by more women skaters in the late 1990s, she is critical of how the skate industry was biased toward women who fit in with and could perform a type of "emphasized femininity" (Abulhawa 2020; Connell 1995). White states, "I felt like I had opportunities, but also I was constantly reminded of what my place was as a girl skater. I would be a token." She also felt resistant to conforming to the type of girls and women the industry wanted to promote, and that, "1999 to 2007 was like this renaissance of women's skating. It was very women-specific but it was very hetero normative. Women needed to have very long hair. It was like that in a big way, and tied into heteronormative likeability." For White, she remembers "keeping my hair long, like it was a really important thing, and that's why I was on Roxy."

She also reveals how, "I remember sitting with dudes and they were being like, 'Oh, the Brazilians…man you've got to see this girl and literally we would be judged by a bar of like, are we fuckable or not? Do we look like a lesbian?" White also states that "The only person I could see reflected back to me was Elissa Steamer at the time, Jaime Reyes too, to a degree but Elissa was more visible in my world at that point. And, like, the industry was like if I'm lucky, I might be the token girl on one of these teams." She adds in frustration, "they've ignored skaters like Vanessa

Torres and Amy Caron, you know, some of the best skateboarders of my generation, my wave."

Kristin Ebeling is part of a newer generation but collaborates and works with Alex White on numerous projects and programs that aim to empower women and non-binary as well as LGBTQIA+ skaters. Ebeling states, "I started skating when I was 12, so I think I got my skateboard like Christmas of 2000. But prior to that. I was like the super jock, girl, and during recess I played football with the boys. I tried to fit in with girls but was bullied a lot." For her, skateboarding was something she became good at quickly, "because I was really good at sports and athletics and I'd snowboarded before… the first summer that I was scared but then I learned how to kickflip, drop in and rock fakie and all that shit." She adds that it was, "after that point, I was going down to the skatepark every single day."

Gender became an issue in adolescence for Ebeling where, "in eighth grade, that's when all the guys at the skatepark, and myself started going through puberty. So that was when things sort of started to turn all of a sudden I was like skateboarding in the beginning, made me feel like I was genderless I was just one of the dudes." Then "within a matter of like a year and a half, guys started calling me JLo because my butt was big." Upon getting sponsored "I remember dudes DMing me being like 'fuck you, you're only sponsored because you're a girl and 'you're such a fucking poser' and harassing me." Ebeling also revealed she then struggled, "for the first five years of my skateboarding, I was like literally don't look at me like a girl. I just want to fit in. And that was how I survived. I had so much internalized sexism." She adds, "I was like what the fuck like, why am I the only girl here, it is so annoying and if I am the only girl I'm gonna wear pants…smoke cigarettes to, and try to fit in. I just wanted to so badly. I just wanted skateboarding to accept me." This was during her middle school years, and then she skated alone.

Toward the end of high school, she states, "it was still fucked up because a couple of guys who were friends of mine helped me make a sponsor me a tape. I submitted it to a sponsor only to be told that I was not pretty enough to ride for the team." This echoes the critique of White who highlighted that men running the industry judged the worth of girls and women on their looks and appeal to a heterosexual gaze rather than their skateboarding, lifestyle, and personalities.

Other barriers that women and non-binary skaters faced included that boys and men firmly believed other genders could not skate well and ranked their styles and trick choices as inferior. Amelia Brodka, whose documentary *Underexposed* featured many of the top women across the history of skateboarding, is another sponsored skater we spoke with. She is also a major figure in its competition scene, including her representing Poland in the Tokyo *Olympic Games*. Brodka started skating when she was 12 years old in 2001, being introduced to it through a male relative, which was common among the skaters we spoke with. She states, "First time I saw a skateboard was my brother's a few years prior to when I started skating. I had never seen a skateboard before. He would just ride around…It just looked fun."

Unlike the boys and men skaters she knew, she was judged due to her gender. She claims, "To this day, I still remember the sidewalk rushing past my face and the wind in my hair and all that, and then the next thing I remember is my brother abruptly taking it from me and telling me that I can't use his skateboard because I don't do it right, I didn't know how." But rather than discouraging her, like White, she felt defiant and more determined explaining, "And that's kind of what sparked it" referring to her journey to becoming a dedicated skateboarder.

In her teenage high school years, despite being good at skateboarding she was not easily accepted by boys who dominated the scene. Brodka states, "I so badly wanted to be friends with the skate crew. I tried to dress the part but instead of being accepted I was called a 'poser' when I showed up to school in an Etnies or Spitfire shirt. It hurt my soul because I just wanted to be friends with the other skaters." To try and prove worthy of acceptance Brodka "thought that if I learned a bunch of tricks that they would allow me to skate with them or to at least consider me a fellow skater. A few months later, I showed them that I learned 360 flips. None of them were able to do those at the time." Rather than being accepted, Brodka reveals "their response was—'well you must be a dude because there is no way that a girl could do a 360 flip' and laughed at me. I felt like I couldn't do anything right, I just wanted to belong." It is important to note however that none of the professional and sponsored women skateboarders we interviewed doubted their skills, and all became more determined to keep skating. Moreover, they would go on to win competitions, start their own, get sponsored, and take up roles in the industry such as brand managers.

Discrimination against women and non-binary skaters also included a range of microaggressions and exclusions in everyday settings, as experienced by many of the women we spoke with who skated for leisure rather than having the goals to get sponsored or win competitions. An interesting effect included a reflexive process where they would also isolate themselves or not take up space in spots like skateparks because they felt their skills were inferior, and because they internalized negative beliefs about non-men skaters. In other words, self-doubts also acted as barriers. Kim Woozy used a skateboard as a child but was more dedicated to skating in college where, "I was like I'm gonna learn to skate, and then the first people I saw were other students on campus who were skaters." However, she still found "it was still the disconnect, as it was all guys so I never saw a girl doing tricks or anything like that." She adds, "it occurred to me, that's very hard, and I don't know how I can try to achieve that. But I admired it for sure."

Most skate locations were described by non-professional women and non-binary skaters as male-dominated and that could be intimidating. For instance, in the 2000s Woozy convinced a woman friend who surfed to go visit a skatepark, and she recalls, "we just showed up, we're like, oh my god like we're so out of place like everyone's so good, everyone was ripping." Woozy adds, "It was super intimidating and we just went in the corner…then we left because it was like, I don't know about this. I don't think we're really a part of this and this is too far beyond our skill level." Later when Woozy started at the *Osiris* shoe company "I think immediately I knew that I was on the outside because I couldn't do tricks…it was very much a separation." Compounding the issue was that the men skaters did not help welcome women into the scene. She states:

> It wasn't like 'hey, can come with us to the, you know warehouse while we skate and we'll teach you and over time you can become a good skateboarder', it wasn't really like that. It was just like you're either cool you're

not, there was definitely a wall, you're either in or you're out. (Woozy in our interview)

The pattern of skateboarding away from where men skaters dominate the space was common among women and non-binary skateboarders who also felt factors such as their age or body shape might make them stand out. This includes Bethany Geckle who reveals:

> I was embarrassed and felt so much older than most people when they start skating, and also felt like I would be more scrutinized as a woman and overweight person, so I mostly practiced skating at home in my garage, with my friend in the parking lot of the campus arboretum on Friday/ Saturday night when it would be empty and isolated while everyone was partying downtown, in my dorm room, and…in the middle of the night after everyone had left.

Adrian Koenisberg started in 2009 and stopped for a while after she reached her teenage years and boys stopped skating with her. But being physically distanced from skating did not mean she did not still try to connect with the culture and feel connected to it. She explains that "basically I would always buy all the Transworld and surf and skate magazines because I loved graphic design. But there were no women in any of those magazines." Although she found other women to skate with, she remained frustrated with the lack of their representation in skateboarding and eventually started *Quell Magazine*.

Denia Kopita who started in 2016 also found that "I didn't know anyone who skated. I didn't have any friends who skated and there were not any parks near me. I stopped because I didn't know anyone who was doing it." She still wanted to stay connected and spoke about watching videos on how to skate on the Internet such as via *YouTube* and following skate platforms on social media. Then "years later, I was like cool, I want to do it again. I started with my friend and it kind of just went from there." Kopita described joining an inclusive and supportive skate scene, plus also volunteering to teach with *Free Movement Skateboarding* where she is able to introduce girls to skateboarding and build their own sense of community. She would also eventually start working as an editor with

Skateism where she is able to share the stories of numerous non-traditional skateboarders.

Izzi Cooper also began to skate around 2016. She states, "I was 16 years old when I started skateboarding. I began skating in the next town over from where I live. A high school male friend of mine who liked me gifted me his used skateboard…It was because of a man that I was introduced to skateboarding." She feels that fortunately for her, "I only was introduced to more diverse skate communities a few months into skating, but before then, I had no idea they existed. I remember being so surprised and intrigued when I first saw two non-male skaters. I ended up idolizing them and we soon became friends." Cooper has keenly embraced the support around her, creating her DIY *Heal Flip* zine that looks at social justice issues in skateboarding, and she also volunteers at *Skate Like a Girl*.

The women and non-binary skateboarders we spoke to who are from a newer generation benefit from the work of forerunners, who have opened up various doors to better welcome skateboarders of all genders into skateboarding. And all of the skaters we interviewed, regardless of age, felt they have benefited from such an inheritance. But they also drew attention to other issues that could intersect and hinder their early journeys to becoming skateboarders and making a space for themselves and others. This includes how forms of ableism can create barriers for skateboarders.

For instance, within masculine interpretations of skateboarding were things such as normalized catch cries to always "send it" and "skate every day" that one interviewee, "Mara" (who requested not to use her last name), emphasized is an example of how that culture is also ableist. Mara is one of the co-founders of the *Doyenne Skateboards* brand that raises funds for a range of skate social projects including disability-focused ones. She also has a personal connection to disability. She describes her journey to becoming a skateboarder as "kind of different because I suffer chronic pain and spinal disorders … I've lived all my life with these conditions. I have a very difficult relationship with skating, which is so hard." She adds, "when you kind of grow up with these problems, you feel very limited and you feel your body is very fragile, and think about all the limitations that you have." However, she also explains that "I have always wanted to skate. I always want to know everything about skateboarding.

It was just a very different time. I was like 23 or 24. I decided 'I'll just buy his skateboard and just like you know skate around. I'm not gonna do any tricks. And, yeah, and then when I started, I didn't realize how much I loved it and how much freedom I felt."

Bäckström (2013) notes that studies of skateboarding and feminism tend to ignore overlapping issues that also impact power relationships, such as class, race, ethnicity, sexuality, and disability and that academics can also be racially homogenous (with exceptions such as Abulhawa 2020; Ahmad and Thorpe 2020; Garcia Marquez 2020; Weaver 2016; Willing and Shearer 2016). Emerging attention to multiple rather than singular biases in society that shape relations of power in skateboarding owes much to theoretical work on intersectionality which Crenshaw (1991) developed to understand things like class, gender, sexuality, and other things that contributed to Black women's disempowerment along-side being marginalized from being racialized.

For example, non-traditional skaters who are Black reveal they not only grappled with feeling intimidated from being the only beginners, but also as a racialized minority in skate spaces. Karlie Thornton of *froSkate* went to her first skatepark at an indoor event for *Vans*. She recalls, "so like they're all around like 'pro-level type vibe' of skateboarders. When I stepped in, and this is maybe my second or third day on a skateboard, I barely knew how to stand on it. And they're like, just zooming past." She describes how "They know what they're doing. They're focused on their tricks. And you know, when you're at the skatepark, and you see people with that kind of focus, they look kind of mean or not the friendliest." She adds that once she got more into skateboarding she understood and that, "I was obviously like in my own head too" but that, "oftentimes, I was still very scared and intimidated by all of the men skating around me. So naturally, I wanted to make space for people who look like me and more beginner-level people, and that's why I created *froSkate*."

Thornton also mentions that most of the time it was White men who dominated the space, which for her felt "like not only am I scared by everyone's level but there's also this innate kind of discomfort of just not really seeing myself in this space…that's obviously not going to make someone feel fully like fully comfortable." She emphasizes "And that's not their fault. It's just like how I was feeling. They weren't like, 'you're Black, you don't belong' but more…We've always been Black women. And so like, always our entire lives, we are bending the rules in these types of spaces, where we don't really see ourselves."

L Brew, also from *froSkate*, feels that as a Black skater, "I often find myself feeling as though I've got to prove myself worthy. Since we're representing and amplifying demographics of skaters that have often been overlooked, there's an extra sort of pressure to be perfect." They add that "BIPOC and Queer skaters come few and far between, and it can sometimes make me feel like I've got to be the best of the best in order to represent my people well. That's a lot of pressure in general and reflects how BIPOC folks must work twice, if not three times, as hard to be seen, respected, or have the same opportunities as our white counterparts." They also reveal that they "lived in a very suburban white neighborhood…There weren't skateboarders around in general." They add, "So there was a combination of being the loud, disruptive skater on the sidewalk, while also being a Black girl, and generally one of the few Black people in town."

Another isolating factor for L Brew was also their being a minority because of their gender. As a result, they felt they "definitely had an isolated start, like in my driveway, garage or backyard." At the skatepark in the beginning L Brew also found, "had very uncomfortable experiences. Not only was I the only black girl, but I was also a beginner, completely alone and unfamiliar. I didn't really know what I was doing and felt embarrassed." They continue "I was eager to get better, but the stares and being ignored were discouraging, so I decided to leave parks alone and just skate by myself. That's what made me love street skating and long cruises."

Latosha Stone who founded *Proper Gnar* had similar experiences and concerns. "I didn't go to the skate park for like, a really long time. After I started skating like when I first started skating, I was super nervous so I would just do it around my block and on the street." She continues, "I didn't go to the skate park for a while…where I live in Ohio, it was like, all white people at the time." This was also the case at school and she adds, "I never knew any Black people that I wasn't related to until I got to high school. I was like, always the only Black person and then they always like, also the only girl so it was like two things I had going against me."

We also interviewed a number of women who were PoC, whose heritage included being first generation or children of immigrants, including skaters of Asian and Latin or Hispanic heritage. Such skateboarders were involved with projects that empowered these communities, such as Kim Woozy being an active participant and supporter of *Soy Sauce Nation* which focuses on Asian Americans in action sports. Norma Ibarra's work with the *UCanSkate* crew from Mexico. Ibarra's experience also offers insight to skateboarding in the US and other North American contexts like Canada as a PoC and first-generation immigrant from a non-English speaking background. She explains how in Mexico, "I used to see guys who kind of skateboards…but didn't feel like it was for me because my family's kind of very strict and in Mexico, there was only one skate shop. I didn't feel like it was for me but I always was captivated. I always wanted to try, but it took 31 years."

Ibarra spends a lot of her time in the US and reveals that "It took years for me to meet another Mexican woman who skated, and they're still not many. It was only in the last couple of years that I started to meet more people that speak Spanish that I connect culturally with." At the same time, Ibarra shares that "I'm a very extroverted person. I like making friends so I always tried to talk to everyone. I always felt however like there weren't that many people or immigrants or people of color."

While we have so far highlighted the external pressures or isolation skaters face, we also want to draw attention to an interesting, invisible process of internalized negative attitudes many skaters felt they had to overcome. The aim is to provide deeper insight into how they could sometimes be further isolated or be complicit in centering hegemonic masculinity as a result.

Internalizing Negative Attitudes

Skateboarding is not a blank canvas and can be inscribed with all kinds of informal rules and conventions that have a gendered dimension that is quite discernable in our interviews. And as Carr (2017: 28–29) argues, "it is difficult to state how much skateboarding remains an intensely masculine gendered activity or the profoundly imbricated nature of space and gender within skate culture." Men can also feel a sense of intimidation at skateparks and within the culture. But in this section, we focus on women and non-binary skaters' experiences to provide some insight into the stereotypes, pressures, and labels that they not only face but sometimes also internalize and reproduce.

Rhianon Bader for instance states that insults based on homophobia were common in skating, and that she "grew up at a time when it was still like, 'You're a tomboy' or 'You're gay' or this or that. Like, all my friends would use it and homophobic slurs." Women were also given a lower status, with Bader describing how "if you weren't going to do something, you're 'pussyfooting' or 'being a pussy'. And I definitely also said it. I didn't want to be seen as if I 'skate like a girl'. That kind of thing. It was a real thing."

Kristin Ebeling also reveals insights into some of the negative attitudes she would internalize. She states, "I had these toxic experiences as a young person, then in high school...I didn't realize how starved I was to fit in in skating, you know, and until you find your community, you're like holy shit, I didn't realize I was missing this. So, I just jumped all in." For Ebeling, this meant holding up an ideal and trying to embody an identity in skateboarding that boys and men created at the exclusion of other genders. She states, "I would say it took a while for me to let go of a lot of internalized sexism that I had because I would go to an inclusive themed meeting and I would say some fucked up shit."

Rather than helping her blend, Ebeling found that "the organizers that became like my mentors were like, 'Yo, like, that's not cool'! She continues that with *Skate Like a Girl*, "they fuckin educated me. Dude, I always say it was like I was raised by wolves. I had the *Lord of the Flies* experience as the only girl and that was a part fucked up experience." She further explains:

All of a sudden I entered this radical feminist intersectional organization. They educated me and through that experience of having people that actually cared about me, I could be myself...I didn't have to prove anything. I didn't have to go hard enough, I didn't have to be pretty enough. (Ebeling in our interview)

Latosha Stone's story also includes that while "I was like a pretty big tomboy growing up…I did internalize a lot of stuff." She explains one of the reasons why "you know like, you just kind of want to fit in with the group. Because you didn't want to be like at the end of those jokes and you just want to be like 'one of the guys. So yeah I did internalize a lot of that stuff when I was younger."

Amelia Brodka reflects on how negative stereotypes about women pushed her to skate in particular ways. She states, "It kind of feels like I have to prove myself sometimes, even though it doesn't really matter…I do think that throughout my life, yes. It always felt I have to kind of be like, 'I'll show you that I deserve to be here'." Even as an Olympian in the present-day she reveals she sometimes grapples with feeling imposter syndrome due. She states, "Throughout my life it has felt as though I constantly have to prove that I deserve to be here. Sometimes it feels like I don't deserve to be sponsored or have my name on a board or call myself an Olympian."

However, Brodka also proposes such internalization can and does shift. Asked about today's generation of young girls she feels, "it has definitely changed for the better. It does feel like this generation can't really relate to what it would feel like to not belong at the skatepark." For her, she also feels younger skaters have more confidence in the degree that, "I honestly don't think that girls coming up today can relate to needing to prove that they deserve to share the space at the skatepark or spot because of their gender." In her own competition, she also reflects on how:

At our Exposure X event we felt like we needed to remind the girls to appreciate how things are now. Because just a handful of years ago they would have been challenged at the skatepark just because of their gender. The girls coming up today don't have to have that experience. It's a reality we would have hoped for future generations to experience and it is wonderful to see it happening now. (Brodka in our interview)

For those who skate for leisure rather than at an elite level like Dani Abulhawa, different framing is created to balance out self-doubts on if they are an authentic skateboarder. She explains:

> Now I am almost accepting that I'm not a super good skateboarder. I'm not even moderately skilled. But that's not a reason to do it or not do it. It's like severing this, this attachment between being good at skateboarding and doing skateboarding and being good at skateboarding in regards to displaying masculine tropes and being good at skateboarding…I've really stopped, I think recently I've really stopped apologizing for myself. (Abulhawa in our interview)

Sarah Huston also describes how for her, "I think the hardest thing, like the thing that I probably struggle with in skateboarding most now is imposter syndrome. I've been skating for most of my life, but I've never been particularly I'm not great at it and I think it can be hard to separate your worthiness from your skill level in skateboarding." On the other hand, she makes space to validate what she does stating "I've earned my stripes," but "the fact that you have to earn your stripes and all of that sort of stuff that can be really difficult. I like it's a constant awareness now that I'm working within skateboarding. I'm hyper-aware." Like Brodka, she hopes it is a generational issue and that today's youth can leave self-doubts behind. She states, "I think there's a lot of self-reflection going on within skateboarding the landscape and maybe that's just part of how our generation is stuck with it a lot longer." Huston hopes, "there's actually that opportunity for reflection over almost like a whole generation almost. And obviously with that comes awareness, comes change."

Kaily Bayr Blackburn reflects on similar themes and resolutions. She states that she now faces "challenges that include the feeling that I don't belong in skateboarding." However, this process co-exists with how she and others have to battle "how some people project and try to gate-keep skateboarding. It is improving every day and I'm grateful for all the amazing people stepping up and making statements in the scene that 'skateboarding is for everyone'." She also expressed how she "can't wait for the day that people forget skaters used to be a**holes to each other."

Joy, Gratitude, Tenacity, and Resistance

Although the skateboarders we spoke with were reflexive about challenges people of various backgrounds can face, they were all enthusiastic to also share what they loved about skateboarding. Their discussions in our interviews included a range of personal benefits they feel is a result of their becoming skateboarders. Firstly, skateboarding was seen as offering a type of salvation or sanctuary to their lives by offering forms of fun and joy. Many described a need to escape or find forms of relief from a range of social issues that impacted their personal lives or social spaces. The gratitude they express was also from how skating assisted them to cope with and respond to needs related to their mental health. Secondly, many interviewees commented on being thankful for having tenacity due to how they built resilience from the physical sacrifices involved with skating, such as enduring pain and injury, and to keep being committed to acquiring skate tricks despite failures and frustrations. Thirdly, the discussions in our interviews included themes of resistance where skaters describe skating as giving them an outlet to be different from and resist elements of mainstream cultures.

Gratitude for the sanctuary skateboarding could offer is evident in Ashley Masters' story, which begins with her starting skating when she was around 11 years old. She states, "When I started using skateboarding, it was like more transportation. Then as I got older, it helped with just dealing with family and some being in and out of incarceration and detention centers. Like, Dad was an immigrant." For her "it was something that was really just healing and it was like a positive option for me to just go and escape. And feel some freedom and some joy." Skateboarding also appealed to her rebellious side:

I was already experimenting with my gender expression and in terms of how I express myself to the world. I already was kind of creating this narrative for my young self, and skateboarding to me felt right. It was just this sort of counterculture, right. And I was always that kid at a young age that wanted to try everything, especially if it was weird or different.

Alec Beck was thankful to how skateboarding complemented his mental health needs such as Obsessive Compulsive Disorder (OCD) and trauma care, which are often not discussed in skating or society due to being widely misunderstood or stigmatized. He states:

> I had a few personal issues. Skateboarding certainly helped me get through being diagnosed with OCD and the related anxiety. I was somehow able to channel that energy into performance cues for skateboarding. One of my compulsions, derived from fear, became something that would help me through other fears. Skateboarding was very helpful, having the type of repetitive activity that was freely creative helped me manage those emotions and give me a renewed sense of purpose. And now a whole lot of services are pointing out that skateboarding and skateparks are great for healing trauma through the neurosequential model and having that type of self-regulating activity on a regular basis. It was big for me in my formative years. (Beck in quoted from our interview)

Beck continues, "Often the best skater has the loudest voice sometimes, but skaters aren't always good at using their voice for the right reasons. That's not why people do skate. They don't do it for the 'clout.' They're doing it because something inside them is telling them that it is meaningful." He describes skating as giving him also a place to channel his sense of conviction and creativity to doing even ordinary tasks. He states, "creative conviction. Practicing conviction is a big part of it. And with skating, you get the reward, and apply that lesson elsewhere in your life"

Kaily "Bayr" Blackburn also conveys appreciation for how skateboarding provides joy which she sees as a crucial experience she needs in her life to balance out various challenges she has had to face. She states, "Skateboarding revived my love and joy for life and learning…To me, it is the only thing that I do 100% for fun, and it has been helping me bring that energy into all corners of my life."

Not everyone who was grateful for the impact skateboarding had on their life linked it to personal struggle. Alternatively, some framed it as something that put them on a positive life path. Timothy Ward for instance states:

My motivation for seeing social change is to hopefully help to get others introduced to something that has been such a positive force in my own life…Skateboarding is directly responsible for all or most of my friendships, most of the trips I've taken, most of the jobs that I've had, etc. And if I didn't have the opportunity to try skateboarding, in a hospitable and supportive environment, I might not like the direction that my life would have taken. (Ward quoted from our interview)

As skateboarders ourselves, we agree that skateboarding can and should be fun and joyful. But we also know sometimes it feels like anything but that. For instance, it can actually be physically painful. As Lynn Kramer in our interview stated, "Skateboarding is about perseverance more than anything. It is also a difficult sport to get good at. You have to be one of those people that thrives on pain. Pain makes some people feel alive because it activates the adrenal gland." Even when not held back or in fear of an injury, skating can be enormously frustrating and involves as much if not more failure than success (Geckle and Shaw 2022). But the idea that skateboarding builds resilience and tenacity from such struggles and failures is another common theme that also inspired gratitude in the interviewees. Kevin Pacella for instance explains:

Skateboarding also taught me the most valuable lesson: shit is gonna take you a while before you succeed. Skateboarding is failure over and over and over and then one glimmer of success. And then back to more failure. Oh, you fell? Get up and try again. Oh, you finally landed the back tail kickflip out after 300 tries? Do it better now. That kinda lesson translates a lot to "real" life…You give up when you've mastered it. (Pacella quoted from our interview)

Pacella also links this type of tenacity with a kind of work ethic or philosophy for everyday life stating:

You will fail a thousand times to succeed once. This lesson can be used in every single aspect of life and the experiences that come with it. It can quite literally be trying a trick and failing over and over just to land it once…You only let it make you better and stronger. This valuable lesson will make you become a more resilient and stronger individual. A lesson you can learn best just by stopping by your local skatepark.

Peggy Oki also proposes that such types of resilience and tenacity are also why skateboarders, in her eyes, are great activists:

> One of the things about people that know how to skateboard is that skate-boarders have tenacity. We are pursuing our passion on a skateboard expressing ourselves, and you're guaranteed to hit the concrete, but you get back up and you skate some more. And that's the thing about skating. And so skateboarders can be great activists because they have tenacity. Women skaters you know. Vert, street skater, whatever. They also fall and hit the concrete and they get back up. And that's a really beautiful thing.

Another interesting theme that emerged in the interviews was resistance and having an affinity with alternative cultures. We recognize that while skateboarding may provide individuals with a way to be resistant to mainstream culture, this opposition needs to be seen as "flexible" (Dinces 2011) as they may also integrate elements of it and even try to carve out "subcultural careers" (Snyder 2017). However, it is important not to dismiss skaters who express an attraction to the types of resistance skateboarding may offer, especially in the change-makers we interview who have clearly gone beyond performative styles to enact tangible changes.

Kramer, who is a veteran of skateboarding, describes this appeal in skateboarding as, "Skaters don't care about what is 'proper.' From our dress to our actions, we are anarchists…For most of my life, my sport has been illegal in some form or other." Her own attitude of defiance and rejecting traditional "feminine" traits of being passive, she feels, also is part of why she was able to navigate things such as sexism in skating stating, "I hear stories from women saying they were made fun of for being a female skater but I never heard anything like that personally. Maybe I was too strong in my personality for anyone to feel like messing with me."

Rhianon Bader also discussed being drawn to skateboarding because of its subcultural traits and association with rebellion. She explains this as:

I guess I linked it with a lot of other subcultures that I was getting interested in at the time. So I was like, getting into politics. And activism, as well. Any subcultural stuff was really interesting to me. I also had friends that were really into graffiti and rave culture and stuff...and at the time, skateboarding was very much an alternative thing. (Bader quoted from our interview)

The DIY culture, which is often seen as a form of resistance to commercialized cultures and ties to capitalism, was also something Bader liked about skateboarding, which places an emphasis on its creative side. She states, "I think the big one is the DIY in general. Not just DIY spots, but like the whole DIY culture in skateboarding." For her, this entails "if you've never done something before, you're kind of willing to jump into it and find a way, usually with a low budget, and just having confidence in yourself and doing something that you had never done before."

Bethany Geckle provides some further reflections which are also careful not to romanticize or reify the idea of resistance in skateboarding. She urges us to see how "skateboarding is a blank or empty tool, its effect on social change is entirely dependent on how it is used." Furthermore, she argues that "skateboarding's association with the subculture, if it can even be considered one anymore, does not make it inherently subversive, despite skateboarding relying heavily on that image." She offers a cautionary counter-view that "the skateboarding industry and culture in a lot of ways confirms dominant hetero-masculinity and centers White, western nations." At the same time, she is optimistic about how:

The way it has been adopted and adapted by women, queer folks, and groups around the world as a tool for empowerment has the potential to indicate social change away from heteronormative, patriarchal, western standards. Ultimately, there will always be multiple versions of skateboarding that, depending on who is practicing which and how each is applied, can both usher in social change and confirm the norms and standards that already exist. (Geckle quoted from our interview)

The above quote by Geckle stands as another important reminder that while we use the term "skateboarding culture" throughout this book, it is simply an umbrella term that we use to cover multiple skate cultures, each shaped by often contrasting people, activities, practices, discourses, styles, and contributions. Nevertheless, in the next and final section of this chapter, we explore types of orientations and outlooks that can assist us to understand why skateboarders, even with vastly different backgrounds, identities, and experiences, can still build a collective sense of care, compassion, and community together as part of their efforts to bring about social change.

Radical Empathy, Everyday Cosmopolitanism, and an Ethics of Sharing

Scholar Terri Givens (2022), who is a Black woman and political scientist, proposes that "radical empathy" offers a way for people facing the specific problem of racism to move beyond "having" empathy to "practicing" it. She argues that it also can reduce the pressure on Black people and others who are the targets of racism to perform "emotional labor" (Hoschild 1979) that operates by erasing their own distress and minimizing the harm White people and others who perpetuate racism can feel. She explains, "Radical empathy allows us to turn those feelings around. We all have a responsibility to let ourselves be vulnerable and practice understanding and compassion for the experiences of those who may be strangers to us" (31). Givens (2022: 31) adds that, "getting to radical empathy requires us all to understand, learn about, and acknowledge the impact of racism."

For our study, we draw upon the concept of "radical empathy" as further developed by Tommy Caroll and Luke Cianciotto (2020) who use it to highlight how individuals learn to sensitively and intuitively relate to each other in skateboarding sessions, anticipating each other's objectives and needs and how to act accordingly. Caroll is a professional skateboarder who has also been blind since birth and writes about how exclusions in skating are shaped by bias and ableism. However, he also argues that through radical empathy, issues of power can be expanded, turned around, and shared, pointing to how adaptive skateboarding and disability activists have worked to co-design spaces to skate as different yet equal, rather than being segregated from and positioned as inferior to other skateboarders. Cianciotto joins him by writing from a position of allyship but also as a fellow skateboarder. Their own interpretation of radical empathy is also one that suggests it leads to pathways beyond the physical act of skateboarding to something used to anticipate, understand, and share values and bonds in much broader contexts, such as activism that brings benefits to a range of communities. Carroll and Cianciotto (2020: 12) described this as a process of "seeing one's self, seeing another, seeing one's self through another, and then re-seeing another through one's self."

We also draw on Michèle Lamont and Sada Aksartova's (2002) research on "everyday" and "ordinary cosmopolitanism," which consists of an empirical, interview-based study of how individuals in everyday situations get on with people who are different from them. Cosmopolitanism is an idea whose origins stem from a traditional philosophy based on the idea of being citizens of the world, but in contemporary research is seen as an orientation and outlook that involves openness and a willingness to engage with people of different backgrounds (Hannerz 1990). The idea of cosmopolitanism has since been studied in a range of populations and occupations, but usually people with a high degree of social and cultural capital such as artists, diplomats, and business travelers, and rarely with attention to people from working-class and less privileged backgrounds.

Lamont and Askartova's (2002) study was based on the experiences of working-class and blue-collar men in France and the US who worked at places like factories, and within a workforce that was racially, culturally, and religiously diverse. Lamont and Askartova (2002: 3) argue that the rationales and strategies these populations use to achieve social cohesion in their jobs consist of particular "cultural repertoires" that allowed them to both construct and navigate symbolic boundaries of us and them, and things they deemed to be universal. For instance, the findings from the US fieldwork reveal that "these men posit that human nature is universal and that one should not generalize about Blacks or any other races since there are so many differences among people."

However, their study also warns that people use the cultural repertoires most available to them, which in other words means context matters.

French workers for instance tended to draw upon ideas that are held up in France such as egalitarianism and fraternity, and ideas of freedom and liberty that were far more collective and influenced by socialist principles. The US workers were alternatively informed by things such as individualism, and "the American Dream" such as anyone, regardless of background, being able to become rich one day. Such repertoires can and do of course change and are not innate or inherent because one is born in one place or another. So, the cultural repertoires that skateboarders may use to bridge differences need to be contextualized and be seen as flexible and open to changing.

Another key framework our study will adopt is one that focuses on an ethical reflexive process that Stefanie Plage, Indigo Willing and Ian Woodward, and Zlatko Skrbiš (2017) observed in ordinary cosmopolitan encounters, which we argue must entail an ethics of sharing rather than giving. For instance, "we insist that for encounters to be deemed cosmopolitan the requirement of reflexive engagement that opens up the possibility of being changed paired with an ethical framework centered on sharing is the essential requirement for the cosmopolitan performance of conviviality" (Plage et al. 2017: 19). Importantly, this non-possessive approach, which can also be applied to change making in skateboarding, is further described as being founded upon the idea that:

> Sharing is different from 'giving' or 'helping' in that it facilitates opportunities for unconditional relationality rather than managing or controlling cultural diversity. This includes the accumulation of cross-cultural knowledge and communication skills, and the ongoing interrogation of prejudices, stereotypes and self. Crucially, such reasoning acknowledges cosmopolitan outcomes as a potential for every encounter with diversity that is uncertain and needs to be worked towards. Both dimensions elaborated here—reflexive engagement and ethics of sharing are mutually reinforcing and both need to be present to realize the cosmopolitan potential. (Plage et al. 2017: 20)

As an example of having radical empathy not just for humans but also for animals, we highlight the duty of care that guides Peggy Oki in her work as an ocean activist for whales, orcas, and dolphins. She describes this stance as, "I think that everybody is individual, just as I believe that animals are individuals." She also feels to move past discrimination it is important to recognize that:

> Every person has something that they resonate with for their physical outlet, and I think it's really important that everybody is physically active. There's quite a lot of appeal with a skateboard and it is very intimate, not like team sports, and provides different ways of expressing themselves. And it is not nice to judge skateboarders, because that's just what makes them happy. (Oki quoted from our interview)

Many of the skateboarders we spoke to expressed having an openness to people from different backgrounds. This includes Latosha Stone who grew up in a mostly White neighborhood and feels her outlook has been informed by her college years in Dayton. It was there that she found it much more diverse but also it was an experience she was open and willing to engage with, stating "I was like the first time where I was exposed to a lot of different types of people, and just being able to talk to different people. And, you know, being exposed to them just kind of opened my eyes to things." Displaying an outlook that is both empathetic and cosmopolitan, she explains:

> I feel those experiences and circumstances make you a more versatile person because you can kind of see things from all points of view. And sometimes people don't really expect that from you. When it comes to Black people. And White people. I guess how I grew up, I got to know both sides, and I feel like sometimes one side doesn't expect someone that looks like me to know this about like the other side, maybe. (Beachy quoted from our interview)

A number of skaters that grew up in mostly homogeneous environments were able to be exposed to greater diversity after they left school or college by continuing to skateboard. As part of that, they not only welcomed new encounters but also began to grow more aware of social issues by being ethically reflexive. For instance, Kyle Beachy recalls, "I don't think that any thoughts about the social side of skateboarding really even clicked for me until after college." From this point he was then more frequently exposed to various hierarchies of power in something he had once turned to for freedom and fun, explaining he "thought like okay, well what is this thing, and what are we up to?" This includes racism which he explains was not always overt, and that "there was a naturalness to it where it seemed to kind of blend with the other sort of hierarchies." Awareness rather than ignorance and evasion of it required a form of empathy and with the diversity, he found in skateboarding he felt, "racially it was a kind of opening."

Rhianon Bader also discusses the different world skateboarding opens up that are not always joyful experiences but offer important encounters to develop empathy and care. She explains that as a teenager, "I grew up in the suburbs and had a pretty sheltered life and then you go downtown, and you see how other people live and you are face to face with things like addiction and homelessness and people that are struggling." She feels that, "as a skateboarder, skating street spots, you often are like, in close contact with people you wouldn't be otherwise." In her view, "we got to know the characters downtown and that was I think a really healthy experience for a young person."

Patrick Kigongo's insights provide something that also assists us to understand a unique side of skateboarding that helps skaters feel radical empathy across racial groups, particularly for the *Black Lives Matter* movement. He argues that "Skateboarders became very intimate with a type of normalized police violence." He is careful not to conflate White skaters' harassment by police as being the same as experiencing racism and racial profiling, explaining that "seems extreme to them. Now, imagine, that's all the time as a Black person. Because you can't rub off your skin." He also points out however that:

I think that's one of the reasons why you may think have little empathy, have really started to stand more certainly in solidarity with People of Color, but specifically Black and Latino people who have been targeted by police for racial profiling and police brutality…even just like that little taste that most skateboarders get with police harassment. It's more than most Americans will ever have, and especially most White Americans who rarely interact with the police.

In our interview with Timothy Ward he also demonstrates the development of a cosmopolitan lens that entails an appreciation of diversity and being open to different people and cultures abroad. At the same time, his insights assist us to not romanticize and reify skateboarders as global citizens who are beyond power relationships and problematic behaviors. He states:

> I think the role of skateboarding in bringing about social change is just that skateboarding becomes the lens which I and many others view the entire world from. This can be good or bad because skateboarding can also be the thing that brings people to drugs, excessive drinking, toxic friends etc. But skateboarding, the act, and the culture, does give people a reason to physically leave their own area, whether it's your own neighborhood, your own state, your own country etc…and culturally it causes us to spend our time reading about and watching skate videos and magazines from other places. (Ward quoted from our interview)

In Ward's opinion, even everyday exposure to difference is transformative, stating, "Even if your motivation is only to see the skating, you're going to learn about those other places regardless of if you're actively trying to." He adds, "as a skater, most of what I know about Europe is what cities are good for skating, but also learning that European countries invest in their citizens by providing universal healthcare informs my politics in my own country." In Ward's conversation here we might see skateboarding as being able to generate a type of "ordinary cosmopolitanism" through cosmopolitan encounters that may never develop into a more substantial commitment but nevertheless offers a range of foundations.

Similarly, our conversation with Keegan Guizard provides more insight into how skateboarding may not always entail radical forms of empathy but can generate well-suited starting points. Guizard explains, "Skateboarding is accessible. It can be enjoyed alone, but also in groups. It is 'not a sport', which creates a lovely loophole to bring boys and girls together when they otherwise wouldn't have, in many cultures around the globe." Rather than wanting this togetherness to be based just on similarities, he also suggests a more cosmopolitan outlook that is aware of differences while also being open to them. He states, "Skateboarding is many things and barely anything, all at the same time. Although skate-boarding can be seen as meaningless, it is the ultimate tool to bring young and older people together in a joyful way. There is just too much good to come from sharing skateboarding to not do so."

Denia Kopita also emphasizes the creative side of skateboarding, which presents an additional layer involved with the development of empathy and openness in skateboarders who become change-makers. Kopita explains that "we don't talk much about racism or social justice, but it's more about the way to see things and how to treat people. With social justice, it is how you treat people. No matter where they're from, and what background they have." But rather than resting on a type of univer-salism and openness that erases differences, she adds, "I mean, of course, we're not all the same, not all skateboarders have the same mind." In her conversation with us she also shares some of the unique things that con-nect skateboarders that can create a type of radical empathy both on and off the board:

> At the end of the day, we all share the same passion and it's a very specific one. It's not like we like drawing, which is something quite broad. It's skateboarding. I think skaters are very creative, and it's not just about the art or the music. It's special how we're looking at a set of stairs and we're thinking of how many tricks we could do there or finding a marble ledge, and looking at it like no one has ever looked at it before. We always just walk around finding new spots and it's because we have such a specific mindset. (Kopita quoted from our interview)

Kopita's insights about what makes skateboarding special also provide some insight into how skateboarders who want change to happen go beyond just performative acts or simply giving, but never sharing power. She explains:

> We (skateboarders) like to make things happen. If we say that 'I want to do this trick', we'll do everything we can to do it. That can lead and also con-nect to social justice, if we don't like something, we'll try to make change. In our world, there's also a strong sense of unity. Like when you go to a skatepark and there are people there that you haven't met before. Your home is their home now, and you can automatically connect and hang,

because of this unity. It means that we can all become a group, and with this feeling of being part of a group, we can try and make things change. (Kopita quoted from our interview)

Across the spectrum of experiences skaters have that can generate radical empathy, our conversation with Rhianon Bader also reminds us that sometimes it is the joy and elation that comes with skateboarding. We propose joy can indeed bring a sense of unity that can also build the groundwork for a cosmopolitan form of togetherness in difference (Valentine 2008). Bader believes, "it's a very supportive culture. And people want to see others succeed…everyone wants to see their friends and people around them like progress." She adds that "I think what's also great is that progression is never the same for two people. It's always like different tricks and different styles, stuff like that." She describes how there is an awareness and respect of difference and the non-hierarchical side of shared experience because in her view:

In skateboarding, no two people's progression is the same. It's really nice to think about. But truly, it's like, the sharing of something right? You don't want to just be the best at skateboarding, it's not fun. Yeah, like we know when somebody learns a trick and everyone's so happy. (Bader quoted from our interview)

Amelia Brodka also conveys the joy skateboarders feel for others, which can offer an even cathartic experience of empathy and connection. She states, "I have to say my favorite moments in skateboarding are when you're skateboarding either with your friends or maybe just with other people at the skatepark and then all of a sudden everyone is trying a trick." She continues, "and then this magical thing happens. As soon as one person lands what they are trying, everyone else lands the trick they are trying. It usually happens in succession, one after another. We call this the 'make train.'" For her, "it's a surreal situation in which your intention is carried on to others and your success gives other people the confidence to succeed. They will usually say something like 'I've got your back!' before they drop in. They saw you commit to something you may have been afraid of and it gave them the courage to commit too. It becomes a joyous occasion and everyone leaves the session elated. It's my favorite thing."

Part of this empathy is something she also nurtures through her work with her *Skate Rising* program partner Callie Kelsey, which gives youth an opportunity to do social activities such as creating care packages for refugees and unhoused people and generally share their time doing things for the community. Brodka states, "I just hope that they could see that there are people in their communities that are struggling in a variety of ways, and they can actually do something relatively simple to help." Her hopes are that "just teaching them that a really simple act of kindness…can really affect not just someone's day but you know, their whole outlook." In addition to a sense of personal growth, she feels that it is:

> Valuable to instill that sense of community, camaraderie and leadership as well, because others tend to follow suit when they see the positive impact that that has. I think it's important to bring context to their own experiences too, as kids. Everybody has their own ups and downs, but then when you can see the spectrum of what people go through, it helps you appreciate the little things as well. (Brodka quote from our interview)

In this chapter, we explored some of the formative experiences of the individuals we spoke to that underpinned their transformation from someone who simply uses a skateboard to their embodying the identity of being a "skateboarder." Within that journey, we also paid attention to specific types of reflexivity, as well as outlooks and values they have formed in their evolution into being change-makers in skateboarding. Next, we shall move attention to some of the challenges, strategies, and reflections that the skaters we spoke to share. As we shall see, these guides and experts on social change in skateboarding provide a number of important insights on how existing problematic power relationships in skateboarding have manifested but can also be turned around, re-engineered, and reconfigured in ways that promote sharing rather than the more conditional and controlled act of giving.

References

Abulhawa, D (2020) *Skateboarding and femininity: gender, space-making and expressive movement* London: Routledge.

Ahmad, N and Thorpe, H (2020) Muslim Sportswomen as Digital Space Invaders: Hashtag Politics and Everyday Visibilities, *Communication and Sport*, 1-20. https://doi.org/10.1177/2167479519898447

Bäckström, Å (2013). Gender Maneuvering in Swedish Skateboarding: Negotiations of Femininities and the Hierarchical Gender Structure. *Young*, 21(1), 29–53.

Beal, B, and Weidman, L (2003). Authenticity in the Skateboarding World. In Rinehart, R. E. and Sydnor, S (Eds.), *To the extreme: Alternative sports, inside and out* (pp. 337–352). SUNY Press.

Bennett, A (2011) The Post-Subcultural Turn: Some Reflections 10 years on. *Journal of Youth Studies, 14*(5), 493–506. https://doi.org/10.1080/1367626 1.2011.559216.

Blackman, S (2005) Youth Subcultural Theory: A Critical Engagement with the Concept, its Origins and Politics, from the Chicago School to Postmodernism. *Journal of Youth Studies, 8*(1), 1–20. https://doi.org/10.1080/ 13676260500063629.

Bourdieu, P (1994) Structures, Habitus, Power. In Dirks, N. B. Eley, G. and Ortner, SB (Eds.) *Culture/power/history*. Princeton, NJ: Princeton University Press, pp. 155–199.

Bourdieu, P (2002) *Masculine Domination*, Stanford, CA: Stanford University Press.

Bourdieu, P and Wacquant, L (1992). *An Invitation to Reflexive Sociology*. Chicago, IL: University of Chicago Press.

Carr, J (2017) Skateboarding in Dude Space: The Roles of Space and Sport in Constructing Gender Among Adult Skateboarders, *Sociology of Sport Journal*, 35: 25–35. https://doi.org/10.1123/ssj.2016-0044.

Carroll, T and Cianciotto, L (2020) Towards Radical Empathy. In Callen-Riley, T and Holsgens, S (Eds) *Urban Pamphleteer #8 Skateboardings*, pp. 11–12, Downloaded 18 July 2022: http://urbanpamphleteer.org/skateboardings.

Connell, R (1995) *Masculinities*. Cambridge, UK: Polity Press.

Crenshaw, K (1991) Mapping the Margins: Intersectionality, Identity Politics, and Violence against Women of Color, *Stanford Law Review*, 46(6): 1241–1299. https://doi.org/10.2307/1229039.

Cutting Stone (2013) Land Mountain Quote, *Cutting Stone* blog. Posted 27 February. Downloaded 22 June 2022: https://cuttingthestone.wordpress.com/2013/02/27/lance-mountain-quote/.

Dinces, S (2011) Flexible Opposition: Skateboarding Subcultures under the Rubric of Late Capitalism, International Journal of the History of Sport, 28, (11): 1512–1535.

Dobija-Nootens, N (2015) Skateboarding as a Career with Ryan Lay, *Jenkem Magazine*. Posted 10 November. Downloaded 23 July 2022: https://www.jenkemmag.com/home/2015/11/10/skateboarding-as-a-career-with-ryan-lay/.

Dupont, T (2014) From Core to Consumer: The Informal Hierarchy of the Skateboard Scene, \ *Journal of Contemporary Ethnography, 43*(5), 556–581. https://doi.org/10.1177/0891241613513033.

Dupont, T (2020) Authentic subcultural identities and social media: American skateboarders and Instagram. *Deviant Behavior, 41*(5), 649–664. https://doi.org/10.1080/01639625.2019.1585413

Garcia Marquez, K (2020) Skateboarding into the Sun, Eds Callen-Riley, T and Holsgens, S, *Urban Pamphleteer #8 Skateboardings*, pp 32–33, Downloaded 18 July 2022: http://urbanpamphleteer.org/skateboardings.

Geckle, B and Shaw, S (2022) Failure and Futurity: The Transformative Potential of Queer Skateboarding. *YOUNG, 30*(2), 132–148. https://doi.org/10.1177/1103308820945100.

Givens, T (2022) *Radical Empathy*, Bristol: Polity Press.

Gutierrez, G (2021) Skateboarding, We Hardly Knew You, *Public Books*. Posted 23 September. Downloaded 23 July 2022: https://www.publicbooks.org/skateboarding-we-hardly-knew-you/.

Hannerz, U (1990) Cosmopolitans and Locals in World Culture, *Theory, Culture and Society* 7(2): 237–251. https://doi.org/10.1177/026327690007002014.

Hill, J (2018) *Mid90s*, A24 Productions, USA.

Hoschild, A (1979) Emotion Work, Feeling Rules, and Social Structure, *American Journal of Sociology*, 85(3)551–575.

Lay, R (2019) Life Lessons from Being a Pro Skater. *Jenkem Magazine*. Posted 24 October. Downloaded 23 July 2022: https://www.jenkemmag.com/home/2019/10/24/life-lessons-pro-skater/.

Lamont, M, and Aksartova, S (2002) Ordinary Cosmopolitanisms: Strategies for Bridging Racial Boundaries among Working Class Men, *Theory, Culture and Society* 19(4):1–25. https://doi.org/10.1177/0263276402019004001.

O'Connor, P (2017) Beyond the youth culture: Understanding Middle-aged Skateboarders through Temporal Capital, *International Review for the Sociology of Sport*, Preview Copy. 1-20

Plage, S, Willing, I, Woodward, I, and Skrbiš Z (2017) Cosmopolitan Encounters: Reflexive Engagements and the Ethics of Sharing, *Ethnic and Racial Studies*, *40*(1), 4–23. https://doi.org/10.1080/01419870.2016.1178788.

Sharp, M, and Threadgold, S (2020). Defiance Labour and Reflexive Complicity: Illusio and Gendered Marginalisation in DIY Punk Scenes. *Sociological Review*, 68(3), pp. 606–622. https://doi.org/10.1177/0038026119875325.

Snow, D (2012) Skateboarders, Streets and Style in R White (ed), *Youth subcultures: Theory, history and the Australian experience (revised second edition)*, ACYS, Hobart, pp. 273–282.

Snyder, G. J. (2017). *Skateboarding LA: Inside professional street skateboarding*. New York University Press.

Schwier, J and Kilberth, V eds (2020) *Skateboarding Between Subculture and the Olympics: A Youth Culture under Pressure from Commercialization and Sportification*. Columbia University Press.

Tedam, P (2021) Radical Empathy: Finding a Path to Bridging the Racial Divides, Review of Terri Givens. *The British Journal of Social Work*, *(20210714)*. https://doi.org/10.1093/bjsw/bcab151.

Valentine, G (2008) Living with Difference: Reflections on Geographies of Encounter, *Progress in Human Geography*, 32(3): 323–337 https://doi.org/10.1177/0309133308089372.

Weaver, H (2016) Where Wounded Knee meets Wounded Knees: Skateparks and Native American Youth. *Alternative: An International Journal of Indigenous Peoples*, *12*(5), 513–526. https://search-informit-org.libraryproxy.griffith.edu.au/doi/epdf/10.3316/informit.523827165207373.

Wheaton, B and Beal, B (2004) 'Keeping it Real': Subcultural Media and the Discourses of Authenticity in Alternative sport. *International Review for the Sociology of Sport*, 38(2), 155–176. https://doi.org/10.1177/1012690203038002002.

Wheaton, B and Thorpe, H (2021) *Action Sports and the Olympic Games: Past, Present, Future*, Routledge.

Willing, I and Shearer, S (2016) Skateboarding Activism: Exploring Diverse Voices and Community Support, Lombard, KJ (ed) *Skateboarding: Subcultures, Sites and Shifts*, London: Routledge. pp 44–58.

Willing, I, Bennett, Am, Piispa M and Green, B (2019) Skateboarding and the 'Tired Generation': Aging in Youth Cultures and Lifestyle Sports. *Sociology* 53(3):503–18.

5

Strategies, Challenges, and Change-Making

Introduction

In this chapter we are guided by the questions: What does change look like through the eyes of people who pursue, initiate, and facilitate it? What meanings and motivations are a part of that? What challenges exist? And what strategies are helping them gain ground? Insights arise from exploring the critical reflections of skateboarders, who share their experiences and cover a range of tactics, skills, and expertise they develop.

The discussion of the interviews ahead is our most extensive in this book, reflecting the richly diverse range of people we spoke to and the various areas in skateboarding they represent. Despite many differences across identities and communities, the types of concepts and themes that arose from our analysis appeared applicable across their professions and disciplines. As we shall reveal, the purposeful (re)actions and motivations that skateboarders share in this chapter reflect many of the outlooks and values we highlighted in the last chapter. This includes their orientations of openness to diversity, and unlike some of their developing stages of becoming skateboarders where they might have internalized and been complicit in negative aspects of skate culture, they now have a stance that is resistant and defiant toward situations of unfairness and

© The Author(s), under exclusive license to Springer Nature Singapore Pte Ltd. 2023
I. Willing, A. Pappalardo, *Skateboarding, Power and Change*,
https://doi.org/10.1007/978-981-99-1234-6_5

discrimination. We also observed that the skateboarders we spoke to demonstrate what is an "ethics of empathy" and sharing over being competitive and individualistic, founded upon the joy skateboarding gives them and their desire to share their love for it in ways that include rather than exclude others.

Our exploration ahead unfolds in three main parts with various subsections. Firstly, we begin with "Part 1: De-centering Established Power" which has two subsections, "Decolonizing and De-centering Whiteness in Skateboarding Culture" and "Evolving Collaborations and Emerging Equity." In the first part of this chapter, we listen to how skaters de-center established power through the perspectives of First Nations, Black, and People of Color (PoC) skaters. We then expand the scope to hear from a range of other skateboarders as well, with a focus on those working with the industry and those involved in the areas of both community and elite skate competitions.

Secondly, we present "Part 2: Change-Making in Media, Creative Landscapes, and Knowledge" which has three subsections, "DIY Approaches and Bringing Change to Skate Media," "Creative Interventions: Humor as a Strategy for Change," and "Supporting Education." In this part, our discussion turns to look at change-making in terms of DIY and alternative skate media, creative ventures, and the area of providing scholarships for skateboarders to attain a college education.

Thirdly, we present "Part 3: Ethical Togetherness at the Micro and Macro Levels" which has two subsections, "Micro-Level Boundaries and Togetherness in Skate Community Spaces" and "Macro-Level Relations: Skate Spaces and Ethical Place Making." In the last part of this chapter, we examine the idea of ethical togetherness at the micro and macro levels. The former is done by considering interpersonal issues such as consent, group interactions, and how people interact together at things like skate camps or through alliances of mostly grassroots and small skate collectives. We then explore how skaters at the macro level engage and relate to others in terms of building and maintaining skateparks and skate spots in cities. The following provides some introductory background to these areas of interest and then examples of our conversations that illustrate key themes.

Part 1: De-Centering Established Power

David Martinez (2013: 383) proposes that "skateboarding represents an iconoclastic surge" against the status quo as well as being fun and creative. He also emphasizes it is something that defies ethnic labels, yet has the power to challenge stereotypes about marginalized groups, including Indigenous skaters. In this first section of Part 1 of this chapter we focus on Douglas Miles Sr. and Douglas Miles Jr. from Apache Skateboards. We listen to how they approach their own representation, leading with innovative thinking, and creativity and with the effect of decolonizing the skate industry, which often denigrates and attempts to erase their presence.

The issue of racism in skateboarding for others is also explored in this first section of Part 1. Williams (2021:291) in his study of Black and PoC professional skaters also argues, "Elite skateboarding has been a battleground for racial and cultural politics from the 1970s to the present day." He also states:

> Furthermore, there have been distinct differences within and among SOC in the ways they embrace the DIY (Do-it-yourself) aesthetic of skateboarding and harness its power toward a progressive agenda. These differences emphasize worldviews based in part on participants' perspectives on the obstacles in their life impacting how they navigate elite skateboarding culture…each of the triumphs and struggles discussed by SOC and their relationships with non-POC conclusively demonstrates how the multiple perspective and histories make skateboarding culture an important site of further racial and intersectional exploration. (Williams, 2021:291)

Our exploration includes professional and non-professional skateboarders, which reflects the multiple ways social change can occur. The expansion from studies of elite skateboarders for us, as authors and researchers, also corresponds with our professional and volunteering experiences and the networks we have developed within skateboarding. Many of the interviewees, even at the professional level, embody a DIY approach through their creating brands, media platforms and podcasts, inclusive networks, new industry roles, creative works, inclusive events, and activism. We highlight the challenges and contributions Black skaters and allies experience and also their evaluations and advice on how to keep up the momentum of the Black Lives Matter movement post-2020. We also acknowledge how PoC skateboarders can also go under-recognized and problematic issues of portraying any populations in skating as static and monolithic communities.

Our discussion in the second section of Part 1 considers how the research conversations shed more light on the flexibility skaters can have toward mainstreaming and commercialization, with a particular focus on how "non-traditional" skateboarders reflect on encounters with the skate industry (Toffoletti et al., 2018, Toffoletti and Thorpe, 2018b). Borden (2001:101) argued in his seminal study over 20 years ago that skateboarding "outrightly rejected commodification." But in later studies, he and others observe a more entangled relationship between commercialism, incorporation, and subcultural entrepreneurship (Borden, 2019, Dinces, 2011, Dupont, 2014, Lombard, 2010, Snyder, 2017). We draw attention to skateboarders whose work includes commercial aspects and a social justice focus. We explore the experiences and advice they share, how they negotiate pay, and industry invitations that are more performative and tokenistic. The interviewees also shed light on how to create empowering partnerships.

We then focus on the social meanings skateboarders attach to community-run competitions and incorporated events like the Olympic Games experience following skateboarding's debut in Tokyo in 202 and in the lead up to its inclusion in both Paris in 2024 and in Los Angeles in 2028. Just over ten years ago Holly Thorpe and Belinda Wheaton (2011) observed strong resistance to skateboarding's incorporation into corporate and institutionally run competitions like X Games and the Olympics, known as "mega-events." But they also suggested attitudes may shift, and a more willing but no less complex relationship is observed by Belinda Wheaton and Holly Thorpe (2021) a decade on. Importantly, the conversations ahead provide a window into how skateboarders do not view skate competitions as pitting individuals against each other, but rather channel hopes they can be transformed by skateboarders into occasions to strengthen the community.

Decolonizing and De-Centering Whiteness in Skateboarding Culture

This section shares insights from change-makers on decolonizing and de-centering Whiteness. To begin, skateboarding has long been perceived and aligned with White masculine culture, similarly to surfing culture where diversity was not absent, but could be pushed to the periphery or erased from how it is represented. We first draw attention to Douglas Miles Sr. and Douglas Miles Jr. from First Nations skateboard company Apache Skateboards who describe a process that recasts and re-engineers skate culture by prioritizing the sovereignty of Native people to the land skateboarders are on, and the Indigenous lens that shapes how they approach skateboarding.

We then hear from skateboarders who discuss racism and their present-day thoughts on the impact of the Black Lives Matter movement, which began in 2013 and was reinvigorated with more urgency in 2020. We focus on what impact the movement had on skaters' lives and what steps they feel will contribute toward its longevity in skateboarding. We also extend our reflections on issues of racism and inclusion beyond Black and White relations by also considering how People of Color (PoC) are a part of the skate culture and their contributions.

First Nations Skateboarding

> Don't tell me to just shut up and skate when you know you're skating on Native land. You know these are not just sound bites. This is the way we think. And they're not just outtakes. Yeah they're hot takes. But they're more than that. It's the way we think. (Douglas Miles Sr., quoted from our interview)

Social justice is unachievable without the presence, positioning, and expertise of First Nations skateboarders across the world (Morgan, 2012, Weaver, 2016). In the aforementioned quote, Douglas Miles Sr. presents a powerful message that goes beyond a critique of power relationships just in skateboarding. His words, art, and social media content creation regularly emphasize an Indigenous standpoint. Themes include custodianship of the land by Native people that everyone including "settlers" skates upon, but usually without acknowledging and respecting Indigenous sovereignty. The term "settlers" refers to the position non-Indigenous people have within colonies that generate colonial encounters, such as in North American locations and Australia (Tallbear, 2021, Watego, 2021). Miles Sr. also builds up a positionality in skateboarding that de-centers the authority of White masculinity in skateboarding that often erases and silences First Nations skateboarders (Miles Snr, 2022).

Miles Sr. has been a strong and leading voice for over 20 years that holds space for Native skaters and asserts Native authority over their own skate culture while reversing a critical gaze back onto non-Native people in skateboarding. His profile as an artist and as a founder of the Apache Skateboards, plus his whole team's skating and projects are gaining recognition by industry such as Etnies, in skate media and films (Buchanan, 2019, Foley, 2022, Gray, 2020), and scholars (Martinez, 2013 Weaver 2016). Miles Sr. has also been actively putting women on their skate team and in a way that challenges tropes in skateboarding that position Native skaters as "exotic" or subordinating them into objects of pity. Di'orr Greenwood, an Apache Skateboards team member, describes this positioning as

> Native skateboarders aren't hungry for your sympathy, we purely want to present our facts and just skate. All skateboarders aren't out to cause destruction. There is a group of us—you all know who you are—that decided to take the notch higher and start investing in our next generation, incorporating skateboarding both as a bridge and a tool. There are Indigenous people in the future. Apache Skateboards is for everyone. (Di'orr Greenwood, quoted from interview with Willing, 2019)

Hilary Weaver (2016: 514), a Lakota woman, researcher, and mother of two children who frequently go to skateparks, also explains how Native people's presence in skateboarding can challenge broader racist stereotypes that "deny complex, diverse identities of Native Americans. As contemporary peoples we exist within multifaceted realities…While many remain rooted…in Indigenous ways, we are also multidimensional human beings in everyday popular pleasures." She observes, for instance, that "skateboarding is the fastest growing sport in reservations" (516). She also adds that skateboarding subcultures are not static or monolithic and Native skateboarders do not always want to adopt the typical traits and images of "core" skateboarding.

This independence or flexible connection between Native and non-Native skating is highlighted in the work of David Martinez (2013: 382), who is an Akimel O'odham/Hia Ced O'odham/Mexican professor of American Indian Studies:

> Indian skaters, it should be noted, are not merely mimicking their non-Indian counterparts. In other words, it would be naive to claim that these skaters are "assimilating" into American society. Instead, skateboarding is providing an alternative means of self-expression that has always been a part of reservation youth culture but that until recently has been hidden in the shadows of more conventional forms of athletic activity. (Martinez, 2013: 382)

Douglas Miles Jr., who also founded his own company Indellica, also emphasized that his own journey into becoming a skateboarder was not shaped by stereotypes and white tropes of skateboarders. He remarked, for instance, how he found the "core" skate culture neither relatable nor enviable. Instead, it was the artists and musicians his father introduced him to who he admired and felt inspired by, especially those who had social messages in their work.

Miles Jr. felt it was important to do something different for skating than what was promoted in mainstream skate media which had "the power to influence the young kids, promoting all that crazy shit. And be brainwashed by it because you're a kid and that's all you're looking at the magazines, the videos." Rather than repeating stereotypes of skateboarding or of Indigenous, Black, and other PoC, Douglas Miles Sr. encouraged his son and the Apache Skateboards team to be innovative and improvisational and to find inspiration in artists, hip-hop musicians, and jazz. His son explains:

I thought it'd be cool to create something more positive and then my pops one day, he told me skateboarding was kind of like hip-hop. I didn't know what the hell he was talking about, but I meditated on it for a little bit. Then I really got into hip-hop and I thought, "Oh shit, I'm learning from this! I'm learning just by listening to all this music." (Miles Jr. quoted from our interview)

As we shall see, both he and his father have their own messages they now promote together in skateboarding that centers on Native innovation and standpoints of Indigenous independence and sovereignty, creating forms of decolonization rather than assimilating into and privileging "Whiteness."

Decolonizing is a popular and widely used term, typically used to refer to processes involving efforts to de-center Western hegemony and cultural dominance founded upon colonization. Nation states such as Australia, Aotearoa New Zealand, Canada, and in focus in this book, the US are all examples where Indigenous peoples continue their battles for sovereignty. This includes legal, cultural, financial, and social standpoints, which also intersect with how knowledge is produced and how Indigenous people are represented.

While many definitions of decolonization exist, we reflect on our conversation with First Nations skateboarders through the framework of sovereignty (Tallbear, 2021, Watego, 2021). Indigenous scholar Chelsea Watego (2021), a Mununjali and South Sea Islander woman, and South Asian settler scholar David Singh (2020) introduce two important angles. For Singh (quoted in Watego, 132) the idea of "sovereign divergence" has the standpoint that "a settler hegemony structured in dominance is ontologically impossible much less total" which means colonization is not totalizing, but it is resisted and, therefore, always incomplete. Further light is shed in his citing Indigenous activist Michael Mansell, who states:

We are the first people of this land. We have suffered every indignity ever meted out to a people. Yet our strength is our determination…our sovereign rights as a people remain intact. By virtue of those sovereign rights we are the sole decision-makers about what we need and what we will accept. (cited in Watego, 2021: 132)

Watego is specifically focused on Aboriginal and Torres Strait Islanders' sovereignty that resists British colonialism and ongoing settler force. But other powerful stances in her work include an explicit rejection of "hope," to which she devotes a whole chapter in her book *Another Day in the Colony* called "fuck hope" (Watego, 2021: 195). This is not a declaration of defeat but declaration of bold resistance, retiring the idea of "hope" as it is an idea that rests on settlers' promises and programs to "change" Indigenous lives. As she points out, "hope" enables only performative efforts, if any at all, and does not place emphasis on action.

A type of emotion and experience that is constructive to efforts toward decolonizing and sovereignty that Watego (2021) introduces as an alternative to "hope" is the idea of "joy." She states, for example, "There is so much joy to be found in turning over the tables that we've been denied a seat at" (Watego, 2021: 229). Joy can also mean self-care, freedom, and being nourished by living the fullest and through, and with love, for fellow Indigenous people. She also provides the powerful quote by Audrey Lorde (cited in Watego, 2021: 299): "I work. I love, I rest and learn And I report. These are my givens. Not sureties, but a firm belief that whether or not living them with joy prolongs my life, it certainty enables me to pursue the objectives of that life with deeper and more effective clarity." Neftalie Williams (2021) also applies the emotion of joy to skateboarding for Black and PoC skaters noting it has political significance as it is a form of agency and points to the full range of experiences that can mobilize, bring freedom, and empower.

> You are skating on Native Land.
> —Douglas Miles Snr, Apache Skateboards (2022)

Douglas Miles Senior (Sr.) has been one of the earliest voices and presence to draw attention to First Nations skateboarding and particularly on their own terms (Borden, 2019, Martínez, 2013, Weaver, 2016). Miles Sr. proposes Native skateboarders are "in a lot of ways they are kind of a new archetype, and especially within Native Nations where Native people are concerned. I never wanted these kids to perform 'Indianness' or perform, you know, their indigeneity for people." He continues, "I didn't want people to look at them as odd or exotic 'other' skateboarders. I just wanted them to skate, and they have fun." While Miles Sr. has always emphasized that those involved with Apache Skateboards are skateboarding because it is fun and a source of joy and creativity, he also acknowledges they are changing the way people view not just Native skateboarding but the more diverse depth and breadth of skate culture itself. This includes what Native and non-Native skateboarders do off the board too.

Also a fine artist, Miles Sr. has had exhibitions and artist residencies around the US. This includes 2022 at the invitation of the Phoenix Art Museum. His exhibit entailed a wall with rows of one of the Apache Skateboards signature deck designs. Set on a white background with a graphic featuring Miles Sr.'s art in bold black text is the statement "You are skating on Native Land." Explaining some of the context and background behind the board's strong message of sovereignty and colonial resistance, he states:

> The skateboard industry is very extractive. And so I thought, well what is a good way to remind skateboard industry slash culture that you're really on Native land? You're skating on Native land. You think like, oh, well, I just can skate wherever I want because it's a free country. But you're not thinking beyond the present. You need to think about the communities you're going into. And you need to think about the communities that you're a part of...It started with one skateboard and the phrase, you're skating on Native land, but I thought this is the perfect way to share with skateboarders in skateboarding and the skate industry...I felt like someone needed to say that and who better than Apache skateboards. (Miles Snr, 2022)

In our interview, Miles Sr. explains that there is often backlash by skateboarders—including those in the industry—for making audible as well as visually bold stances on Indigenous sovereignty and resistance to performative efforts at inclusion. He explains, "Skate bigotry is real. It's kind of a nod to the industry. We expect them not to understand the weight but that doesn't mean I hate them." He adds, "I'm not anti-White, I'm anti-racism. So, I'm anti-systemic racism."

Miles Sr. also critically draws attention to how his and other First Nations peoples' insights have relevance throughout the US, stating,

"You know, as landlords and original inhabitants and citizens of America/pre-America, who is more qualified than the Native American to talk about these issues in any industry, including skateboarding?" He further reminds how, "in fine art, street art, Hollywood films and film genres we know, as Native Americans, [] we have been portrayed and betrayed. So we are most qualified." He adds:

> Don't get me wrong, when I say we are the most qualified. I'm saying we are overqualified. We're just as we are. We understand and empathize, of course, with Black, Asian, and Latino communities as well, because they too have been marginalized and criticized in the US and the American media.
> (Miles Sr., quoted from our interview)

When reflecting on skateboarding, Miles Sr. explains that it is also their refusal to assimilate into the image of skateboarding that's been determined by legacy media and industry.

> The gaslighting by the skateboarding industry is real in a lot of ways. I think it's partly and possibly because they don't see us as part of skateboarding. After all, we don't adhere to the rules that the owners of the industry have made for themselves: to keep skateboarding "pure." This idea of "pure" skateboarding for "pure" skateboarders. (Miles Sr., quoted from our interview)

This leads to questions of positionality and of non-Native skaters attempting to exclude Native skateboarders on their own lands. Miles Sr. describes this by asking, "Where does that leave us out here in America, deep in the heart of real America? What does that make us? Some strange exotic anomaly?" Also reversing the tables on a legacy of skateboarding that prides itself on consisting of outsiders while also excluding First Nations skaters, he states, "If skateboarding is truly free, if it is really unique, rebellious and radical, then essentially we are the core of what true skateboarding really is and has been." On social media, Miles Sr. has also shared the phrase he coined as a hashtag #YouAreSkatingOnNativeLand and adds, "I created the hashtags #ImSkateboardingToo, #SkateandDestroyRacism, and #NativeKidsSkate. The point I was making is that I think that they (the industry) don't really see us as part of who they are, therefore, they don't really include us."

Some of the messages Miles Jr. shares (see Foley, 2022) is, "Whatever you want to do, make it your best and push it to the limits…keep going and outdo yourself every single time…That's basically what *Indellica* is and where I am at right now with the *Apache Passion Project*" (Foley, 2022). He adds that this can include things like fashion, skateboarding, photography, and filmmaking, and he adds that his projects are making stuff for people in his community, but also people from around the world (Foley, 2022). He also encourages collaboration, stating, "There are many different ways, but the best way is to work with us and to hire us and if they want to do some native stuff. Hit us up and let's collaborate on something. Let's make something cool and dope, and useful" (Foley, 2022).

His father Miles Sr. states, "What skate brands don't understand is that if they brought a skater like Doug Miles Jnr to their company…who is a part of Native America, and has worked hard in his communities…they would become part of the change that we represent." Miles Sr. also emphasized how "we are decolonizing skateboarding…we are." But also that companies like Apache Skateboards and his son's company Indellica are doing things on their terms rather than hoping that the industry will rapidly change. With phrases such as "You are Skating on Native Land" he is also reversing the gaze back on a culture of skating that has often enabled colonialism and racism. Miles Sr. states of his work and the Apache Skateboard team, "It's like decolonization. That's what some call it. But we go further. We're reverse engineering skateboarding because we're Native and predominantly, there are mostly White-owned companies."

Black Lives Matter and Windows onto Longevity Post-2020

Some of your favorite companies don't give a f*ck about the Black Man - Na-Kel Smith, professional skateboarder, from a 35-minute video posted in *Jenkem Magazine*. (Jenkem Staff, 2020)

Skateboarding has always had Black skateboarders from African American and Black African diasporas (Yochim, 2010). Pioneering figures have been featured in the documentary *The Spades: History of Black Skateboarding* (Grimes, Brown, and Chilli, 2011), contemporary elite and professional skateboarders in the academic work of Neftalie Williams (2020, 2022), and the women, non-binary, and queer skate scene in essays such as by Kava Garcia Marquez (2020) and in magazines such as *Skateism*. The "core" skate media from *Thrasher* to *Jenkem Magazine* are also making efforts to celebrate Black skaters' history and explore the issues they face (Brown, 2022; Corporan et al., 2021; Foley 2020; Jefferson, 2020; Jenkem Staff, 2020; Lanza, 2020). While not an exhaustive list, some of the figures who have been influential across these areas and eras include Don Hillsman, Stephanie Person, Ray Barbee, Sal Barbier, Alfonso Rawls, Marty Grimes, Stevie Williams, Clyde Singleton, Harold Hunter (1974–2006), Kareem Campbell, Antwuan Dixon, Brandon Turner, Ishod Wair, Samarria Brevard, Tyshawn Jones, and Dashawn Jordon. There are also influential and creative high-profile figures such as Briana King, Beatrice Domond, Yasmeen "Yaz" Wilkerson, A Klass, Kava Garcia Vasquez, Kane Caples, Myles de Courcy, Arin Lester, Brianna Holt, Mike Brown, and Ibn Jasper.

In the contemporary era, a cover has been taken off instances of exclusion from racism and more overt incidents of anti-Blackness toward Black skateboarders (Jenkem, 2020, Williams, 2020, 2021). In the wake of George Floyd's murder at the hands of police in 2020, the Black Lives Matter movement provided the energy and momentum to tackle racism and anti-Blackness in skateboarding head-on. Strategies included calling out racism through things such as protest marches, fundraising, and social media messaging, but also de-centering Whiteness by challenging brands and media to represent and equally include Black people in skate teams, in skate media, and in more industry roles and to increase knowledge of things such as Black-owned skateboarding businesses.

Neftalie Williams (2020: 288) has observed that while studies of race and skateboarding provide useful windows, there is a general lack on Black and PoC "lived experiences," and he proposes "a broader agenda into race scholarship (incorporating ethnicity) focused on the lives of SoC" (skaters of color). His own study is based on the experiences of 50 elite skateboarders who consist of professional skateboarders, photographers, and editors from Black and various PoC backgrounds. His study highlights things such as mico-aggressions in everyday encounters to structural issues such as the unquestioned homogeneity of those in power in the industry, namely White men.

Williams (2020) also warns about colorblindness, which is a process that acts to normalize Whiteness. Whiteness is a process that upholds the idea White people are neutral yet also the superior group that everyone else is measured up to (Bonilla-Silva, 2012, Frankenberg, 1999). In skateboarding, it also makes it appear as if the dominance of White people in key roles of power and the main ways skateboarding is represented is something neutral, central, and "authentic" while failing to recognize how this de-centers and erases Black and SoC skaters. The cause of certain populations being erased is also then assumed to rest on those who are excluded rather than systemic racism. For studies of race that intervene in this process, he states:

> What I propose is a move beyond either accepting a utopian 'color-blind' rhetoric of equality or the assumption of SOC as outliers without power, and instead dive into those differences and similarities with a critical, yet reflexive lens to investigate how POC experiences informed, and continue to shape, their lives as SOC. (Williams, 2020: 291)

Our study is guided by this call to focus on skateboarders' lived experiences and we extended our conversations to include skateboarders who are part of the industry and formal structure of skateboarding, including allies. As we conducted interviews from 2020 to 2022, we were able to hear what impacts they feel the intense period of protest and change in 2020 had on them. This includes what kinds of springboards they feel the momentum of 2020 provided, as well as what kinds of things are at risk of waning off and steps they feel will help keep up longevity.

Highly charged incidents of racism for photographer and director Atiba Jefferson includes: "When I was 15, there was Klu Klux Klan rally on Martin Luther King Day in Denver and we all went to protest and it turned into a riot, cop cars got broken and I ended up getting tear gassed." It was an incident that would shape his creative work as an adult. Jefferson explains, "I was able to be really creative, you know through that time and then George Floyd happened. Being here in Los Angeles, I was able to go in and use my camera as my voice and I wanted to document this movement that we've never seen in our lifetime."

Jefferson was also at the Black Lives Matter protests in Fairfax District, California, in June 2020, which started with peaceful protests and then escalated (Buchanan et al., 2020). Jefferson recalls, "The big Fairfax thing…I was there at the protest, then went skating and started seeing everything happening on social media. I was driving home and it seemed like things had settled." He continues, "A lot of my friends work on Fairfax at Supreme so I figured I'd check in on everyone on my drive home. When I got down there it was like a straight war zone. Fires in the streets, stand-offs with cops, we were getting sprayed with rubber bullets, you know, it was intense."

Due to the escalation, Jefferson began to critically reflect on what resonated with him and what troubled him about the effects it was going to have. He states:

> It was pretty wild and it was negative energy and it was actually really sad and depressing. That's what was cool about participating in the protests that were peaceful and intelligent and documenting those. That's what's really rad about that movement. Now that we've all had some space from the George Floyd protests, that stood for him and so many other Black people who have been mistreated and even killed by police officers. And with the recent storming of the United States Capitol by White supremacists, we have more context.

Jefferson describes a type of "defiance" that we discussed in an early chapter along with how all individuals can respond to situations of oppression within a spectrum of reflection and reflexivity that ranges from ethical to complicit (Sharp and Threadgold, 2020). What is powerful in Jefferson's unpacking of the situation is his wisdom that both ethics and defiance need to co-exist. That is, there is a need to be defiant but with ethical boundaries, including acts of resistance that may end up entirely destructive, rather than being subversive and enacting constructive change. He states:

All summer and into the fall we saw millions of people across the globe peacefully protesting and there was a lot of good and positivity that not only came out of it, but that continues to resonate. Whereas a mob of mostly White people caused chaos at the Capitol to take selfies and try to illegally change the results of the election. Nothing good will ever come out of that and it's a really stark contrast. (Jefferson quoted from our interview)

Jefferson recognizes the transformative legacy and power that was generated by the events of 2020 after a surge of exposure to police brutality and racial violence leading to massive protests. He explains, "I will never say 'Fuck 2020,' as much as we lost people, and it was difficult. This was the first time you saw the world make a change for the better, especially in our country." Jefferson also provides an openness and willingness to engage across populations in this pivotal time that has everyday cosmopolitan traits while avoiding the pitfalls of colorblindness. He states, "It's also got more White people and People of Color. That's a good thing. Now you have allies, whereas before you didn't have that many allies. To me the best part of the whole movement in that sense."

Another important insight into Jefferson's experiences is how he sheds light on an ethical stance that is not just personal but also socially connected. We must remember our ethical outlooks and actions are not something that "just happens," but rather one has to start to "become" socially engaged, similar to one having to "become" a skateboarder. There is also no set timeline or measuring stick. Jefferson describes his journey as the following: "I started to volunteer at this community center in Watts. Why did it take me until I was 44 to give back to the community? I've always been a politically correct person, I don't litter, I'm vegetarian…and it's not a competition." For him, it was a journey that was assisted by "being single and not being so hyper-focused on my career during the pandemic. I was able to stop and think about how I could give back to the people around me. Now it's literally my favorite thing to do every Friday." He adds, "I'm happy to be able to do it now. I don't think I would have taken that time if I didn't have all this happen to wake me up."

Jefferson also credits being into punk rock as giving him earlier experiences of being "anti-establishment and anti-government." However, he believes that "the thing with skating is that a lot of people just don't care.

They just skate. They'll say they don't know enough about politics or even voting." He reveals, "I was surprised by the number of skaters that were so indifferent. I think it's just a lack of knowledge in general because voting is kind of scary if you don't understand it." He sums up the mixture of fear and ambivalence skaters can have toward being socially engaged: "I never really got people saying 'keep skating out of politics,' it was more that they didn't care. All they're thinking about is what trick they're going to get."

In the role as the photographer for *Thrasher* magazine's September 2020 issue which featured portraits of Black skaters exclusively on both the front and back covers of the magazine, Jefferson was able to channel his own creative talents and social concerns. Along with the obvious visual statement, it's noteworthy that *Thrasher* eschewed selling advertising on the back cover as it typically does in order to amplify the message. He states:

> It felt as if everyone looked at what they can impact, what their network is, and how they can use it to make things bigger. It felt like there was a shift or at least an intention with *Thrasher* Magazine to use their platform to be more progressive and give people a voice. I think it's just an evolution of the magazine. The Black skaters cover idea was great…I was really honored. (Jefferson quoted in our interview)

Fashion and streetwear is another area of skateboarding where Black people have been a central influence, yet with only a few rising to attain the power of Stevie Williams who co-founded Dirty Ghetto Kids (DGK) in 2002 with Troy Morgan through the Kayo Corp. Even less so for Black women, but this is changing. Other examples of Black skaters taking up space in the skate industry include Ron Allen who owned several brands in the 1990s and Sal Barbier who co-founded both Aesthetics Skateboards and Elwood Clothing, as well as having one of the earliest and most successful "pro model shoes" after Steve Caballero and Natas Kaupas. Alfonso Rawls was also able to build on his skateboarding career with his art and in shoe design, including with DC Shoes. Ibn Jasper has also built his career in the world of art such as with Diamond Supply Co. and as a hairstylist to high-profile musicians.

In our interviews, we spoke with Latosha Stone about her experiences as the founder of Proper Gnar, the first Black woman-owned skate company that enjoyed a spike in business in 2020 when singer Beyoncé added her to the *Black Parade Directory of Black Owned Businesses* and her apparel was also used in HBO's television show called *Betty*. Of that time she states, "Honestly, that was unexpected (the inclusion on Beyoncé's list). It was not expected at all either. I still don't know how that happened, but I'm super thankful for it."

Stone feels that despite the momentum in 2020, it also took some of the brands "a very long time to speak about racism." In her view, they lagged due to fear of backlash, and "it was almost like, okay, so this major brand's talking about Black Lives Matter so now we can because it won't affect our brand because other brands have already taken heat for talking about it." With the careful navigation Black people have to do in terms of speaking up against racism, there is also a dimension of both "defiance" and "emotional labour" (Hochschild, 1979) that can be unspoken about. Stone explains that for her, "because I'm like a Black-owned company it's hard because you have to say something but at the same time it's draining. It's sad that I even got to the point where the industry had to say something. It shouldn't have been like that."

Despite the fatigue that can occur, Stone expresses why she feels she and other skateboarders stay committed and keep momentum, stating, "As a Black woman living in America my identity is a challenge, but I feel like skaters are unique with what they do too because skaters also have a similar history." Here she indicates the type of "radical empathy" we discussed in a previous chapter on the values and outlooks skaters develop. Stone explains, "In America, authorities really fuck with skaters a lot. Almost every guy I know that skates have received a ticket or something from (alleged) trespassing or vandalism—for skating somewhere they weren't 'supposed' to skate or something like that."

While it is clear that Black people can become provoked to act through blatant injustice, there is also frustration and exhaustion as their forms of defiance and resistance are a matter of survival as well as an ethical orientation. This raises the question of what may move potential allies from ambivalence or forms of complicit reflexivity over to more sincere commitments toward anti-racism and tangible actions. We spoke with Kevin

Pacella, a White cisgender man, on his co-organizing a skating for the Black Lives Matter march with Ben Jones from the Kinetic Skateboard shop in Delaware (Pappalardo, 2020a). Pacella states, "Unfortunately, it took the horrifying murder of George Floyd to get our heads out of our asses and force that change. Once that happened, we sought out ways to confront the systemic problems within our community."

Through Pacella's discussion we can see how the subcultural attitudes of resistance and belonging can help motivate White people into action and also others outside of skateboarding to take notice. He states, "Skateboarding is a culture that has a huge effect on the world, whether people like it or not." As an example, he points to how "you see it in fashion and music and art. We are trendsetters and influencers because we have a do-whatever-the-fuck-you-want attitude and it's contagious." He also adds, "When you see a group of skateboarders out in the streets protesting for the betterment of Black lives it makes you feel some type of way. It makes you want to join in and learn more about the cause."

What started as a semi-organized grassroots protest for skateboarders turned into hundreds of skaters, BMX riders and cyclists, roller skaters and rollerbladers, and "regular-ass citizens marching on the streets of Philadelphia." Pacella also explains that the promotion of the protest was shared by wider-focused sports platforms and other non-skate-related social media as it was a collectively joyful and less-structured way for people to gather who may not see themselves as activists but wanted to get out and oppose racism. Pacella feels, "This is a perfect example of the role skateboarding plays in bringing about social change. We see the wrong and we call that shit out and we provide a platform for others to join in and call that shit out, too." He adds, "A lot of times they are just people influenced by our culture and wanting to be a part of something great."

Patrick Kigongo demonstrates another way the ordinary public can be supportive of Black Lives Matter. He is the creator of *The Black List* which promotes Black-owned skate businesses. Kigongo is a skateboarder and the child of immigrants from Uganda. He grew up in New York and now lives in Los Angeles, California. In his view, there are multiple ways that everyone can do something. He explains:

In 2020, skateboarders of all backgrounds have been involved. You have seen fundraising for parks or getting folks to donate clothes. You've seen skaters all over the world participating in pushes for peace. Some folks been doing stuff like myself putting together *The Black List* or trying to get people to organize. There have been folks who have been writing editorials in skateboarding magazines and talking about their experience.

Beyond the momentum of 2020, Kigongo has faith that things have kept changing. He states, for instance, that even in the immediate years after, "this moment occupies a distinct place in popular culture because skateboarding is no longer simply seen as, 'Oh, that's that White boy shit.'" What the Black Lives Matter movement was able to also achieve was that "skating is no longer something that is dismissed as a small segment of suburban White teenagers." He adds that this joins a more global outlook occurring in skateboarding where "kids all over the world skateboard and people who knew absolutely nothing about skateboarding now see skateboarders everywhere."

For Kigongo, this adds to more opportunities for unity across differences in skating, which is when he feels skateboarders who want to make change happen are at their most powerful. He states, "You saw such a diverse rank and file and that shows how skateboarding is able to make a dent." He also feels that "because skateboarding is also made up of a younger generation who are much more aware and actively engaged now, people are coming to the understanding that skateboarding is no longer just a one-way street where the industry dominates and dictates it."

Beyond Binaries of Black and White: PoC Experiences

Racism can often be viewed in binary terms of Black and White. In skateboarding culture, this can lead to a lack of recognition of other forms of racial and ethnic diversity. This includes skateboarders with Jewish ancestry or who are Jewish American but whose religious and ethnic identities are a lesser-known feature (Quarter Snacks Staff, 2012, Moldof, 2022). While there are many notable skateboarders of Jewish heritage such as Alan Gelfand, known for introducing the ollie, and Spike Jonze, a prolific skate video and filmmaker, we also acknowledge that Jewish American identities are not static or homogenous (Frankenberg, 1999) and some may only identify symbolically (Gans, 1979). Even so, it can be noted that Jewish skaters in the US are rarely discussed in skateboarding studies (O'Conner, 2020, Quarter Snacks Staff, 2012, Murrell 2018).

However, more awareness is beginning to emerge about non-Jewish high-profile skateboarders who express anti-Semitic slurs. There is also wider critique on the adoption of some of the imagery associated with the Nazi Party on skateboard products and clothing and as seen in statements made by professional skateboarder Jason Jessee (Beachy, 2018, 2021, Murrell, 2019) who later apologized in a hand-written statement at *Boardrap* (2018). As scholarship on skateboarding continues, more studies of ethnic and also religious diversity will grow (O'Conner, 2020), and we encourage more dedicated research on this population to be included.

Asian American skateboarders, and especially those with East and South-East Asian ancestry, have many influential, well-known figures from the 1960s to the 1990s. This includes Peggy Oki, Judi Oyama, Shogo Kubo, Christian Hosoi, Lester Kasai, Danny Supa, Willy Santos, Steve Caballero, Tommy Guerrero, Eric Koston, Jerry Hsu, Don Nguyen, William Nguyen, Spencer Fujimoto, and Daewon Song (also see Grosso, 2017a,b). They are followed by a new generation of elite skaters from the 2000s like Sean Malto, Jenn Soto, and those whose presence also advances Asian representation in skate videos, filmmaking, fashion, and art such as Eunice Chang, Kat Sy, Mitch Buangsuwon, Grant Yansura, Oorbee Roy, Jilleen Liao, Pat Sison, and Van Nguyen. There are also many Asian Americans who are influential behind the scenes in the skate industry like Jeffrey Cheung (Grosso 2020), Bing Liu (2018), Kim Woozy, and sports agent Yulin Olliver who have helped elevate their history (Willing, 2014, 2019a).

In 1998 the subversive and satirical magazine *Big Brother* also published the "Yellow" issue highlighting Asian skateboarders exclusively. These efforts join a pivotal and in-depth two-part series of interviews with numerous Asian American skateboarders from the 1970s to the 1990s as part of Jeff Grosso's (2017a, b) *Love Letters to Skateboarding* (also see Costa, 2017). Asian American skaters are also acknowledged in broader studies about race and PoC skaters (Williams, 2021, Yochim, 2010) and as being influential in skateboarding in Asia (McDuie-Ra,

2021, Willing 2021). Common themes across this literature include how skateboarding offered a way for Asian Americans to express an identity that went against traditional expectations often placed on them by migrant parents (Grosso, 2017a,b) and to have fun with and push against Asian stereotypes (Willing, 2014, 2019a). Yet there is little research specifically about Asian Americans in skateboarding history (Sueyoshi, 2015).

The skateboarders of Asian backgrounds we spoke with in this book took up some occasions to talk about their strategies for coping with xenophobia and anti-Asian racism. For instance, Peggy Oki's strategy to encourage anti-racism included everyday cosmopolitan gestures, such as sharing multicultural-themed memes on her social media accounts to show "the beauty we all share." Kim Woozy also spoke of how important it was to have Asian American "possibility models" in sports growing up, as Asians were often stereotyped as not being into the sport, let alone action sport. This led her to create Mahfia and later work on projects such as ones focused on the Japanese skateboarding scene with people like Chihiro Uchida "Chihi Rock" and Yulin Olliver to work toward ensuring individuals of Asian ancestry could be recognized as part of action sports like skateboarding and also able to inspire others (Willing, 2014, 2019a).

Contributions to skateboarding also include immigrants and diasporas from Middle Eastern geographies and skateboarders who identify as Muslim (Williams, 2021). Existing studies include Nida Ahmad and Holly Thorpe (2020) who note that Muslim American women in sports including action sports have to negotiate Islamophobia but are turning to social media to build their narratives and break stereotypes. This includes combatting stereotypes that link Muslims to terrorism or framing women as passive and oppressed because of their faith. Ahmad and Thorpe's (2020) study points to how social media has opened up platforms for Muslim girls and women to combat racism by documenting their own lives and framing their own sports narratives.

We also spoke with academic and SkatePal Ambassador Dani Abulhawa, whose heritage includes being British and Palestinian. Support for SkatePal extends over to the US, with professional skaters like Ryan Lay also being involved as a volunteer. One of the challenges Abulhawa raises is that for people in the West like those in the US who only view violence-based media images of Palestinian people, "there's a kind of problematic gaze around that." One of the issues is that Palestinian people can feel dehumanized and made spectacles of, which, Abulhawa states, "a lot of people want to also resist, so it's Western audiences always consuming this voyeuristic encounter with the people." Rather than just "seeing what's happening at these hot points," she proposes that it is vital to "actually having a relationship with people and gaining a sense of what the everyday experience is like." This can include visiting programs overseas, but also following Palestinian skateboarders and programs on social media, reading and engaging with online and offline content.

The history of Latin and Hispanic skateboarding is also yet to be more fully acknowledged. We acknowledge that some use the term "Latin" and "Latinx" as a general umbrella to refer to people who may also identify as Hispanic, Latino, Latin American, Mexican American/Chicano, or Indigenous Latinos, Afro-Latinos, and, more broadly, as immigrants or children of immigrants from Portuguese- and Spanish-speaking countries in Central and South America. Although we use the term "Latin" and "Hispanic," we do so with an awareness that all ethnic labels can be contested and shifting (Campos, 2021).

There are many examples of famous skateboarders like Stacy Peralta, Cindy Whitehead, Mark Gonzales, Paul Rodriguez, Stevie Perez, Leo Romero, Tony Alva, Socrates Leal, Louie Lopez, and Vanessa Torres, but the focus is not so much on the Latino or Hispanic community but rather on their successes generally as skateboarders (Snyder, 2017). Efforts to highlight more such histories include by Abel Macias, who is a skateboarder and professor of Chicano Studies at San Diego State University. Also recently, insight into Hispanic experiences of skateboarding is covered in the evocative memoir *Interstate* by Jose Vardi (2021). Skate media has also been a source of overviews and homage articles (Kerr, 2019, Lapchick, 2009, Lupine, 2015, Ramiez, 2016). In Part 2 we include some reflections by Norma Ibarra, who is Mexican and works in Canada and the US, about her experiences as a photographer.

We also spoke with Christian Kerr (2019) who wrote about "Latinx" skateboarders for *Jenkem*. His experience is an important reminder of how even the terms to use for ethnic communities require knowledge that they can involve shifting language and sensitivities to how members position themselves historically, politically, and geographically. Latinx arose as a gender-neutral way to refer to skateboarders from Latin America, Mexico, and Spanish-speaking nations where immigrants and following generations have made lives in the US (for more discussion, see Hernandez, 2017). Kerr felt even with language and using the term Latinx "I don't know if I made the right decision on that one, you know, considering kind of like how the language debates are so quickly changing." He explains, "It almost overshadowed the point of the piece in general. That was a tough one because I wrote it at a time where Latinx was still at the forefront of what people were using."

Kerr also emphasizes the need for more stories about various ethnic communities and children of immigrants, stating, "I think that the 'skating's for White boys' culture is not the only truth that stands." He also stresses that no one culture is monolithic, adding, "It's important to show that you can tell lots of different kinds of stories about the origin of skating and the Latin history of it." Kerr also warns, "I think the Latin community is so diverse with its nationalities and also politically. If we're thinking about an entire group of people, you're not getting this unified response because there are a lot of internal tensions between all these different people." As Kerr emphasizes, "There are a million different stories and none of them are mutually exclusive from one another." In his view, "in a way, it's sort of a convergent evolution where it's happening all in different places around the world…sort of at the same time."

Evolving Collaborations and Emerging Equity

This second section of Part 1 of this chapter will now turn to explore the changing nature of how skateboarders interact with the skate industry and view the social benefits of skate competitions. This includes hearing about how change-makers think the industry can change from a position of control over to being open to collaboration, and with more balance between large brands' focus on profit and what it can do for communities who are also potential and existing consumers.

We then consider what meanings skateboarders place on competitions by speaking with Kim Woozy who in 2019 advocated for California State Bill AB 467 (Equal Pay for Equal Play) which was signed into law in 2020. We also talked with Amelia Brodka who founded the Exposure

Skate competition in 2012 which with Lesli Cohen in 2013 and others has gone on to become a major annual competition and has the biggest women's and non-binary prize purse for a skateboarding contest in the world. Brodka was also a representative for Poland at the Tokyo Olympics. As we shall see, rather than prioritizing the act of winning, she throws light on issues such as the importance of standing up for pay parity, inclusive competition, and open-minded outlooks.

Pushing Industry to Share Power

The rising power of the skate industry has shaped much of what is considered normative in skate culture, often revolving around White masculinity and heteronormativity (Beachy, 2021; Delardi, 2021; Dinces, 2011; Geckle, 2022, Grosso 2020). Challenging this, Douglas Miles Sr. states:

> Cool dudes and cool music and rad skateboarding are awesome but what else is skateboarding offering to communities? What else are you offering in terms of opportunities to Black, Asian, Latino, and Native skateboarders? Are you paying Black, Asian, and Latino skateboarders to be pros? Are you putting Black, Asian, Latino, and Native skateboarders in as team managers or filmers?

Miles Sr.'s critique is also important in revealing how "all these opportunities are closed because you don't hear about it…they keep it to themselves." He also calls for industry figures in power to think about how "you're not hiring Black, Asian, Latino, and Native American people, and yet we're some of your biggest core supporters buyers. Where is the inclusion?"

Industry exclusion was one of the key themes raised in our interviews as was frustration over token gestures and being exploited. We explore these issues but also where skateboarders feel they have gained more power and better interactions. Karlie Thornton from froSkate provides us with some insights into how it can be helpful for "non-traditional" skateboarders to look at strategies outside the skateboarding world to negotiate what is fair within the skate industry. This includes her background in advertising as an art director and creative strategist. She states, "I come from multicultural advertising. I used to work for a Black-woman-owned agency as well, so I've been able to take what I've learned from advertising into skateboarding." This includes being aware that "exposure is not enough" and that skaters need to be paid properly and have a say in how they want to engage. She states, "There've been plenty of brands that we turned down collaborating with. I can tell if they're being disingenuous. I have high standards for us."

Thornton explains froSkate's busiest time of the year is *Black History Month* and explains, "It's hard because we do want to be represented by big companies. We got to be on an *Apple* billboard. Something like that gets me excited, but at the same time, we're trying to not only spread our mission but become a representative for our race. Unfortunately, we feel like we have to." Yet for Thornton, "the reason I got into advertising was to be able to bring more Black and Brown people into these representative spaces and just be able to see ourselves doing things or just being areas in which we've never seen ourselves before."

At present, Thornton feels: "we are now in a good place where we can ask that question of why are you coming to us? When we speak to brands I'll say, 'Okay, let's not make this a one-off campaign and then we never hear from you again. How can you promise that we're gonna hear from you in the future?'" On their partnership with Nike SB, which includes a shoe collaboration launched in August 2022, she explains, "It has been pretty good because we've worked on some different campaigns with them and they continue to communicate and help us out with things that we need and sponsor some events." For her "that's an ideal partnership for me because I can tell it's not just because we're Black. They do still need our support and our community but also they care about what we're doing."

L Brew from their experiences with froSkate argues that there needs to be an ethical rather than just financial dimension that they would like to see built into collaborations with skateboarders. They state, "These brands need to have an understanding that equity is more important than a dollar amount." They add, "If you're investing in us—if you're investing in our ecosystem if you're using the thing that we built from the ground up to give some authentic to your brand—I'd rather you stick around and be a partner than write me a check because the check goes away." In light of the Black Lives Matter movement, L Brew also explains, "I think that's a positive change from in the past. Basically, in the wake of George Floyd and Black Lives Matter, these brands have to re-evaluate their relationships." They reflect, "I'm not saying it's a sweeping positive change but understanding that they have less power than they think and they have to evaluate how these relationships work." Key to this is acts of resistance and defiance to industry norms where she states that "the more they're pushed back on, the more the power shifts."

While having sustainable business practices and being profitable are key goals, not all support "from above" has to be financial. Latosha Stone from Proper Gnar emphasizes how encouragement from higher profile identities and bigger brands can also be valuable. For instance, Stevie Williams from DGK reached out to support her. She talked about how "he founded the first Black-owned company that I ever knew and seeing him do that inspired me to do what I do." While the proposed collaboration has not eventuated as yet, Stone adds it raised her confidence to believe in her work and says, "It was the highlight of my life. I didn't even respond to him until the next day because I was like, 'oh my god like Stevie messaged me!'"

Moreover, the exposure Beyoncé gave her increased her sales so much that she rapidly went from a small DIY brand to a formal business. While the effect overall was positive, Stone also had to learn how to deal with increased business demands and harassment on social media. She states, "I don't get as much hate now as I used to get online but a few years ago it was ridiculous." Stone hired an assistant who checks her social media and email. For Stone, it also helps when "I do get in moods where I don't want to get online because I can get social media burnout. When you own a business, you feel like you have to be there every day interacting." Balance, she proposes, is important because "if what you have to do in business interferes too much with your overall life, it's gonna fail."

One of the important changes that smaller businesses can do is to create more socially responsible brands. Stone donates to various charities including ones related to Black Lives Matter and with a rainbow range, gives profits to The Trevor Project that supports LGBTQIA+ youth. She adds that being smaller gives her more freedom of expression as well, stating, "Some people feel so constrained that they can't address anything political in skateboarding because it will affect their business, whereas I run the business so I speak as I like."

Stone also works with models who represent a greater diversity than many bigger brands. She states, "I try to use all types of models and things that you don't typically see when it comes to skate brands." She feels that she has seen the most change since 2020 and that before that "I feel like all skate magazines and videos and stuff were all White guys—all regular looking White guys." For Stone, her motivation includes how she lacked role models growing up, stating, "I think diverse role models are important for little Black girls, to have that representation and to see themselves, because when I was younger I didn't have anybody like that to look up to." She argues that when they see "somebody that looks like me that does skateboard, they think, 'maybe I can go do that now.'"

The Doyenne Skateboards company also builds its brand image in a way that customers "can see themselves represented by our brand or knowing that our brand cares about the world." "Mara," who is one of the founders, adds, "We also keep working on understanding how to do things better for the environment. We grew organically, and it was slow and not very ecologically sustainable at one point, but there was like a turning point of feeling part of a bigger thing." After that, Doyenne Skateboards incorporated recyclable materials. Mara also explains their business model, "We always remember that part of the money will be reinvested into the brand, but also we always donate to the skateboarding charities out there we believe in."

The fundraising that Doyenne Skateboards does includes various campaigns, including ones on awareness of neurodiversity with Hart Club, consent with Consent for Breakfast, Consent Is Rad, and Hera Skate (Huston 2022), and on awareness of disability and issues of recognition, equity, and well-being. Mara explains, "We also donated to a local brand for people with low visibility and blind people. We made a t-shirt that had our logo in Braille embroidery. It was a way to raise awareness about the fact that people with a disability are excluded in fashion." The brand's mission statement includes that "we want everyone, skateboarders and non-skateboarders, to know this brand is for them, and we don't care how hardcore their heelflip is" and that Doyenne Skateboards "channels inclusivity and intersectionality by questioning ourselves and our environment, but most importantly by opening conversations with our community, listening to them and trying to constantly reflect it in the work we do."

In contrast to small skate brands, NHS Inc. is a major skateboard manufacturer and distribution company that was established in 1972 and oversees brands such as Santa Cruz, Creature, Mob Grip, OJ Wheels, Independent Trucks, and Krux Trucks. We spoke with Alex White who joined them in 2019 and is the Krux Brand Manager and became the first Women's and Non-Binary Rider Relations Manager at NHS Inc. (2022). When approaching issues of equity and inclusion, she is now able to combine her experiences as a former professional skateboarder, video maker, and part of the women's DIY culture and work with groups like The Skate Witches with her increasing industry knowledge. She recalls that rather than waiting for the industry to change, "we ended up building our ladder, our mini industry to prop up the talent, and that's valuable."

Acknowledging the power that can come with working at NHS Inc., White describes it as "the longest standing legacy brand. I can't say they've always had a perfect track record, but I negotiated this position where I'm like the women's and non-binary writer relations manager." Her objective "is just like trying to help the brands change with the times though they were already on that trajectory." An example she shares is how Independent changed its logo from an Iron Cross, which has in the past been adopted by punks and bikers but is also associated with Nazi iconography. White states, "During the BLM protests, it was like this total revolution that we were having this awakening around racism in the country. They decided like right then like we're changing the logo." She describes their willingness as being "like, I don't care if it's tattooed on everybody in our creative departments back, if people are perceiving this logo as being racist and if like racists are adopting this logo, we need to cut it, because it doesn't matter what our intentions are anymore."

An important approach at NHS Inc. for White is that they "really ask the questions and pay attention to how they're being perceived and want to be perceived, better and correctly." But it is also not a case of them giving more power but rather, they are experiencing the kind of engagement and ethical reflexivity (Plage et al., 2017) where the emphasis is on sharing. White explains, "The biggest positive change in skateboarding I've seen is this understanding that women or non-traditional skaters are beyond tokenized, they are a viable part of the marketplace or the community."

Tommy Guerrero as co-founder at Real Skateboards is someone who has been able to bridge activism with the need to sell things in the marketplace for many years. The company has a history of taking bold stances on things such as racism, notably with the "hanging Klansman board" (Dobija-Nootens, 2017). Their priority was not so much activism but to do their own thing, and he states, "That was putting new ideas out there. And really fun shit too like…it doesn't all have to be heavy." However, he adds that with the Klansmen board which was Jim Thiebaud's idea, it "was throwing a monkey wrench in the works of government and, and so forth. You know, these are very heavy messages and Jim got a lot of flack for it. *Real* got a lot of grief for it."

On provocative and political messages, Guerrero states, "It was all very, at the moment by the seat of our pants, and trying to do what we felt was something a little different." But he also explains, "I'm just trying to grow the company as well, at the same time, in any kind of meaningful way. I'm just trying to make some changes, you know, trying to do some good stuff with the vehicle that we have." He adds, "Some initiatives are brought to the table by Jim (Thiebaud) because you know, Jim is trying to be helpful in an actual, tangible way to different communities." This includes the ActionREALize (https://actionsrealized.com/) boards which are brought out by Real and with profits going to different social projects such as Unity Skateboards dedicated to LGBTQIA+ skaters, Jaime Reyes collaboration with Skate Like a Girl to raise funds for mental health support for skaters, and the Ben Raemers Foundation addressing suicide prevention.

For Guerrero, it was a "way to help those who were in need at the time. And it was direct, which I dig is, you know, sort of, it's not a roundabout way." For him, it is most effective to be "giving the person the money and just doing types of things to make a little difference, a dent in the need of what is out there." In his following statement, we can see how the ethical foundations of such projects that are built into his and Thiebaud's business are guided by valuing a sense of collective purpose and sharing profits rather than just accumulating wealth:

> I think the thing is you can't constantly just live for yourself. It's unfulfilling, it's not something that you're sort of after it's not, it's not like that, the end game result is to line your pockets and, you know, have the stuff. It's not that it's just, you know, it's to keep the lights on, you know, and do some good. (Guerrero quoted from our interview)

The emphasis by skaters in the discussion above where the industry is concerned is on thinking about the importance of collaborations, being mentored, and having more powerful people share their platforms and profits. It is not enough to make a space inclusive by adding Black models to a one-off photo shoot or giving money or visibility once a year when it is a heritage month. The emphasis is on substantial relationships and reciprocity. This also opens awareness of issues of financial compensation and how and with who profits are shared.

Non-traditional Skater's Outlooks on Skateboarding Competitions

In the period leading up to skateboarding's inclusion in the Summer 2020 Olympic Games (postponed to 2021 due to Covid-19-related restrictions), Neftalie Williams (2022: 8) highlights how much of the discussion on whether competitions help or hinder skate culture has been dominated by "White, Western males." He also highlights research by Belinda Wheaton and Becky Beal (2019, 2021) who argue, "The Olympics offered a unique opportunity to create gender equity within skateboarding culture for women and girls because of the enforced gender equity of Olympic events" (Williams, 2022: 8). His study presents a critical inquiry on how intersectionality affects the meanings elite Black and PoC skateboarders place on the Olympics. Importantly, his study reminds us of how Black and PoC skateboarders and various "non-traditional skateboarders" along lines of gender can use competitions as a tool for awareness, highlighting underrepresented voices, and as spaces to accomplish not just sporting achievements but also social change with varying degrees of success.

The Olympic Games still uphold a range of exclusions, with many inconsistencies in its rules and structures that can reproduce inequality. In disciplines such as track and field races, for instance, the exclusion of some women athletes over others has shed light on a series of trans-exclusionary and racist decisions (Pape, 2019). Concerns are also raised over gendered divisions that uphold a gender binary of men and women, which rests on false beliefs about biological advantages, not any scientifically confirmed fact, and works to deny the inclusion of non-binary, intersex, and gender-diverse participants.

The gender binary is also argued to be part of "the colonial project" (O'Sullivan, 2021) that has imposed the idea of only two genders over Indigenous and non-Western frameworks that are continually resisted. Processes of anti-Blackness are also often in operation in decisions to exclude Black athletes while allowing White athletes also on a gender spectrum to compete (Pape, 2019). Research on transgender skateboarders and the Olympics is only beginning to emerge (Willing and Barbier, 2020), but the impacts can be observed in non-binary and trans-athletes decisions such as Leo Baker's withdrawal from the USA Skateboarding team and Alana Smith, who uses they/them pronouns and had written that on their skateboard deck being misgendered at the Tokyo Games by announcers during their run.

At the time of writing this book, there was also a critical turnaround from USA Skateboarding (USAS), which is the National Governing Body for skateboarding in the US, and its Olympic team. On August 6, 2022, social media ignited with a series of posts featuring white text that stated "We quit. Effective immediately" on a blue background and with a small US flag at the top. Each was announcing a group resignation by the High-Performance Team of USAS, which included Mimi Knoop from the Women's Skateboarding Alliance (WSA), Micaela Ramirez from The Poseiden Foundation, and Oscar Loreto Jr, an elite athlete, filmmaker, and disability activist.

A sports industry news article by Duncan Mackay (2022) also revealed that Gary Ream, who was the USAS Chair, resigned following an audit conducted by the United States Olympic and Paralympic Committee.

The article alleges this included a lack of transparency, only meeting 12 of the 48 compliance standards required, and falling short of expectations of progressing in the areas of diversity and inclusion.

As we can see, skateboarding's incorporation into the US national structures required for competing in the Olympics in the lead-up to its debut and following it has not been a smooth road. Yet, despite the barriers, conflicts, and setbacks in its short history so far, the attention the Olympic Games is capable of generating, positive and negative, has pushed some organizers of big competitions to consider how equality should be built into their structures but often is not. This includes a turn-around by competitions previously offering higher prize money to men that have not always had divisions for other genders. We shall soon highlight how competitions run by "non-traditional" skateboarders are a growing community solution. But in the first part of this section, we hear about some of the strategies that can make larger competitions embrace pay parity.

In 2019 Kim Woozy was invited to advocate for the California State Bill AB 467 (Equal Pay for Equal Play). This equity bid was initiated by people in the surfing world when women wanted to participate in the Mavericks Surfing Competition. Woozy explains, "They have to pull permits and as some of the women surfers were advocating for a women's division and getting denied, they ended up connecting with local government officials who realized this is beyond surfing, this is a human right issue." She adds that "the whole idea was that if they're pulling state permits to hold an event and it's occurring on state lands" which means they see the competitors as how the state would pay an employee in any job where all genders would be making the same amount.

Although they faced significant resistance, the World Surfing League that oversees Mavericks eventually backed the campaign and even promoted it as a way to build inclusivity into their image. Woozy describes the turnaround as the following: "They went from saying there's no way to, yeah, look at us, we are into gender equality." As a leader in the women's action sports community, Woozy was invited by Tasha Boerner Horvath and Cori Schumacher to act as a witness for the "Equal Pay to Play" Bill. The Bill was successfully signed into law in January 2020 and mandates female athletes receive equal prize money for athletic competitions held on state lands (Barbier, 2020).

Woozy explains there is still work to do as the Bill does not say there have to be multiple gender divisions, so contests can continue with only men. However, she shares the following advice:

> What I learned is in the legislative process it's a lot easier to just make it simple. When you start to add layers to all these conditions people start to be like 'oh we don't know we don't, we don't know.' So the plan was to focus on equal pay first and then participation at the next level. You have to go one step at a time.

The appeal skateboarding has to officials and the public is also something Woozy also feels can be underestimated. She explains, "One of the senators was an older gentleman and he said, 'I used to skateboard back in my day like this is amazing.'" She also describes how "a lot of them were just excited because the other bills are about very mundane stuff. They were so excited that there was something cool to see." Another tactic is empathy and holding up a mirror to officials. Woozy recalls an example she heard of putting oneself in the shoes of a parent who has to explain to their daughters why girls and women on a podium would hold checks of lesser value. She states, "You have to explain to your kid, 'Well, girls are worth less' and you're perpetuating that narrative that existed 50 years ago when women were perceived as less valuable than men."

Outside of official competitions, the influence of DIY culture in skateboarding can be seen in the rise of women's, non-binary, and queer-led competitions. One of the largest is Exposure Skate which was founded in 2012 and also has maintained the biggest "prize purse," totaling $60,000 for their 2022 event. We spoke with Olympian Amelia Brodka about Exposure Skate who describes the competition going from 24 participants at its inaugural event in 2012 to having 230 participants from 23 different countries in 2020. She states, "The growth has been exponential." She also explains how the impacts are social, including "new friendships blossoming between girls who live in separate parts of the world and to see kind of the joy and the support that they all bring each other in skateboarding." The competition also removes barriers and gatekeeping often held up in men's competitions. She states, "No matter what level they skate or what they like to skate…it's been cool to see the community grow globally."

Brodka and her team had to move the competition online to a video part contest in 2020 and 2021 due to Covid-19 restrictions. However, they looked at the situation from a skater's perspective, which includes a love for "stacking clips" which is a colloquial term referring to skateboarders filming their progress and tricks to share online, often to gain or at the request of their sponsors. The video format was therefore seen as having positives. She states, "I think it's really important for skate culture and for these non-traditional skaters to have that space to be incentivized and supported and to be putting out legitimate video parts." The competition covered vert and transition but also street parts, which "non-traditional" skaters have traditionally lacked representation in skate media (McDuie-Ra, 2021, Yochim, 2010).

Emphasizing the collective benefits of the competition, rather than just on individual accomplishment alone, Brodka was eager to see "non-traditional" skaters "getting in the streets and progressing their skating and progressing our community skating as a whole." The video competition was also a way to reach a wider audience beyond just the people able to attend the screening of finalists held in Encinitas, California. She states, "It was great to be able to do that virtually and then to have people watching it live together…it created collective support, collective admiration, and collective acknowledgment."

The competition was also designed to encourage skateboarders to feel a connection with the judges who consisted of major icons and breakthrough figures in skateboarding. These were Elissa Steamer, Vanessa Torres, Alex White, and Jaime Reyes. Brodka states, "Elissa Steamer was just such an icon to me growing up" and "Vanessa Torres…I watched her video part *Elementality Vol 1* almost every single day before I went skating in high school." She also adds, "Everything that Alex White does and has done is super inspirational and Jaime Reyes' Thrasher cover and contributions to skateboarding are legendary." Although she is a high-profile, professionally sponsored, champion vert skateboarder and Olympian, she jokes how she was no different from other skaters who meet them and "fanned out," explaining, "I was thinking, 'Be cool, like, totally normal. I'm chill' and laughed."

Brodka expressed how the environment of conviviality and support that skateboarders brought for each other into the Tokyo Olympic Games was one of the positives. This reflection supports studies that suggest that despite the shortcomings, the Games could be an occasion for social good when it is skateboarders who influence it and not the other way around (Wheaton and Thorpe, 2019, 2021, Williams, 2022, Willing and Barbier, 2020). Brodka states that at a personal level she was "very grateful to have made it that that was a dream come true. A dream I never even thought could exist. When I started skating it wasn't even a possibility. So that part feels amazing." But she also looks at the situation in a pragmatic way, stating, "I think it's helped women skateboarding…it's not just a coincidence that as soon as skateboarding's inclusion in the 2020 Summer Olympics was announced, then all sudden, competitions had prize purse parity and every competition had a women's division." She feels that pushed competition organizers reflect on how

> as an Olympic sport, it means there have to be equal medals. You know, that means there has to be equal support for the men and the women. All of a sudden we actually had more events and then because we had more events, we had more support, and then there were more girls and the level was getting higher.

Another area Brodka felt was positive from the Tokyo Games was how the women's division coverage in "core" skate media and podcasts like *The Nine Club* that "rarely ever talk about any 'non-traditional' skaters, or even any transition skaters for that matter," were "being totally blown away by the level of skating that the women are doing." She feels that the Games helped a broader audience to have "that shift in perspective and awareness of how much women have been progressing." Another point she makes is how there was positive coverage of Alana Smith, who is a non-binary skateboarder. Brodka states, "Skateboarding is for so many people." She adds that this includes how she and girls and women of all ages "got to participate, as well as non-binary folk and others who just really show the diversity and inclusion that skateboarding brings."

The skateboarders at Tokyo in 2021 also fostered a type of cosmopolitanism that transcended nationality. Brodka recalls how non-skaters watching the camaraderie that skaters showed regardless of what team they were on "were all like 'Why was the Brazilian cheering for the Australian and the American was hugging the Japanese skater? What is this?'" While these values can be seen in other sports, interesting insights also arise from skateboarding due to how skaters do not tend to practice in teams, but in crews or independently or with anyone who may be around during a session. This leads to conviviality and openness that is being possibly embraced, rather than suppressed in their Olympic experiences.

Empathy and everyday openness is also embodied in moments such as when Misugu Okamoto was lifted up and carried on the shoulders of fellow competitors Poppy Starr-Olsen and Bryce Wettstein after she'd fallen on her last run. Brodka explains, "It meant absolutely the world to her. It turned into this moment where they said, 'Hey, your community is here to lift you up, literally.'" For Brodka this illuminates how

> if you fall, that's the beauty of skateboarding. At the end of the day, the thing that I was most proud of was how that shone through and how skateboarding was presented to the world—that we support one another. We're in a competition but it's not necessarily "us against them." We want to see each other succeed.

However, Brodka does not just restrict these observations to "non-traditional" skaters and also includes how men also demonstrated such connections. This included for her "watching Cory Juneau and Keegan Palmer on the deck having fun with each other after each other's runs." She continues, "I don't know if that was shown on TV, but it was beautiful. Sometimes in the past, for men to show their feelings, it was maybe questioned which is ridiculous, right?" But, she explains, "for them to not only not be competitive, but hug each other in such a gleeful way in front of all of these cameras and people watching, that was beautiful in a lot of ways." In her observations, we also see more of the "alternative masculinity" that studies suggest skateboarding can foster in place of more hegemonic and toxic forms ingrained in many mainstream sports (Atencio, M, and Beal, B, 2011, Willing et al., 2020).

Part 2: Change-Making in Media, Creative Landscapes, and Knowledge

Next in focus are skateboarders who are storytellers, creatives, and future knowledge produces. Snyder (2017: 176) in his reflections on "subcultural media and the digital turn" states that "skateboard media are not simply about profit but are essential for the continued progression of the subculture." This includes also defining what counts for "good skating," such as trick choices, spots, styles, and behavior. The curating of skateboarding culture does not just fall into the hands of writers but also consists of a "visual literature" (Snyder, 2017: 176) where photographers, video makers, editors, and other creative fields all play an important role. We also consider education pathways as another area where a lack of equity can be an issue.

Our exploration in the first section of Part 2 begins by sharing insights from individuals who work in skate media, podcasting, academia, and various creative areas. We reveal how the DIY approach has been pivotal to the rise of independent magazines and online platforms by "nontraditional skaters." Through podcasts, photography, editorial, and video skaters are carving out a place outside of the "core" masculine culture. In the second part of Part 2, we highlight examples of men showing allyship by using various forms of satire as a self-critique of dominant forms of masculinity. We then explore the area of education and future knowledge producers in the third section of Part 2 by focusing on a scholarship program that assists skateboarders to gain college degrees. Skate culture has only recently paid attention to what role education can play in skateboarding (Kerr, 2018), but professional skateboarders have noted that such avenues—while not available to everyone—can be beneficial for self-development as well as broadening their options (Lay, 2019). However, access in the US can be expensive and out of reach for many.

We talk to skateboarders about what motivates them to provide scholar-ships and how they may keep the program growing.

DIY Approaches and Bringing Change to Skate Media

This section explores what change-making means to those behind how skate culture is documented, spanning areas that encompass expressive and creative practices such as writing, research, photography, and satirical content. Some of the content that these change-makers produce is meant to simply inform or bring greater representation or provoke critique and ethical reflection. We highlight the perspectives of people who are involved with various creative and artistic projects which also promote skateboarders to think about issues of inclusion and social equity.

Skate media has not always been a welcoming place for "non-traditional" skaters. This is especially the case in print and videos. Over 20 years ago, Becky Beal and Lisa Weidman (2003: 349) were critical of the typical ads and images of women in skating magazines such as *Thrasher*, which were often invested in "the core value of masculinity" that "specifically appealed to male, heterosexual desires, while others appeal to skaters' admiration of toughness and risk-taking." When women appeared, it was "through the use of female models who possess a number of feminine characteristics" (349). They also describe how:

> The models sometimes function as trophies or adornments for fully clothed (and usually recognizable) male skateboarders. In other cases, the female models appear only with the products being advertised (or even without the products) and function as sexual enticements to the young male read-ers. (Beal and Weidman, 2003: 549)

Skateboarding Hall of Fame inductee, Cindy Whitehead, who won multiple skate championships in the 1970s and now runs the skate plat-form Girl Is Not a 4 Letter Word, felt that early on, men also had a lim-ited view of what women could achieve when skating due to the types of skating they were most visible and promoted doing. She explains how: "I think before when women were doing freestyle it was deemed feminine and pretty and it was okay to go do those gymnastics maneuvers on a skateboard, people were like 'oh, isn't that pretty and cute and fluid,' and it's not a threat to anybody." However, she states, "When you start skating pools and vert and then later the girls skating street, it becomes more of a threat—you're in a male world."

Emily Yochim (2010: 28) also outlines how, "The various moments at which particular mythologies of the skateboarding culture are solidified and disrupted, demonstrate skateboarding's flexibility as both a discourse and a practice built into and outside of mainstream culture." And as Whitehead's conversation shows, the mythology of skating as an exclusively White, heterosexual men's activity is repeatedly disrupted, even if from the margins of skate culture. Whitehead recalls, "When an all-girls issue came out, whether it was *Thrasher* or *Transworld*, I remember talking to a CEO in the skateboarding industry and going, 'God is this great.'" She continues, "Then he said something that I should have thought of: 'yeah it's great but wouldn't it be better to see equal coverage of the girls, every single month instead of one issue devoted to girls?'" Despite special issues, however, Whitehead feels "core" magazines still have a long way to go in terms of inclusion going from token to normalized. She states, "In reality if you flick through every issue, are you still seeing those things? Not so much. I mean I picked up *Thrasher* yesterday and I don't see any consistency at all."

Yuliya Kulynych's (2020) contemporary study of women skateboarders assists with outlining how persistent socially constructed hierarchies of gender can be. She builds on Raewyn Connell's (1995) concepts of "emphasized femininity" and "hegemonic masculinity" to see how gender hierarchies are still naturalized in many portrayals of skate culture. At the same time, the participants in her study also expressed defiance and resistance to oppressive beliefs in skating around gender and "viewed their femininity as a discourse that could be actively redefined, in relation to conventional masculine and feminine cultural expressions" (Kulynych, 2020: 82).

One of the major issues in skate media in the past has been a lack of "non-traditional" skateboarders holding the roles of editors, particularly in print media. But skate media is also evolving to include not just print magazines and videos produced by skate companies, but also social media content, online magazines and blogs, Internet video channels, podcasts, and other broadcast platforms. With these expansions, "non-traditional" skateboarders have taken up more powerful and influential roles in various media, and often ones they create via a DIY approach bolstered by accessible and affordable technology.

In many ways, skate media is currently experiencing what could be called an era of democratization (Willing 2020a). For instance, feminist studies of sport more broadly explain how platforms such as social media have assisted women and girls not only to share their activities in ways they want to be represented, but also to draw attention to and gain support for social issues that affect them (Ahmad and Thorpe, 2020, Thorpe et al., 2017, Thorpe et al., 2018, Toffoletti and Thorpe, 2018a, 2018b, Toffoletti et al., 2018). But there is also a legacy of writings and zines forged by women and other "non-traditional" skaters from older generations from the 1960s to the 1990s, which were at risk of becoming what youth studies scholar Christine Feldman-Barrett (2014) calls a "lost history of youth culture" but are now being documented by sites such as documented by the Instagram account Womxn's Skateboarding History @womxnsk8history.

Lynn Kramer, who is a champion skateboarder, was one of the earlier change-makers to get women represented on the pages. She states, "In 1988 I took over the Women's Skateboard Network…I created quarterly zines for distribution by mail and to skateboard shops. By 1990 we had 200+ women members on three continents. Our message is 'Women Skate.'" Kramer points to how dedication is needed to gain any ground in advancing gender equity and to keep the momentum, "Things need to be turned around. I mean, physically. It won't just happen. You have to work at it. Like my promotion of a zine dedicated to women included road trips to visit and connect women skaters."

Pivotal moments of change that Kramer acknowledges include "the subsequent women's contests like Exposure and also pioneering women with pro model decks, wheels, and shoes." She adds, "The people behind these, opened the door for others. They decided that it would benefit the scene." Kramer states that she is thankful to various "women who have helped the women's scene including but not limited to Amelia Brodka,

Patty McGee, and Cindy Whitehead." Kramer also acknowledges "an alternative skateboard magazine for several years called *Concrete Wave*. This magazine opened up skateboarding. They featured plenty of women, as well as downhill, pools, freestyle, and slalom. It was everything *Thrasher* was not." She hopes a newer generation of skaters of all genders will be taking up space and stresses, "Now that we have the web…people can just see what they want to see. If you want to see 'women skateboarding' you can just type that in and up it pops."

Kim Woozy's reflection on her experiences creating skate media bridges the era where print magazines and videos on DVD and YouTube were the main ways to view skating over to the new era of social media. Her motivation was after working on Osiris and growing up being both a customer and a fan right but seeing people she felt were "super rad humans" not get elevated based on shoe sale figures. However, rather than being a situation of women not being able to sell shoes, she felt they needed to give the whole women's scene more exposure, support, promotion, and time to raise those sales. She states, "I get it, that's the reality of business and capitalism. But then I shifted to media because that's also what I went to school for and before I even worked in the skate and action sports industry." She then created Mahfia with a focus on elite action sports women's lifestyle as much as their skills. It was after Woozy went to Japan that she then saw a scene where skateboarding was comparatively new, and a lot more people were having a go, not just ones who were at the advanced elite level. For her "that was the first real-life example of being an adult beginner and just going for it." She now feels that "with the evolution of technology we started seeing more of that."

Woozy's work with Skate Like a Girl, for instance, uses social media to encourage women and/or transgender and non-binary skaters to feel validated that they belong in skateboarding. The importance, she explains, is that "I think before you had things like Instagram all you saw was the best. It just felt like it was out of reach or it felt like these people are just naturally talented; they must have been born super good skateboarders, and clearly, I'm not. So therefore I'm not even gonna try." Woozy feels that, unlike traditional media, "when Instagram came along, it was a different story because you can post anything and everything, whereas before it was very curated."

While it is clear that print magazines are no longer the most dominant mode that skateboarders consume the culture's news, images, and opinions, they still have a certain prestige and appeal. Many traditional magazines such as *Thrasher* keep their flagship, hard copy printed monthly magazine while also having various online content posted daily. A much smaller operation, *Skateism* also prints a traditional magazine as well as its online version and social media. It is based in Europe but has an international circulation and engages regularly with US content and audiences. *Skateism* began in 2012 and has had various writers and staff. Alternative media platforms are not without critical feedback from various community perspectives. This has included calls for better representation of transgender, non-binary, gender-diverse, Black, and PoC skaters. Independent magazines have best responded to include more diversity across their editorial pages and creative staff.

Skateism's cover photos have included Brian Anderson, Briana King, Myles de Courcy, and Chandler Burton, as well as publishing work by photographer Samuel McGuire who, like Brian Anderson, was part of a turnaround in 2016 of challenging the industry's heteronormativity by discussing their experiences as gay men (Geckle and Shaw, 2022). The style and target audiences are not unique to *Skateism* and follow progressive zines such as the ones by Kramer as well as *XEM* and *The Skate Witches*. But as a full-size magazine, it competes with traditional ones like *Thrasher* and has become one of the largest publications of its kind that specifically aims to be inclusive.

We spoke with Denia Kopita who, when we were conducting interviews, was the editor of *Skateism* until 2022. Rather than the magazine emphasizing the biggest stair sets or the latest never been done (NBD) trick, she states, "I think a conversation is the most important thing we can do, sharing stories." One of the reasons for her is that can build understanding and empathy. She states, "If someone is called racist, or if they have very specific ways of seeing things you can be like, 'Okay, go watch this interview, be open, and listen to what others are saying…' you have these opinions because you've never experienced going outside your own life and world" and that it helps to dismiss fears through "listening to other people's stories."

The representation of diverse genders in skate media is also an area still lagging for Kopita which she describes as "we need to have more women…we're not just five girls skating anymore. There are so many different women and non-binary people skating everywhere, not just in Europe or the US, you know." However, at *Skateism*, she also states, "it is not about a quota but more what the skater is about." Kopita describes the process of selection as depending on things such as "if we like someone, if we think that they're cool, a very good person, and they're doing things in the community. They might be owning their style or be different. We are a diversity skate magazine." She explains further, "This is the first thing that we try and see. If we like someone because we like to support everyone…we just try to support what's different, like the *Skateism* motto, we are all 'for the weird and wonderful.'" The content online and in print magazines reflects this with stories not just on the "good skaters" or professional ones, but on skaters such as Cher Strauberry and Peach Sørenson who are as Bethany Geckle and Sally Shaw (2022: 11) describe "two of the most visible trans women in skateboarding…each notable for their unique styles and unconventional tricks. If skateboarders see and use the world differently than most people, Strauberry and Sørenson see and use it differently than most skaters." These skaters and others in the magazine in her view also "point to a new iteration of skateboarding being born by this generation of queer-skaters that is redefining what it means to be 'core' or authentic" (Geckle and Shaw, 2022: 12).

Some interviewees conveyed that skate media for "non-traditional" skaters can exist as something that is both complementary and alternative to magazines and platforms considered "core" rather than in competition or inferior. Sarah Huston, who is the founder of Yeah Girl Media, reflects on the role of "women's media" and the smaller platforms, stating, "It's hard to try and how do you compete with *Thrasher* or any of the big outlets that have been built up over like decades, but it's also not necessary. It's not to say that you should not go and do your own thing with the goal and expect to be like Thrasher one day, but I'm really into more of the DIY sort of thing." Huston adds that with the "non-traditional" skate scene "it is like '90s DIY skate culture—just doing it for ourselves. You don't have to follow the rules with the rest of the industry because we're making our own. That's what makes it special."

Huston also feels that embracing a DIY approach does not have to mean being separate from corporate brands in the industry. She explains for instance that it can build a situation of "making them come to the table than the other way around. I think when you do it yourself, you get recognized for what you're doing. The big brands are always looking for a way to stay relevant at a grassroots level so if you're doing good work in that space, they'll want to align themselves and invest in what you're doing. It's like The Skate Witches, for example. They do it all themselves and now they've got partnerships with brands and do a lot of stuff with the big guns in the skate world." There have also been outcomes for Yeah Girl Media, which includes Vans, which also has sponsored one of their exhibitions of women's skate photography and event zine, and recently Red Bull that sponsors events such as art, zine making, and learn to skate workshops.

Adrien Koenigsberg who co-founded *Quell Magazine* agrees that most skateboarders favor *Thrasher* and want to be featured there. But she also demonstrates how publishing articles on smaller platforms or in print can also gain attention and be distributed by larger "core" media. For instance, when *Quell Magazine* published an article about the groundbreaking all-women's team and owned Rookie Skateboards, written by Jessica Roechoudt (2020), it was later published by "core" magazine *Jenkem Mag* which has a more sizable following and audience. However, Koenigsberg expresses some frustration, stating, "People want to get their big break on *Thrasher* because they get the most views." She reveals, "I tried to inter-view people all the time and…I'm trying to add your story to the heart to the like narrative of skateboarding, but *Thrasher* is trying to just get con-tent…like that this bad example but not that bad of an example."

Cindy Whitehead emphasizes the importance of capturing women within narratives of skateboarding, in print or other mediums stating that they can easily become excluded from skate history. Of her era and docu-mentaries, she explains that for her and other women, "it's hard to find the footage. There's very little footage for us." And for skaters from par-ticular generations, it becomes hard to retrace that history. In her experi-ence she states, "On the women's side, I'll be honest with you, I'm tired. I'm like, Man, cuz somebody else I help out here, from the 70s…not with interviews and things, but more like creative magazines. I'm one person, but every woman I know has a busy life, has had children, and now has grandchildren."

Whitehead also feels women especially are lone wolves and need to support each other more, including "shouting out" and acknowledging those creating and contributing content to alternative media. She states, "When you're in a magazine, if somebody takes the time to do an article on you, I was always taught when I was pro skateboarding…if somebody ever writes an article on you, you talk about it." Additionally, she feels "now with social media, you, you should post that, you should give back to the people who are singing your praises." She is concerned when skateboarders get a certain level of fame and become professional skateboarders that they take the attention for granted but states, "Okay, I get that. But when you're coming up the ranks, and these people are taking the time to write about you, and sing your praises or put you on TV or whatever, you need to give a little bit back." She continues, "I don't care where, but to act like it just doesn't happen makes you look ungrateful."

While Whitehead also understands the strategic benefits of being in "core" media traditionally run by men that have much larger audiences and industry "clout," she offers the analogy of it is like trying to keep getting attention from a bad rather than supportive love interest. She states:

> Why are we constantly grasping at the, you know, banging on the door that doesn't want you necessarily? It's like why aren't you not wanting to date the guy who wants to date you for the right reasons? It's like we go for the asshole guy. You've got all these women and other folks supporting you, but you keep banging on the door, the one that doesn't want you, and rewarding the bad behavior.

Despite Whitehead's frustrations with attitudes of ambivalence or a type of subcultural snobbery toward smaller, DIY, and women's and other "non-traditional-"created skate media, it is one of the most effective ways to change the culture. This includes her platform that has a blog (https://www.girlisnota4letterword.com/blog), social media including an Instagram with 37 K followers, and a YouTube channel that does regular interviews.

Our interviewees also include change-makers doing things at the grassroots level. Izzi Cooper who created the *Heal Flip* zine feels that the smaller medium has allowed her to devote the pages to a range of lived experiences that inform approaches to healing and social justice. She states, "Skateboarding has been a unique puzzle piece connecting my interests of healing and social justice…Through my recent research, I have discovered the many ways skateboarding can be used as a vehicle for individual and social change." Explaining further she states, "This includes accessible healing through regulation, social cohesion, and topics such as Indigenous sovereignty and consent."

Cooper believes zines allow her to express, "The more I learn about skateboarding and all of the ways it can be used for social justice issues, the more I enjoy my experience on the board." Benefits include having more patience when she feels frustrated with her progress to being able to better understand the lives of those who skate alongside her. She states, "It has been wonderful to be able to combine my interests and passions. Skateboarding has allowed me to see amazing connections on and off the board."

The visually creative side of skate media, including photography, is also an area where social change is occurring and counters how skating has long been portrayed through the lens of hegemonic masculinity. Norma Ibarra started as a photographer for community events but is now also approached by companies like Vans and Nike SB as well as covering competitions like the World Skate Olympic qualifier Street Skating Rome. She has a collective rather than individualist outlook on her progress; she reflected in her statement, "If I can help other people too, to show them that there's a place for them, I will." Ibarra does not promote exceptionalism or elitism, nor does she emphasize authenticity as a criterion for a career in skateboarding, things all observed to uphold gatekeeping in "core" skate culture (Atencio et al., 2013, Dupont, 2014, 2020, 2021, Snyder, 2017). Her approach provides an alternative to gatekeeping, stating:

> Every time I go on a panel I try to say there's a place for you in skateboarding and you don't have to kickflip or you don't have to do rails. Skateboarding is an activity, but also there's an industry that needs journalists, photogra-

phers, accountants, lawyers, everything, so if you're scared but also a designer or something else, there's a place for you to skateboarding. I always try to talk about that. (Ibarra quoted from our interview)

Ibarra's insights offer support to feminist scholars who argue social media is democratizing sports (Ahmad and Thorpe, 2020, Thorpe et al., 2017, 2018). She states, "With social media, we can reach to more people…and get to make our Instagram posts and it can be seen by people from all over the world…it's just more sharing and documenting so more people can see each other, spreading their words and content." Her approach is also grounded in the idea of having tenacity, stating, "I'm stubborn; I'm gonna stick with it, whether, you know, they want it or not," and she extends this to social interactions where "even though I had bad experiences with people sometimes, we have to be able to mentor other people. I share my experiences so that people can relate." Highlighting the importance of empathy she also states, "I didn't have anyone that I could relate to when I started, so if I can help other people to show them that there's a place for them I will every time."

Shari White has also been able to work across the community and industry with The Skate Witches, and *Mess Magazine*, and her videos like *Credits* with Vans express similar values and outlooks. She states, "I grew up not seeing anybody like me in magazines, etc., and now you can see this momentum of it happening around me, so it gets me excited to keep working on it." She emphasizes how power can be gained independently from industry, "I think it starts at the grassroots community and grows in numbers. Doing things DIY until they are noticed, not waiting for big companies to take action." White also feels that "skateboarding isn't conservative, so it has the power to make changes fast. I think the power is with us and the Instagram 'personal brand movement?' or whatever you'd call it, of being able to show brands people are interested and want certain content or certain people."

While social media has opened the gates for various perspectives to be heard and have influence, "core media" can still be closed off. It can also close conversations down, such as when figures who are famous do problematic things and are "given a pass" or quietly tolerated. One of the pivotal articles to throw light on such maneuvering and evasion is

"Primitive Progressivism" by Kyle Beachy (2018). It was created to draw attention to the ongoing support skateboarder Jason Jessee received despite making various racist and anti-Semitic statements in public and in the media. Beachy's article was offered to and declined by *Jenkem*, then posted on *King Shit* but taken down, and then finally published in *Free Skate Magazine* (2018), and given a deeper exploration in his memoir *The Most Fun Thing* (2021).

In "Primitive Progressivism" Beachy (2018) writes that "it inhales our silent complacency like oxygen, and its exhale is poison" as a reflection on instances where industry continues to try to profit from problematic figures. This includes when those figures may seek redemption, but where questions continue as to the substance of their regret or commitment to do better. However, Beachy is careful not to separate himself and other skateboarders from, at times, being complicit with pervasive but not always overt problematic views and behaviors in skateboarding. His own journey to writing critically about skateboarding arose when he was injured and had more time to reflect. In our interview, he shared, "I was thinking to myself basically like 'Don't be a pussy, like why are you crying a little pussy, toughen up,' then thinking where does that come from?" He then realized in what he describes as a "watershed moment" that "oh that language comes from my 20 years on a skateboard. And so I was trying to kind of interrogate that."

Beachy also explains that as a professor in English and creative writing, he was not dependent on writing about skateboarding as a living, so had more freedom to be vocal about issues in skateboarding culture regardless of any repercussions in skate media or industry. For him, it was more a case of questioning his and other skateboarders' own "economic complicity" and power to effect change. Beachy revealed he thought about how "much fucking money have I given to these people" and "it just seemed like...wait a second, we don't have to do this!" He adds:

> It was a kind of perfect storm of feeling empowered to speak angrily, and it was kind of the first time that I allowed myself to speak with an authority that included judgment and disdain and a strong sort of ethos that says, this is not how it should be.

Beachy's insights above further support Sharp and Threadgold's (2020: 618) proposal to understand and bridge the difference between a complicit form of reflexivity that holds the belief that "it is what it is" and the ethical action-focused orientation of "it is not what it could be." Beachy's stance of defiance through his article on Jessee also assisted others whose careers did rely on skateboarding so they were not alone, such as Ryan Lay (Beachy, 2018). In our interview Beachy highlights, "Ryan is such an interesting character because he has always sort of been this sort of not marginal but liminal character in the industry where, you know, he's never in the center of its conventions."

Lay and Beachy have collaborated and co-created on a number of occasions to keep conversations in skate culture open to "real talk." This includes as co-hosts on the *Vent City* podcast with other co-creators Kristin Ebeling, Ted Barrow, and Ted Schmitz and with the addition of Alex White who joined later. The expanding team purposely broke away from a pattern seen in podcasts like *The Nine Club* whose co-hosts are all men. Beachy states, "At the time it was sort of radical to have girls and guys having conversations about skateboarding together." The podcast also tries to have regular guests. Beachy states, "From the get-go, we recognized, 'Hey, there are some key ways we're not diverse right? We are all White.'" He adds, "The impulse from the beginning was that we would be a collective and that we would regularly rotate out and bring in other people…to try to have conversations with people who don't look like us."

Beachy credits Ebeling and White as key influences in checking his own privilege and being an ally. Of Ebeling's influence, he states, "I have probably learned more from Kristin Ebeling on a practical level than I have from any single individual in the last five to ten years." He continues, "Her approach to activism, her own mental health, in her own care, her approach to forgiveness and openness and harm reduction, I cannot overstate how much I've learned from her." Key to being an ally for him is also revisiting the episodes they record together and "just listening."

Beachy also discusses how "Alex brings this sort of radical industry awareness" to the podcast. He describes her as sharing "like extremely street level, biting wit right and, you know, the balance is so important. Being able to have people who have enough of a distance from the industry to be able to critique it." He also notes, "There are people in the roles now who can help the industry stop being what it's always been. And not only that, but become something cooler and radder, and newer and bigger and more open." Reflecting on the increasing power that "non-traditional" skaters have through being employed in more significant roles, he states, "I get so hyped on that, it's the coolest thing in the world. I don't want to have to keep writing things like the Jason Jessee piece."

Creative Interventions: Humor as a Strategy for Change

In the push for social change in skateboarding, there is a tendency to overlook and downplay the role that humor has had in shaping skate culture. In this second section of Part 2 of this chapter we explore how satire is being incorporated into the creative works of skateboarders as a way to simply make fun of the more serious side of skateboarding, but also sometimes as a springboard for social commentary, self-critique, and self-growth. More light-hearted examples include in the *Tired Video* where older skateboarders who no longer being "youthful" or be "good" skaters have fun and make jokes at their own expense while maintaining a sense of inclusion by demonstrating forms of "subcultural capital" through dress style, skate spots, and trick choices (Willing et al., 2019). There are also the hyper-masculine, albeit absurd stunts and pranks seen in films like *Jackass*, and *Thrasher's King of the Road* challenges, with male skateboarding teams doing over-the-top dares (Thorpe, 2007). There have also been highly controversial uses of humor that include shock tactics, such as using themes of rape or racism to sell boards (Jenkem Staff, 2014, Willing, 2020b).

For Peggy Oki, humor can help keep people engaged rather than be fearful of the serious nature of her work on ending the harm, captivity, and killing of whales and dolphins by humans. Long-term activists like Oki are joined by a new generation of skateboarders addressing their impact on the environment who also have to overcome challenges such as audiences getting compassion fatigue or feeling the issues are too overwhelming (Kerr, 2022, Willing, 2020b). Oki believes in finding a balance, revealing, "So far, I've been mainly striving to raise awareness and I really try to avoid posting graphic images. I don't post images of the slaughter" because she does not "want people to just turn off. I'd rather hopefully engage people in appreciation." One strategy she has also found useful is that "I've been posting things on Instagram that are not even related." This includes fun-natured clips that are humorous such as cute animals and babies having silly interactions. She adds, "And you know, it's okay we need a little break. We need to laugh because there's a lot of crap going on in the world right now."

Kerr, whose first skate writing work was at *Jenkem*, points to a tradition of humor in skating that was also able to be subversive by holding up a mirror to industry. He states, "I like their funny stuff that they would do…like fun to poke fun at the serious side of skateboarding, which was too prevalent in the industry, especially at the time when I started working with them." He also feels humor can be one of the best tools of persuasion, stating, "The best way to get skating skateboarders to change is to get them to laugh at themselves. I think because, otherwise, we'll get really defensive and prickly and stuff like that."

Rhianon Bader whose main work with the Goodpush Alliance is to draw attention to serious issues of social justice also feels, "I think that skaters are also just shit talkers. And I think it's funny." However, Adam Abada, an artist who uses illustration for critical social commentary but also to make fun-natured observations, raises the issue of setting boundaries. He states, "It's very much been, let's make a joke about this person, and it's like this weird hierarchy…like you'll make it about one famous guy but not others." Informal rules include that it is acceptable to punch up but not punch down, meaning leave those who are more disadvantaged or with less power alone. However, Abada feels the lines become blurry and arbitrary and that it is not fair to "clown people, and I'm guilty of all that stuff too." He feels that humor highlights "how we can be so progressive but then we can be so nasty. Why is it okay that we laugh about Tony Hawk? Is it because he does so many commercials? Still not cool. You know what I mean."

A key issue that Timothy Ward, who with Ted Schmitz is behind a number of satirical accounts including *The Nut Daily News* (@

thenutdailynews), sees the main problem as one of escalation. He states, "Everything has to escalate and escalate and escalate…they keep having to do it over and over but then upping the ante." He applies this to skateboarders who gain big social media followings and profiles by making fun of other skaters without their consent and being in on the joke.

An example Ward gives is "Weck," also known as "Wecking Ball" (@ weckingball), who has 120 K followers from playing up his muscular physique and "roasting" other skaters by saying derogatory and overly critical things about their skate videos. Ward feels he "went from funny and goofy to troll. He had some pretty funny ideas. Like he would call people out on something like relatively harmless like touching on a manual." But Ward observes, "Now he's like gone to this full other side where he's like an 'edge lord,' and a lot of people have turned their back on because his sense of humor just isn't it…he had to escalate up and up and up until he finally got to the zone where it's like, well, who can I offend next?"

Ted Schmitz who we interviewed with Ward agrees with his opinion of how Wecking Ball crossed a line in making fun of people's skate lines (where they put several tricks together in a skate clip), stating, "Is this a bad comedic strategy? Probably fine in my late teens or something. Like triangulating Danny Way's scrape from footage that's 300 feet away is like pretty funny." But for Schmitz, "somehow turning jokes into blatant transphobia is pretty rotten…it is a turning point."

Another underlying ethical framework that emerged in skaters' discussions of humor was that, along with not punching down, it is better to get people to laugh with, not at, others. This includes turning the comedic gaze back on men as seen in some of the memes from *The Nut Daily News* (discussed in Willing, 2019c). One example features a stock photo of a man sitting by himself in a skatepark with the text "Park local just waiting for a woman skater to turn up so he can tell her what she's doing wrong with her kickflips" (Nut Daily News Team, 2018). Another features a stock photo of a woman at a skatepark with her hands in her hair looking excited and the caption "Local skaters day made by finding out that guy in the skatepark 'can't even do that'" (Nut Daily News Team, 2019).

Schmitz explains, "Yeah, I don't even think we really wrote that, we were learning about it. It was probably from a dinner conversation with Kristen (Ebeling)." Ebeling once posted a humorous video on her Instagram about a fictional "helpline" for men who see a woman doing a trick they cannot do, featuring herself humorously answering men's calls. Ebeling has followed this with more videos about fictional helplines that are posted by Skate Like a Girl (@skatelikeagirl) on Instagram with skateboarders including Alexa Berriochoa (@trans.sender) also answering calls by boys or men with questions that c may be well-intentioned but are patronizing and re-establishes a gender hierarchy that positions men as superior.

The punchlines in *The Nut Daily News* memes are interesting in how they illuminate a type of "defiance labour" (Sharp and Threadgold, 2020) consisting of men making fun of themselves on issues women have usually had to take up alone. This includes when men tend to only validate women based on how they measure up against men's skills and the shock they feel when women surpass them. Schmitz jokingly describes how the meme really amplified the issue through the exaggeration of how "…she's like, what? You couldn't even do that. Oh my god, this is the best day of my life. I totally thought you could do that. But now he told me you can't even do that. What a fucking Wow, awesome…he thinks that is such a compliment." He then explains how humor for men, by men, can be used to educate and de-center themselves, "Yeah, that's always fun to like, when you kind of learn something about yourself when you're making fun of it. Like 'yeah, I kind of did that shit too. Oh, that's a nice teaching moment.'"

Our interview turned to the issue of rape jokes and misogyny in skate advertisements and onboard graphics, usually trying to appeal to heterosexual men and teenage boys. Ward feels that both age and encounters with people who may be the subjects of offensive jokes are important. He considers, "I'm speculating that a 14-year-old me I'll just throw myself under the bus and say, I might have thought it was funny when I was 14…And when you get older, and it's like, well, now I'm 19. And a good friend of mine has been sexually assaulted. I don't think this type of joke is funny anymore." He continues that it can also be a turning point: "I'm older now and I realized my friends have been affected negatively by racism. So that racist joke is not funny to me anymore, because I get it now. I mean, it was never funny." Ward clarifies, "I think those jokes that are offensive…They always were inappropriate. But personally, to me, they became clearly inappropriate when I understood the context of what they meant."

Ward is critical of the ways people can try to defend and excuse harmful humor rather than apologize and change it stating that "back to comedians, they always have a choice" and that "it is not enough to say 'it's just a joke. Don't be offended.'" Ward recommends a more ethical response might be, "Okay, I hear you, I'm gonna go back to the drawing board. We'll erase that. And when we come back to this, we'll try to find a better or funnier or more creative way to do it. And that probably should be how it goes across a lot of media." Schmitz also demonstrates how humor can be seen as a type of "defiance" that takes work, rather than giving into complacency or being complicit. He states, "Tim had this concept that you're paid to be good at writing, or you're paid to be interesting, or you're paid to be funny at making fun of skating or having good ideas about skating." And for Schmitz, "[that] always kind of resonated with me…you're supposed to write workshop this shit. Like, come on, like, you know, we're meant to be funny."

Creative humor can have the ability to critique things like hegemonic masculinity rather than reproducing its status and power. We spoke with Brian Glenney who is co-creator of "Manramp" with Worble who gave us more insight into what this can look like. Manramp (@manramp) is a fictional character played by a skateboarder who is a White man who keeps his identity anonymous, has blonde hair and a mustache, has a very muscular physique, and wears a construction hat and overalls. While fictional, he is treated as a real skateboarder, has a large social media following, appears in Worble videos, and is interviewed in character such as in *Thrasher* (Mull, 2017). Glenney explains, "I actually inspired Manramp accidentally when Worble was paid for ten videos on skating different elements like water, snow. And…in Vermont. And we could barely move, but we had to put something together." He continues, "There was a piece of plywood inside, so I just grabbed it and put it over my body. And everyone just started skating it." He jokes, "Sometimes you have to hold the plywood to help the homie."

A couple of years later Glenney and the Worble created a costume, Manramp. The Worble is a crew of skateboarders from Vermont consisting of the Mull brothers Tom, Steve, Chuck, Dave, and friends such as Chris Colburn, Eunice Chang, Andrew Harris, and Sarah Rayne. Glenney describes Manramp as "he is a very nice thing to look at, right? I mean, he's so muscular and everything. So, he's like the perfect YMCA construction worker." Through humor, Glenney explains, "what we've been trying to push is really this deconstruction of masculinity…call it the Village People, deconstructed masculinity by over masculinizing, so to speak." However, in the "core" skate scene with its unspoken expectations of compulsory heterosexuality, the joke can push too far for some. He recalls:

When we did the Manramp series with *Thrasher* six episodes, and our initial intro was…I had men dressed up shirtless…inspired by The Chippendales (a men stripper dance troupe), we tried to oversexualize Manramp to push the deconstruction of masculinity even more. But *Thrasher* thought it might be misinterpreted. So we scaled that back a little bit. (Glenney quoted from our interview)

Glenney describes how a parody like Manramp can also be mistaken or appropriated as a source of homophobia, stating that "the whole point is to kind of disrupt, like, common sense notions of masculinity in skateboarding…you can't overdo it," as "people can easily misinterpret it, given the masculinity it centers."

Later in the interview with Schmitz when asked what he thinks of Manramp he was positively energized, responding, "What do you think about Manramp? Well, I'm clad in his fucking gear (and he stood up in the video call to show he was wearing a Manramp t-shirt), I'm a fan! Manramp and what the Worble does has always been the stuff that I'm excited about." He continues that what they do "will always be the perfect combination. What they have to offer is really awesome skating. Some of it is really hard. Some of it is really dorky. All of it is for a good time."

Ward in the same interview with Schmitz agreed, stating, "I'm a huge fan. I like what they do, because similarly to what Ted said, they're generally very wholesome, and playful, but not in a way where they're performing it." Having met some of the Worble crew he feels, "they legitimately are very nice, friendly, people who are really good at skateboarding, you can tell they really like skateboarding, and they really have fun with it." Ward also explains how the Worble creates an atmosphere of allyship, inclusion, and representation, "They seem to kind of effortlessly be kind of doing right by some of the stuff that skateboarding is confronting. Like 'we skate with a lot of women in this game. We have a lot of queer and trans people.'" He continues, "They have some of that diversity in their crew, but it doesn't feel tokenized…it doesn't feel like they're trying to correct any wrongs that they've made in the past. They're just made up of interesting kinds of diverse people. They're skateboarding right."

Supporting Education

In this third and last section of Part 2 of this chapter we now expand our focus on equity and a turnaround from "skate and destroy" to "skate and appreciate" to what might be seen as a "skate and educate" ethos. Skateboarding has traditionally not placed much emphasis on education and, in many ways, often scorned it as the antithesis of being "core." Pappalardo (2020b) notes, "If you look at skateboarding as an industry and a community, there's historically been very little value on education." He adds that "if we think of skating as some type of sport, it's one that really hates learning" with a "Fuck college, you can go later. You gotta ride this out now! You're not even in your prime!" attitude. Yet the emerging view that education can lead to careers for skaters across many areas, both subcultural (Snyder, 2017) and beyond skate culture (Corwin et al., 2019), is gaining ground and becoming more embraced as more surveys and research are done by hearing from a range of skateboarders.

Some professional skateboarders such as Ryan Lay who is a CSEF Advisory Board Member (also see 2019) and embodies the more reflective and "alternative masculinity" encourages individuals to look beyond skating alone for life satisfaction, social networks, and personal growth. He states in our interview, for instance, that with social media, there is "more opportunity for people to be a little more dynamic as pro skaters. You have skaters that could finally kind of offer different parts of themselves as opposed to the hold days when, if the companies didn't really have a place for it, they wouldn't market it." As part of this he explains that "there's a market of skaters who are interested in college or specific social causes and they can find community through that."

Skateboarders in the US and overseas are also encouraging school-aged children to learn by incorporating things like skating into the curriculum. This includes John Dahlquist who is Vice Principal of Bryggeriets Gymnasium (https://bryggerietsgymnasium.se) known as the "skate high school" in Malmö, Sweden, and programs like Hull Services (https://hullservices.ca) run by Joel Pippus in Canada that are trauma-informed, and skaters calling attention to adaptive designs and programs that consider cognitive and physical disability or general pathways to self-efficacy (Ball, 2018, Rubin and Nunes, 2020). Other programs bring skateboarders to talk in schools, often to youth facing various intersectional disadvantages, such as The Harold Hunter Foundation (https://www.haroldhunter.org) with their In the Classroom program.

The College Skateboarding Education Foundation (CSEF) scholarship program encourages skateboarders to get into and complete college through awarding small grants, with Exposure Skate and also Rollin' From the Heart recently partnering to offer an additional two scholarships worth $5000 each year. CSEF co-chair Thomas Barker explains that the program wants to offer support to all kinds of individuals who are part of the skate culture, not the typical college high-achieving "sports jock" or traditional student. He describes "that kid who's skates and is angry at school and doesn't like get along with his school but is still smart and intelligent" and "maybe they get into filming or like whatever it is, and they don't always have the best grades" but "we want to inspire that kid, if not get them a scholarship." For Barker, "that's my original vision of the CSEF. It was just flipping skateboarding on its head."

Sharing personal insight into how education can help skateboarders as a community, he offers, "I always said if Andrew Reynolds could have told me to do anything in the world when I was 17, I would have done it. That's my ethos behind CSEF." He adds, "I'm trying to connect these people that are skaters that these kids look up to and just do some positive messaging." For Barker, "then the kids are good at school, they just get to feel like they're not alone—that they're not the only skater that's out there." He continues, "It shows them the agency that they have in the world."

Keegan Guizard who is the executive director at CSEF also is dedicated to changing the "'fuck school' to be cool narrative." He met Barker when he arrived in Los Angeles in 2015 and describes himself as "kind of like this college skateboarding guy already" so he felt he had lived experience that gave him motivation as well. He states, "Historically the faces and stars and people that skateboarding looks up to aren't really telling others to live a well-balanced life—to be an educated human and as part of that, maybe have a backup plan. You know, eat well, take care of yourself."

What Guizard wants is not just for skateboarders to get an education in terms of a degree but as part of that "Try to be the best human. Skateboarding is just one really awesome part of your life" rather than only being given the narrative of "fuck the world we skate, that's all that really matters." He emphasizes, "Skateboarding shows us the world and there's all these really awesome things about skateboarding but also not to throw away every other aspect of life, especially for a dream that half a percent of us will achieve."

Guizard explains that the CSEF program has seen its applications rise rapidly and that they are not fully able to meet the demand. At the time of interviewing him in 2021, they had 276 applications and needed to get a list of finalists down to 12, which he states, "And that's really difficult." While not able to pay their full tuition, he lists the microforms of assistance the scholarship offers such as "supporting the skaters financially to accomplish their goals. Thus far, we've only given out relatively small amounts." This covers things like housing, books, daily expenses, and maybe relief from working a second job, where "it's really up to them."

Some scholarship holders use the funding for studying for careers outside of skateboarding in fields as diverse as environmental science, biology and genetic science, counseling, visual design, and special education. Others, such as in the area of urban planning, apply their studies to skateboarding projects. In a later next section, we move our attention to both leading and emerging change-makers in skatepark advocacy. This includes Chris Giamarino, one of the 2021 CSEF recipients who is working toward his PhD in Urban Planning.

Part 3: Ethical Togetherness at the Micro and Macro Levels

In this third part of this chapter we explore a process which we call "ethical togetherness" which refers to skateboarders' efforts to build more respectful, safer, and aware ways of relating to each other and other people. We do this in two subsections, looking at the micro and macro levels of skateboarding. The first section of Part 3 includes listening to how skateboarders define things like consent, boundaries, and constructive ways of relating to each other. Our conversations highlight how community-based strategies are an effective way for skateboarders to build social awareness, allyship, and empathy toward situations and topics that are often silenced and ignored (Willing, 2020b). We also look at how skateboarders interact together as individuals through exploring in-person gathering at a summer camp for women and/or transgender skaters. Our focus then looks at how organizations and groups interact under the umbrella of an alliance.

Our attention in the second section of Part 3 for this chapter is then dedicated to individuals who advocate for skate spaces and what ethical considerations they have as part of this work. Gary Bridge and Sophie Watson (2000, p. 251) argue, "Differences are constructed in, and themselves construct city life and spaces. They are also constituted spatially, socially, and economically, sometimes leading to polarization, inequality, zones of exclusion, and fragmentation." With an interest in what we call "ethical place making," we pay attention to issues that the experts in these areas raise that is not just spatial but also social in the spaces they inhabit.

Micro-Level Boundaries and Togetherness in Skate Community Spaces

Corwin et al. (2019: 25) in a national survey of skateboarding in the US observed what they call a "critical consciousness" in skateboarders that was part of the "ways they recognized and resisted the dominant culture." These authors also state, "Skaters spoke to the importance of inclusivity and diversity in skate communities. They explained that common love of the activity often forces people to see everyone as a community member" (Corwin et al., 2019: 25).

In this first section of Part 3 of this chapter we will focus on micro-level ways of relating such as interpersonally, virtually, and group interactions, and we aim to explore this idea of how skateboarders relate to each other further with an emphasis on what respectful boundaries might look like. This includes how skaters may foster empathy and perform care as a part of that. However, we also point to how skateboarding is not a utopia and that problematic attitudes and harmful behaviors exist too. We explore the critical consciousness that skateboarders develop when confronted with things such as sexual violence and the need to build a culture of consent within their scenes and skate culture itself. Our discussion reveals that a key way to even out power and equity is when there is a commitment to change at a personal level while also doing so as a community.

Bringing Consent into Skate Culture

The term "sexual violence" refers to acts of a sexual nature causing physical, social, and emotional harm, from sexual harassment that is not physical to forms of physical sexual assault (Willing, 2020b). The term "rape culture" places an extra emphasis on the social and cultural dimensions of things that can be used to excuse and perpetuate sexual violence. This includes "rape jokes, sexual harassment, cat-calling, sexualized 'banter'; the routine policing of women's bodies, dress, appearance, and code of conduct; the re-direction of blame from the perpetrator in an assault to the victim" (Keller et al., 2018: 24). Keller et al.'s (2018: 23) definition is that "rape culture is one in which sexual assault is not only seen as *inevitable* in some contexts, but *desirable* and *excusable*." As part of this, entitlement is also an issue, "where men not only feel they have a right to access women's bodies but feel confident they can access them without fear of consequence" (Keller et al., 2018: 27).

Skateboarders have a number of community and survivor-led campaigns dedicated to educating skateboarders about consent such as Fatta in Sweden, Consent for Breakfast and Safe Skate Space also in the UK, and Consent Is Rad which is based in Australia but has an international focus and was launched at the "Pushing Boarders" conference in Sweden in 2019. Consent Is Rad has collaborated with a range of skateboarding groups in the US and abroad. Key collaborations include being invited to collaborate on the Break the Cycle campaign. A call to action and guidelines for change, it was sponsored by Grant Yansura at WKND Skateboards after they reached out to a woman leader in the skate community (who asked to be anonymous) wanting to do better after they had originally supported a problematic skateboarder and not the survivor (covered in Pappalardo, 2020a). The Break the Cycle campaign (https://consentisrad. wordpress.com/break-the-cycle/) was overseen by the same woman leader in the skate community who held a focus group made up of professional skateboarders and members of community groups. A call to action was then co-written by an international writing team. Since its launch in 2020, it was posted on the WKND website and has shared with an international readership, including audiences of young cis-men who are not often prompted to think about rape culture in skating and how to shift to cultures of consent. The campaign features in the pages of *Thrasher* in the US, *Free Skate Magazine*, and *Skateism Magazine* in Europe, *The Skateboarders Companion* in the UK, *Solo Magazine* in Germany, *Dolores Magazine* in Spain, and *Slam Magazine* and *Grassfires Magazine* in Australia.

While the momentum to address sexual violence and "rape culture" in skateboarding is growing, it was for a long time largely neglected or avoided in research and skate media. Because of this, serious discussions of social, emotional, and physical boundaries in skateboarding are often ignored, while bad behaviors can go unchecked, excused, and be forgotten (Liu 2018; Murrell 2019). It is not that skateboarders are more likely to commit sexual violence, but rather, the lack of regulation in skateboarding and its insularity due to being a subculture can make many hesitate to directly condemn it (Dobija-Nootens, 2018, Ebeling and White, 2019, Willing, 2020b).

The silence around sexual violence in skateboarding is particularly a problem when allegations of harassment or rape are made about men skateboarders who are well-liked, well-connected, or profitable public figures (Dobija-Nootens, 2018, Ebeling and White, 2019, Pappalardo, 2020a, 2022b, 2022c, Willing, 2020b). It is important to note that the perpetrators and victims of sexual violence are not restricted to a gender binary of men and women, nor constrained to heterosexuals, but sexual violence within LGBTQIA+ communities is even less reported. An article by Murrell (2019) about a predatory skate shop owner in Atlanta also draws attention to how issues of shame and homophobia can impact the ability of sexual violence victims who are boys and men to report and seek help. He also argues:

> As skateboarding matures, we need to acknowledge that the existing support system tends to fail the survivors of sexual assault. Too often accusers aren't believed, and their accounts are discredited by those in positions of power. Even more often, the stigma around discussing these issues results in them going unreported, sometimes leading to mental issues, addiction, self-harm, and other long-term trauma for the affected. (Murrell, 2019)

Skateboarding studies on sexual violence include a sociological study (Willing, 2020b) of rape culture depicted in the fictional film *Kids* (Clarke, 1995). The film was controversial but has reached cult status. It was directed by Larry Clark and written by Harmony Korine who is a part of skate culture and features actors who were real skateboarders. The study proposes that while fictional, *Kids* provides examples of how hegemonic forms of masculinity become naturalized in skateboarding through things such as hero worship. This is portrayed through the character of Telly, played by Leo Fitzpatrick, who calls himself the "virgin surgeon," reducing girls' value to their potential as new sexual "conquests" and pressuring them into having sex with him. Another one of the characters helps unpack notions that "good guys" cannot be problematic. The character Casper (played by Justine Pierce), who rapes a girl at the end of *Kids*, is portrayed the rest of the time as likable.

There is also the breakthrough article on "coping with creeps" (Ebeling and White, 2019) with an emphasis on abuse and power and steps toward making safety and sports integrity central to skate camps, competitions, and the culture more broadly. These join grassroots efforts in the form of DIY publications about sexual violence and fostering consent, such as Tessa Fox's (2016) *No Consent = Sexual Abuse* zine, Amelia Bjesse-Puffin (2022) *Time's Up: No More Rape Culture in Our Skate Culture* zine and the *Ask Zine*, which was edited by Bella Borgers as a collaborative publication for the *Ask Manifesto* (2022) collective consisting of the skate groups and initiatives Doyenne Skateboards, Consent for Breakfast, Consent Is Rad and Hera Skate.

The skateboarders we spoke to for our exploration provide insight into the personal frustrations and challenges change-makers face in addressing issues of consent. This includes their feelings that people fear consequences for speaking up. We can also again return to the idea of "complicit reflexivity" (Sharp and Threadgold, 2020) where people may recognize an issue exists but resign it as unable to be changed being a common response in skate culture. Kaily "Bayr" Blackburn who volunteers with an informal skate network that arose in response to individuals in her scene experiencing harassment and abuse states, "I do feel disappointed in a few big brands, who still support known abusers with evidence when they have such power to make the change and set a precedent that is not okay in skateboarding." Part of her sense of feeling unsafe is that skateboarding lacks leadership, explaining, "I just want to feel safe in skateboarding and certain brands seem to say you can get away with anything as long as you are good at skateboarding."

Timothy Ward feels skateboarding is well behind other subcultures in terms of addressing sexual violence, stating, "I think other non-skate communities can look to skateboarding as a cautionary tale for how long a culture and an industry can develop without ever looking at or acknowledging its flaws." Blackburn advises that the best strategy is not to wait for powerful people in the industry to step in and instead to find community-based solutions. She states, "My biggest motivator is all the strong survivors amongst my friends and in the scene as a whole, who are speaking out about injustices, in skateboarding, and in society." The effect for her is that "it motivates me that I can use my resources and connections to help to stop negative experiences for my friends and the future skaters coming into the scene." She adds:

> I think that we can use the negative experiences we skaters have gone through to help bring awareness that these issues are happening. We need to keep talking about it and providing solutions like teaching consent, teaching people how they can speak up when they see someone else being bullied or harassed, teaching people how they can speak to their friends without "canceling" them—so that everyone feels supported in moving forward…no matter how much pushback there is to "keep skateboarding core." (Blackburn quoted from our interview)

Brian Glenney feels the best way of being an ally is to keep making space and supporting ways to ensure strategies are led by survivors. He states that men need to find ways to "orchestrate the women to take over the scene." In his own scene, he helped to facilitate a Consent Is Rad–themed video by the DTVT crew filmed by Wyatt Cunningham using the campaign's stickers and saying "consent is rad!" to the camera (Consent is Rad x DVTV 2021). He states that the goal is to create "a power shift. Like this DTVT thing. I think the power shift is the best thing, not sharing power. Putting women in control. If there are any issues, they cancel the individual." He further clarifies what this means for him stating "it's similar to you know, punching a Nazi. What do you do when someone does a Nazi salute? You don't talk with them. You just knock them out. That's a form of action, and then maybe you make sure they leave your space."

A more formalized effort in recent times that is partly inspired by Consent Is Rad is the Skate Like a Girl's educational program called AllySk8. Ashley Masters states that it is about "creating safety, like we normalize the conversation of consent, and every emotion possible, every moment possible, and really taking it beyond what a lot of people think." She explains that this includes sexual violence but also recognizes "consent happens everywhere from a high five giving somebody a trick tip on their skateboard, like saying I wanted to make sure this is OK to share with you." Masters also feels that "Consent Is Rad has been a huge influence in us creating AllySk8 and it is a program or workshop that we do with partners, other organizations, and businesses that are aligned and are part of the skate industry in some regard."

The AllySk8 program consists of three main components that participants complete. The first is focused on how to be welcoming and inclusive and how to be authentically inclusive. The second is on how to receive feedback. In the second part, Masters describes this as "so when somebody tells us something that we maybe aren't excited to hear or wasn't our intention and we hurt them or caused harm like we can be constructive with that feedback and we can see what a gift that is in our growth." She adds that another aspect is recognizing "the fact that they communicate that and then have a conversation about that and be responsible and clear up or get to hear the other side of any breakdown."

Then the third part, Masters states, "is really around consent and really continuing to normalize the conversation of consent in general but also broadening how we think about consent." Masters emphasizes that consent is something they get people to see is relevant to how they interact "with your coworkers, the folks that you serve your boss, your supervisors, your family, everybody. From a hug to…venting to somebody about a situation to anything of intimacy." Masters believes the responses have been positive, "I mean it's, it's pretty incredible to get to facilitate. A space where folks can truly show up and ask difficult questions. The ones we were scared to ask for fear of getting canceled."

Skating and Relating

In this section, we explore the idea of "skating and relating" which refers to how skateboarders can encounter, co-exist, and interact with each other in a way that is empathetic and respectful of boundaries. The change-makers we talk to shed light on a range of strategies that are oppositional to and stand in defiance to attitudes that skaters should "shut up and skate" that "non-traditional" skateboarders feel has long been normalized in "core" skate culture (Willing 2019b,c). The strategies discussed ahead include forms of reflexive engagement, radical empathy (Caroll and Cianciotto 2020) and an everyday type of cosmopolitan openness in skaters which encourages them to engage with differences in a way that nurtures an ethics of sharing rather than giving space (Plage et al., 2017). Put differently, we look at how skaters do not try to control situations when they encounter others who are different to them and instead try to create a situation where power is shared.

We also have an occasion in this section to consider forms of radical empathy in skating that Tommy Carroll and Luke Cianciotto (2020) introduce in their reflections on ways of bridging lived experiences without erasing them, such as in disability and allyship, but also other forms of equity and companionship in skateboarding. Throughout the chapters featuring our interviews, we have made efforts to be attentive to when this open and attentive way for skateboarders to relate to each other can be seen and developed in a variety of populations and micro and macro contexts.

An interesting example of how people can relate to each other in a way that considers differences yet also ensures cohesion and community exists is Ashley Masters' discussion of the Skate Like a Girl women and/or trans annual summer camp for 18+ adults. Although postponed in 2020, it returned in 2021 and required special consideration due to it being the first time many people had gathered after Covid-19-related lockdowns and with related health and safety steps still a requirement. Masters states that as the organizers they were well aware of the "criticalness of creating safe spaces, but especially coming out of a pandemic." This included reflection on "how important people's mental health is and was at the time and how we were confident and being able to navigate putting on a camp like this with Covid in the background and like doing it safely."

Far from the haphazard and spontaneous road trips depicted in the "core" skate video, Masters described, "we also did a lot of communication prior and was really clear on what's expected of campers, like a camper code of conduct" which ranged from "asking people to not wear cologne or perfumes or fragrances because of people's sensitivity to like what we don't tolerate." Masters states how their aims were to ensure "a space of creating safety for folks to show up as they are, their authentic selves." This included "everything from asking pronouns on a registration sheet and making them optional to breaking down cabins and making sure that we're thoughtful and intentional about how and who we were putting in what cabins and giving people space to share." To ensure people could have continual input, she also explains, "We created some basic outlines, we use a lot of community agreements, and we get together to run all of these ideas by and to check in with the community."

Moving the focus from large, in-person group gatherings, our exploration also considers innovation and technology. As part of this research, we explored how virtual reality (VR) can be an emerging way to reflect on how skateboarders relate to each other and build empathy. We spoke with Brennan Hatton who runs a VR company Equal Reality. Hatton is a White cisgender heterosexual man who conveyed that he feels more of an affinity with "non-traditional" skateboarders than "core" skate culture and also a responsibility to be an ally. As part of this, he has been a volunteer who co-organizes and coaches at inclusive skate meet-ups. He also always is purposeful in wearing a helmet and safety gear when skating, which, in studies of masculinity and skateboarding, is observed to be cast as "feminine" and symbolically oppositional to traditional hegemonic masculinity practices of eschewing protective gear (Willing et al., 2019, Willing et al., 2020, Young, and Dallaire, 2008).

Hatton points to how an important part of creating empathy in VR is through having conversations and listening and making it a shared process. He states that with his design work in VR, "what we do is we very actively make sure that we have the right people in the conversations and through a process that we call co-design that is making sure that you know you have people with people with lived experience." In short, he states that they are "the people with expertise on the topics." Hatton also highlights the importance of how understanding diversity and inclusion can be different from group to group and person to person. For him it is crucial to listen to "different minority groups and what works for them. So like people of color or Asians and people that are particularly targeted right now. And LGBT."

Another pitfall that can happen in designing empathy programs in VR is that it generates "pity" in users rather than growth and constructive reflection. Hatton describes how his team is "like okay, how do highlight the problems that these people are facing without creating pity for them." He is adamant that "you don't want to just create pity for them and then make things more difficult because you can raise awareness but you can do it the wrong way. And it will not be helpful." There is a need to get past what he sees as a scenario "where you will like okay, well now I know this person struggles and I pity them and I'm not actually gonna be able to contribute to helping."

Hatton is also careful about how "you don't want to feed the stereotypes…like needing a strong Black woman to come and talk…and this assumption that because she is female and Black that she's in that environment, able to be strong for that." The best strategy for building empathy in VR is co-design. He describes how: "This doesn't come from our technology, this comes from our pre-design, and so this is why it's so important to have these people with lived experiences in a discussion about the design." The reason he highlights is "because they will not only tell us what they're facing but also what their concerns are, if any, with what we're doing."

Skate Like a Girl emphasizes the role of listening to feedback too. Kristin Ebeling states, "A while ago we got feedback on an event we use to call 'Ladies Night.' And we called it that because it was a funny joke. We were like making fun of that term in the same way that Skate Like a Girl isn't that we think we skate a particular way. It is all literally just talking shit about gender norms. We were making fun of 'Ladies Night' at the bar. But someone in our community was like 'Yo, I'm a trans man and I don't identify as a woman. I don't like that I'm welcome, but also it's called 'Ladies Night.''" Ebeling explains, "So we had a whole process where we changed the name. I think it's important to be receptive and open to new ideas and again like I could have been, wait, I think it's funny because I came up with the name, but like it's more important to progress."

The last strategy of relating in this section that we shall look at is how skateboarders can work together under an alliance to address social issues in skateboarding and also broader society. We spoke with Rhianon Bader from the Goodpush Alliance, which is the knowledge-sharing network of Skateistan. The Goodpush Alliance runs autonomously from other groups so is not an alliance in a traditional sense, but it encourages a variety of groups, from grassroots and industry levels, to come together to create best practices in skate culture. Rhianon Bader explained that the idea emerged from seeing skateboarders in the networks Skateistan had made being involved in social projects, but operating independently, often lacking support and becoming isolated. Bader states, "It clicked that maybe we can connect with all these different projects. We can actually find ways to collaborate and do stuff together."

An example of how the Goodpush Alliance brings skateboarding groups together can be observed in their "Pushing Against Racism" campaign that was launched on May 25, 2021, on the first anniversary of the tragic murder of George Floyd. It is a campaign that involves a working group made up of over 20 representatives from skateboarding including Deluxe Distribution from industry, Harold Hunter Foundation from the non-profit sector and was co-created by Sandi Alibo from Surf Ghana, informed by hers and others' experiences as Black and PoC skateboarders. The campaign hosts webinars, shares resources, organizes a fund, and encourages members of the skate community to become a signatory of its Commitment to Anti-Racism in Skateboarding.

Reflecting on the campaign, Denia Kopita, who chaired one of their online panel sessions, states the benefits: "There were so many different people from different backgrounds, like from the States, Ghana, Australia, or from anywhere. You have to let people share their stories. And you see a pattern. Usually in those stories, even if they're also different." She continues, "We usually just like to skate. And that's okay. At the end of the day, we are skaters, but we also are people and we have to have conversations; we have to share our opinions." In her view, "we are smart people, we are creative, and we're unique when it comes to us having a very specific kind of hobby, but we also have so much more to offer than a kickflip. I think it's good to have these panels to actually talk about things."

Bader explains, "Basically we can all help each other leapfrog over different challenges, sharing what resources we have and stuff." She also observed, "A lot of the social scale projects are quite small. They don't have that much staff capacity, volunteer capacity, or budgets and stuff. So it just makes sense to try and make their job easier somehow." From her own perspective she also feels that "it is in the spirit of skateboarding because skateboarding has always been something where people are really down to support each other and collaborate." Another aspect of skateboarding that Bader believes can assist their efforts together is its embrace of a DIY culture where she says it is "not just talking about DIY spots, but like the do it yourself culture in skateboarding. Even if you've never done something before, you're kind of willing to jump into it and find a way."

There is a range of positive skills and outlooks that Bader feels skaters bring to social projects, especially as they are not typically held back when doing something on a low budget or none at all. Instead, they become more adaptive and resourceful. She explains, "I think it is exciting because innovation brings critical thinking and awareness of what you're doing and not just doing it the same way that's already been done…Encouraging creativity is a big one. And perseverance." Bader also emphasizes the value of relating to issues in a collective way, stating, "I think the community aspect of skateboarding is something we bring into social skate work. A lot of what we do is based on relationships, and being able to work and be together with all different kinds of people." She adds, "People that are maybe not always similar to you and how you think, but we know that to really get stuff done, you need a wider community on board."

Macro-Level Relations: Skate Spaces and Ethical Place Making

In this final, second section of Part 3 of this chapter we explore skateboarders' efforts to build and preserve places to skate and their impact on the broader public they need to engage with. We do so by reflecting on interviews with Alec Beck from The Skatepark Project (formerly the Tony Hawk Foundation), Paul Forsline from City of Skate, and Chris Giamarino, one of the 2021 CSEF recipients who is a doctoral student in Urban Planning at the University of California, Los Angeles. It has been over 20 years since Iain Borden published his pivotal study on skateboarding and the city (2001) with its special emphasis, informed by the theory of the social production of space by Henri Lefebvre (1991), on how skateboarders reimagine and repurpose the built environment. For Borden, the presence of skateboarders is transformative, changing urban spaces from a binary of commerce and convention to ones of creativity, capitalist resistance, and counter-culture. He argues, for instance,

"Skateboarding is constantly repressed and legislated against, but counters not through negative destruction but through creativity and production of desires" (Borden, 2001: 1).

Borden's (2001: 253) study outlines how "urban managers have declared skaters as trespassers, or cited the marks skateboarding causes as proof of criminal damage." In defense of skateboarding, he argues, "skateboarding can only be rendered criminal through the most petty-minded laws. This is largely because skateboarding is aimed at the appropriation—and not domination—of time and space, and so cannot readily be represented as a truly illegal practice" (257). He urges city planners and authorities to see the creative and socially transgressive potential that skateboarding has in terms of its contributions to the city.

More recently, researchers including Borden (2019) recognized that skateboarding culture does not involve a wholesale rejection of society and that "contemporary skaters are not necessarily attracted to resistance" (Lombard, 2010: 475). For instance, skate activists often draw upon the positive social benefits that a new skatepark will bring (Willing and Shearer, 2016) to convince councils and authorities to fund them. At the same time, what Borden calls "spatial censorship" (2001) which consists of fines, bans, and even imprisonment for skating in private and public spaces remains an ongoing issue for skateboarders. Various studies now consider the "ecological" (Glenney, 2018), "hybrid" (Glenney and O'Connor, 2019), and flexible nature of skateboarders' inclusion and exclusion in the city, to gentrification (Howell 2001) and how they might inhabit public space and common space in ways that may be seen as trespassing to creative and convivial (Callen-Riley and Holsgens, 2020; Cianciotto, 2020; Chiu and Giamarino, 2019; Dickson et al., 2022; Giamarino et al., 2022; Glover et al. 2021; Pushing Boarders 2019; Ruddick 1996; Ruiz et al., 2020).

At the same time, the rise in skatepark activism and advocacy is gaining ground, sometimes with millions of dollars injected into developments by city authorities often wanting to rejuvenate "problematic areas" (Chiu 2009). As Howell (2005: 33) warned, it is in such situations that skateboarders can also act as the "shock troops of gentrification." Lawton (2020: 36) raises an interesting question of "what if skaters can exercise sufficient agency to mitigate the social harm of regeneration policies by being critical and radical, rather than malleable, 'good partners' to the city?"

Our exploration includes hearing from established advocates and emerging skate activists on what meanings they attach to skateparks and skate spots and their thoughts on how skaters relate to those around them such as homeless or unhoused people. Paul Forsline from City of Skate states, "My wish is, by creating amazing skateparks and spaces, barriers to understanding and accepting differences will be broken down as we discover our mutual interests and experiences." He describes his own scene as positive, but felt in contrast "the fact that the skateboard scene was so poorly supported via public skateparks was a mistake that needed to be corrected." Providing a woman's and youth perspective, *Heal Flip* zine creator Izzi Cooper in her interview with us adds the supportive insight that for her, "Wherever a skatepark exists, it will be filled with people from all different backgrounds whether they live nearby or are visiting. Even if people have nothing else in common besides skateboarding, friendships can blossom."

The strategies that Forsline employs are ones that promote the positive effect skateparks can have, but he points out that other types of sport are much more supported in comparison. He states, "City of Skate and myself have been working to change the dynamic of how public skateparks are funded and viewed within our urban fabric." This includes funding a quality skate space. It has "as much positive impact on our community as other public recreational assets, such as ballfields, pool, playground, court, etc." He feels frustrated that "most public skateparks are completed after ten plus years of advocacy and community fundraisers, mostly a begging dynamic." To counter this, he states, "City of Skate works to create an avenue and model where skateboarding and skate spaces are funded and valued equal to other traditional youth/adult recreational activities…and serve the variety of skate users, and creates spaces that are community assets beyond the skate community too." Furthermore, in his view "by skaters voicing their actions for better public space, it shows the need for more spaces for youth to feel they belong and a sense youth are integral to our society. Non-skaters can also learn to view spaces and the urban environment as multipurpose, not static."

Change often only happens from years of lobbying and building skills on how to navigate political issues and crafting arguments for people who are often ignorant, or have misconceptions about skating. Forsline states,

"City of Skate worked for years to find political allies who were open to learning the positives of providing skate spaces for the mental and physical health of youth and community at large." One of the problems, he states, is that "skateboarders have been easy to ignore by community leaders because of the nature of skating as an unstructured activity and a core demographic of teens, early 20s who are not always present in the political processes." He emphasizes that with increased interactions with skaters who can educate them, "elected officials have tremendous power to provide more spaces and opportunities for skateboarding to happen in safe and inclusive spaces and environments."

Urban planning researcher Chris Giamarino highlights that in California, "it has been well-documented, that skateboarders use public space and architecture more creatively and interactively. This use of space ascribes it a 'use value,' rather than an 'exchange value' to be marketed for private use or requiring an entry fee." But as Gary Bridge and Sophie Watson (2000, p. 25) observe, "Differences are constructed in, and themselves construct city life and spaces. They are also constituted spatially, socially and economically, sometimes leading to polarization, inequality, zones of exclusion and fragmentation." Giamarino proposes, "Most skaters would agree that what others deem as subversive is actually just a fun activity and a way to make new friends." But he also sees the value in skating in the streets as a powerful "form of protest, such as during the George Floyd uprisings across the country during the summer of 2020." For Giamarino:

> Non-skaters can learn from skateboarders that public space is not a static, homogeneous commodity to be used for commercial activities like shopping. Public space can and should be a space for play, sustenance, and survival that is contested and conflictual, politically active, and open and inclusive for different social groups. (Giamarino quoted from our interview)

Giamarino's research for his doctoral dissertation explores how unhoused people resist and rethink privatization of public space, increased policing and surveillance, and hostile architecture. It consists of photographically cataloging hostile designs and conducting 30 semi-structured interviews with unhoused people in Los Angeles. His research investigates how DIY co-production of public spaces are grassroots ways that marginalized communities can bring about "social change at a municipal level through more equitable municipal ordinances and public space design." In public skateparks, he has also helped locals run workshops that "teaches kids construction techniques, avoid policing and destruction of the ramp, and increase the overall flow of space." In other research, he explored the campaign to save the West LA Courthouse (Chui and Giamarino, 2019), which he feels "demonstrates skateboarders' ability to organize, pool industry money, lobby local politicians, peacefully coexist with other 'undesirable' public space users, and reach agreements to decriminalize skateboarding." He observed how skaters gained success not from resistance alone, but by also "exhibiting neoliberal characteristics lauded by cities, like being entrepreneurial with Nike SB, engaging civilly in political meetings, and getting creative with social media to ensure that skateboarders respect other public space users and organize clean-ups to show that they belong in the space."

Giamarino states, "My personal philosophy that public space should be open, accessible, and inclusive for different user groups and activities motivates me to see skateboarding progress." But for him, "the smaller, temporal tactics that skateboarders engage in to attain their right to the city" can be the most satisfying and effective. He explains that "these tactics can be hosting pop-up skate events in public spaces, using plazas until being kicked out by security, or expropriating objects like school benches and bringing them to poorly designed skateparks. These are more subversive forms of social change."

With an emphasis on intersectionality as a requirement to achieve equity, Giamarino states, "Skateboarding takes advantage of the city and public space by bringing people from different social, racial/ethnic, and gender/sexuality backgrounds into casual contact with one another. The plethora of architectural objects and spaces for appropriation enhance social learning." However, he warns that "with exclusionary regulations and hostile architecture, these opportunities to advance socially, spatially, and racially just discourse and actions are less likely to happen." However, going beyond a "complicit reflexivity" of "it is what it is" (Sharp and Threadgold, 2020), Giamarino has been involved with on the ground campaigns, such as efforts to reduce policing on his campus and "in public spaces where homeless and unhoused people are criminalized for performing life-sustaining activities like sitting, sleeping, eating, and going to the bathroom."

Alec Beck is an experienced activist who played pivotal roles in building Stoner Park and preserving access to skate at the Courthouse in West Los Angeles (Snyder, 2017). It was following a meeting with his future mentor in City Council Chair Jay Handal that helped guide Beck into seeing the need for greater communication and teamwork between skaters and local government. "Skaters learn early on that skateboarding functions as both a culture and as a community." He states that when advocating for the building of Stoner Park, it was foreign for skaters to know "what was needed from the powers that be," but at the same time, skateboarders knew how to "work together collectively to achieve their goals." Beck adds, "This experience of skater teamwork, when directed toward skatepark advocacy, leads to a more functional public space for all stakeholders, along with greater stewardship of the space."

Beck states that after his success with Stoner Park, he then focused on the West LA Courthouse, which is a world-famous skate spot. Nike wanted to hold a Go Skateboarding Day event in 2015 and had "spent a bunch of money to get all the legends there," eventually committing to spending $50,000 over five years to help maintain it (see Beck interview in Snyder, 2017: 255–257). What Beck then had to do was get skaters to show considerable restraint by not skating in the area after Go Skateboarding Day when skate knobs were added while they lobbied to get skaters access again. He explains, "We had to knob the ledges with pieces of paper that said, 'Please don't stay here.' We were basically saying 'Don't blow it.' We need to get work in the city for a couple of months. We'll work it out. We may have a legal free skate spot after this if everybody plays cool." And to his surprise, the skate community left it alone because "they knew that they needed to demonstrate their respect for the space and they did. That was critical to the city being like, 'Okay, cool. You can have the space for now.'" For Beck this was the motivation for him also to "continue to work towards advocating for good skate spaces that are meaningful for the community."

While activism can take many forms, "the meaning and nature of public space is constantly produced, reproduced, contested, negotiated and reconfigured" (Nemeth, 2006: 316). Beck's ongoing strategy is one of trying to build empathy and collaboration rather than escalate protests, and a type of skate diplomacy and activism that is transformative rather than aggressively "transgressive" (Nolan, 2003). In his current role with The Skatepark Project, he conveys how this also needs to be practiced on social media. He states, "We're trying to teach people not to drag people on social media, not to push too hard if you can help it, but if you do need to, do a peaceful protest to get attention." His guiding advice is that there is more power "in working together." With a view to what helps the community most, he argues, "you have to come at the constructive process with constructive energy." As an advocate in an organization with a high profile and reach, he also feels the need to understand "what your notion of duty of care is, especially considering we wouldn't want anybody to be in a position that puts anybody in elevated risk situations." He confirms, "That's not what we're recommending. You don't want people to be like, 'Oh, we should protest cool. Okay, go set the city on fire.'" Instead, he wants to encourage activists, and particularly younger ones, "to reposition that energy and that experience."

What Beck sheds light on is a type of defiance labor that also rejects more hegemonic forms of masculinity and fosters a more creative and empathetic style of activism that is founded upon resistance, but evolves into something more collaborative. The effect of this style of change-making is that it can build bridges rather than burn them. Through The Skatepark Project, he and others working there have created resources (https://skatepark.org/start) for ordinary skateboarders to adapt to their own campaigns, such as information on "best practices" for grants. In 2022 they also launched their first round of fellowships for young people who identify as Black, Indigenous, and People of Color (BIPOC) skaters to work on skatepark advocacy projects in their local areas.

While activism in the area of skate spots is growing and evolving, many populations who have some of the sharpest insights on what can seem intimidating or impractical and how to build inclusive, well-designed parks are overlooked (Willing and Shearer, 2016). Design issues are raised, for instance, by Kristin Ebeling and others in the "Bad Design Is a Crime: Skate Friendly Cities" talk at the Pushing Boarders conference (Pushing Boarders 2019) conference panel with Leo Valls, Dr. Karin

Book, and Fredrik Angner and chaired by Ocean Howell and Gustav Eden. Key themes in panel discussions and emerging studies on inclusive designs often make calls for architects and planners to consider how spatial features can be more adaptive and how existing obstacles can often be unsuitable or restrictive for people like beginners (Abulhawa, 2020, Bäckström, 2013, Carroll and Cianciotto, 2020, Ruben and Nunes, 2020, Ruiz et al., 2020, Sayers and Griffin, 2020). Accordingly, we also propose it is important for future planning to also take into account the views of both BIPOC, adaptive skaters and other "non-traditional" skateboarders.

To summarize, in this chapter we focused on the critical thinking of skateboarders, which is revealed in their discussion of key challenges they face and how that leads to a range of strategies and actions. Rather than being exclusive to skateboarding culture, we propose that many of the social issues that these change-makers grapple with are seen to have relevance and can be entangled with wider society. As such, the insights above on challenging things like structural inequality, colonialism, racism, and gender discrimination offer useful guides for a variety of communities, subcultural scenes, and sports.

References

Abulhawa, D (2020) *Skateboarding and Femininity: Gender, Space-making and Expressive Movement* London: Routledge.

Ahmad, N and Thorpe, H (2020) Muslim Sportswomen as Digital Space Invaders: Hashtag Politics and Everyday Visibilities, *Communication and Sport*, 1-20. DOI: https://doi.org/10.1177/2167479519898447

Ask Manifesto (2022) *Ask Zine*, collaboration by *Doyenne Skateboards, Consent for Breakfast, Consent is Rad* and *Hera Skate*. Released April 2020. https://doyenneskateboards.com/collections/ask-collection/products/ask-zine-ask-manifesto-riso-poster

Atencio, M., Beal, B., & Yochim, E. C. (2013). "It Ain't Just Black Kids and White Kids": The Representation and Reproduction of Authentic "Skurban" Masculinities. *Sociology of Sport Journal*, 30(2), 153–172.

Bäckström, Å (2013). Gender Maneuvering in Swedish Skateboarding: Negotiations of Femininities and the Hierarchical Gender Structure. *Young*, 21(1), 29–53.

Ball, B (2018) *Social-Emotional Learning Through Skateboarding: A Gateway to Self-Efficacy*. Honors Thesis. Department of Sociology, University of Colorado, Denver, USA.

Barbier, E (2020) Fighting for Equity: Your Efforts aren't Worthless, *Skateism*. Posted 29 March. Downloaded: https://www.skateism.com/fighting-for-equity-your-efforts-arent-worthless/

Beachy, K (2018) Primitive Progressivism, *Free Skate Magazine*, posted 5 June. Downloaded 8 July 2022: https://www.freeskatemag.com/2018/06/05/primitive-progressivism-by-kyle-beachy/

Beachy, K (2021) *The Most Fun Thing: Dispatches from a Skateboard Life*. Grand Central Publishing.

Beal, B and Weidman, L (2003). Authenticity in the Skateboarding World. In Rinehart, R. E. and Sydnor, S (Eds.), *To the extreme: Alternative sports, inside and out* (pp. 337–352). SUNY Press.

Bjesse-Puffin, A (2022) Times Up: No More Rape Culture in Our Skate Culture, Smash the Skateriarchy, Microcosm Publishing. Released February: https://microcosmpublishing.com/catalog/zines/7501

Boardrap (2018) Jason Jessee Nazi Apology, *Boardrap*. Download 4 August 2022: http://www.boardrap.com/wp-content/uploads/2018/05/jason-jessee-nazi-apology.jpg

Bonilla-Silva, E (2012) The Invisible Weight of Whiteness: The Racial Grammar of Everyday Life in Contemporary America, *Ethnic and Racial Studies*, 35:2, 173-194, DOI: https://doi.org/10.1080/01419870.2011.613997

Borden, I. (2001). *Skateboarding, Space and the City: Architecture and the Body*. Oxford: Berg.

Borden, I. (2019). *Skateboarding and the City: A Complete History*. London: Bloomsbury Visual Arts.

Bridge, G and Watson, S (Eds) (2000) A Companion to the City (Oxford: Blackwell).

Brown, A (2022) Honoring the Lineage of Black Skateboarders, *Nosesliders*, Posted 15 February. Downloaded 18 July 2022: https://nosesliders.substack.com/p/honoring-the-lineage-of-black-skateboarders?r=z8hv9

Buchanan, L, Bui, Q and Patel, J (2020) Black Lives Matter May Be the Largest Movement in U.S. History, *New York Times*. Posted 3 July. Downloaded 18 July 2022: https://www.nytimes.com/interactive/2020/07/03/us/george-floyd-protests-crowd-size.html

Callen-Riley, T and Holsgens, S (Eds) (2020) *Urban Pamphleteer #8 Skateboardings*, Downloaded 18 July 2022: http://urbanpamphleteer.org/skateboardings

Campos, A (2021) What's the Difference Between Hispanic, Latino and Latinx? *University of California News*. Posted Downloaded 31 July 2022: https://www.universityofcalifornia.edu/news/choosing-the-right-word-hispanic-latino-and-latinx

Carroll, T and Cianciotto, L (2020) Towards Radical Empathy, Eds Callen-Riley, T and Holsgens, S, *Urban Pamphleteer #8 Skateboardings*, pp. 11–12, Downloaded 18 July 2022: http://urbanpamphleteer.org/skateboardings

Chiu, C (2009) Contestation and Conformity: Street and Park Skating in New York City Public Space, *Space and Culture* 12: 25–42.

Chiu, C and Giamarino, C (2019) Creativity, Conviviality, and Civil Society in Neoliberalizing Public Space: Changing Politics and Discourses in Skateboarder Activism From New York City to Los Angeles. *Journal of Sport and Social Issues*, 43(6), 462–492. https://doi.org/10.1177/0193723519842219

Cianciotto, L (2020). Public Space, Common Space, and the Spaces In–Between: A Case Study of Philadelphia's LOVE Park, *City & Community*, 19(3), 676–703. https://doi.org/10.1111/cico.12454

Clarke, L (1995) *Kids*, Excalibur Films. Fullerton, CA. USA.

Connell, R (1995) *Masculinities*. Cambridge, UK: Polity Press.

Consent is Rad x DVTV (2021) Consent is Rad! DVTV video, *Consent is Rad*, Posted 21 June: https://consentisrad.wordpress.com/dtvt-gals-x-consent-is-rad/

Corporan, A, Serra, I and Razo, A (2021) Full Bleed: New York City Skateboard Photography (10th Anniversary Edition), New York: Salamander Street Ltd

Corwin, Z, Maruco, T, Williams, N, Reichardt, R, Romero-Morales, M, Rocha, C and Astiazaran, C (2019) *Beyond the Board: Findings from the Field*, Pullias Center for Education, University of Southern California.

Costa, M (2017) A Love Letter to Asian American Skateboarders. *Character Media*. Posted. Downloaded 30 July 2022: https://charactermedia.com/a-love-letter-to-asian-american-skateboarders/

Delardi, C (2021) *Pushing Boarders, Creating Alternative Futures: Resistance and Radical Inclusion in the Production of Non-Traditional Skateboarding Culture*, MA Thesis, Gallatin School of Independent Study, New York University

Dickinson, S, Millie, A and Peters, E (2022) Street Skateboarding and the Aesthetic Order of Public Spaces, *The British Journal of Criminology*, (62)6: 1454–1469. DOI: https://doi.org/10.1093/bjc/azab109

Dinces, S (2011) Flexible Opposition: Skateboarding Subcultures under the Rubric of Late Capitalism, *International Journal of the History of Sport*, 28(11): 1512–1535.

Dobija-Nootens, S (2017) Revisiting the Hanging Klansman Board, *Jenkem Mag*, Posted 14 August. Downloaded 5 July: https://www.jenkemmag.com/home/2017/08/14/revisiting-hanging-klansman-board/

Dobija-Nootens, N (2018). Understanding the Neal Hendrix allegations and power dynamics in skateboarding, *Jenkem Mag*. Posted October 29. Downloaded 5 August 2022: http://www.jenkemmag.com/home/2018/10/29/understanding-neal-hendrix-allegations-power-dynamics-skateboarding/

Dupont, T (2014) From Core to Consumer: The Informal Hierarchy of the Skateboard Scene. *Journal of Contemporary Ethnography, 43*(5), 556–581. https://doi.org/10.1177/0891241613513033

Dupont, T (2020). Authentic Subcultural Identities and Social Media: American Skateboarders and Instagram. *Deviant Behavior, 41*(5), 649–664. 10.1080/01639625.2019.1585413

Dupont, T and Beal, B (2021) *Lifestyle Sports and Identities: Subcultural Careers through the Life Course*. Milton: Taylor & Francis Group.

Feldman-Barrett, C (Ed) (2014) *Lost Histories of Youth Culture (Mediated Youth)*, London: Peter Lang

Foley, Z (2020) From BLM Protests to the Olympics: Are Skateboarders Capable of Creating Social Change, *Skateism*. Posted 1 October. Downloaded 20 July 2022: https://www.skateism.com/from-blm-protests-to-the-olympics-are-skateboarders-capable-of-creating-social-change

Foley, Z (2022) Skate Tales Goes Deeper: The Douglas Miles Jr Interview. *Red Bull*. Posted 24 May. Downloaded 25 July 2022 https://www.redbull.com/ca-en/doug-miles-junior-interview

Fox, T (2016) *No Consent = Sexual Abuse*. Brisbane, Visible Ink. Published: https://consentrequired.wordpress.com/

Frankenberg, R (1999) *White Women, Race Matters: The Social Construction of Whiteness*. Minneapolis: University of Minnesota Press.

Gans, H (1979) Symbolic Ethnicity: The Future of Ethnic Groups and Cultures in America, *Ethnic and Racial Studies, 2*(1): 1-20

Geckle, B and Shaw, S (2022) Failure and Futurity: The Transformative Potential of Queer Skateboarding. *YOUNG, 30*(2), 132–148. https://doi.org/10.1177/1103308820945100

Giamarino, C, Goh, K, Loukaitou-Sideris, A, and Mukhija, V (2022) Just Urban Design Scholarship?: Examining Urban Design Theories Through a Justice Lens, *Just Urban Design: The Struggle for a Public City*, (eds) Kian Goh, Anastasia Loukaitou-Sideris, Vinit Mukhija. MIT Open Press. pp 21-46.

Glenney, B and Mull, S (2018) Skateboarding and the Ecology of Urban Space, *Journal of Sport and Social Issues.* https://doi.org/10.1177/019372 3518800525.

Glenney, B and Paul O'Connor, P (2019) 'Skateparks as hybrid elements of the city', *Journal of Urban Design*, 24(6): 848–849.

Glover, T, Munro, S, Men, I, Loates, W and Altman, I (2021) Skateboarding, Gentle Activism, and the Animation of Public Space: CITE – A Celebration of Skateboard Arts and Culture at The Bentway, *Leisure Studies*, 40:1, 42-56, https://doi.org/10.1080/02614367.2019.1684980

Grosso, J (2017a) Loveletters Season 8: Unleashed the East- Part 1 | Jeff Grosso's Loveletters to Skateboarding, *VANS*, Posted June: https://www.youtube.com/watch?v=_tAtBb6U9rI

Grosso, J (2017b) Loveletters Season 8: Unleashed the East- Part 2 | Jeff Grosso's Loveletters to Skateboarding, *VANS*, Posted 10 June: https://www.youtube.com/watch?v=B6BnbXUZYrs

Grosso, J (2020) Love Letter To LGBTQ+ | Jeff Grosso's Loveletters to Skateboarding, VANS, Posted 12 June: https://www.youtube.com/watch?v=kqD4xfNwd6k

Hernandez, D (2017) The Case Against Latinx, *LA Times*, posted 17 December. Downloaded 4 August 2022: https://www.latimes.com/opinion/op-ed/la-oe-hernandez-the-case-against-latinx-20171217-story.html

Hochschild, A (1979) Emotion Work, Feeling Rules, and Social Structure, *American Journal of Sociology*, 85(3)551-575

Howell, O (2001) The Poetics of Security: Skateboarding, Urban Design, and the New Public Space, *Urban Policy*. Posted http://urbanpolicy.net.

Howell, O (2005) The 'Creative Class' and the Gentrifying City: Skateboarding in Philadelphia's Love Park, *Journal of Architectural Education* 59 (2): 32–42.

Huston, S (2022) Creating the Ask Campaign: A Collaborative Project About Consent, *Yeah Girl*, Posted 30 June. A collective interview with Doyenne Skateboards, Consent for Breakfast, Hera Skate, and Consent is Rad, Downloaded 28 July 2022: https://yeahgirlmedia.com/creating-the-ask-campaign-a-collaborative-project-about-consent/

Jefferson, A (2020) Cover, Black Lives Matter Issue. *Thrasher Magazine*. September 2020.

Jenkem Staff (2014) A collection of some of the most offensive board graphics. *Jenkem Mag*. Posted 10 October, Downloaded 4 August 2022: http://www.jenkemmag.com/home/2014/10/10/a-collection-of-some-of-the-most-offensive-skateboard-graphics/

Jenkem Staff (2020) Listen to Na-Kel Share His Experience as a Black Pro Skater, *Jenkem Magazine*. Posted 1 June, Downloaded 20 July 2022: https://www.jenkemmag.com/home/2020/06/01/listen-nakel-share-experiences-black-pro-skater/

Kerr, C (2018) What I Learned from Skating's First Academic Conference, *Jenkem Mag*. Posted 31 July. Downloaded 18 July: https://www.jenkemmag.com/home/2018/07/31/learned-skatings-first-academic-conference/

Kerr, C (2019) Appreciating Latinx Immigrants that Shaped Skateboarding. *Jenkem Magazine*. Posted 9 August. Downloaded 28 July 2022: https://www.jenkemmag.com/home/2019/08/09/appreciating-latinx-immigrants-shaped-skateboarding/

Kerr, C (2022) Imagining a Sustainable Skateboard, *Village Psychic*. Posted 22 April. Downloaded 28 July 2022: http://www.villagepsychic.net/blog/imagining-a-sustainable-skateboard

Kulynych, Y (2020) Resistant Formations of Alternative Femininities within Skateboarding an Exploration of Gender at a Time of Feminist Transformation, *Masculinities Journal of Culture and Society*, 14: 61-86.

Lanza, L (2020) Black Skateboarders Share their Experiences, *Jenkem Magazine*, posted 31 July. Downloaded 18 July 2022: https://www.jenkemmag.com/home/2020/07/31/black-skaters-share-experiences-skateboarding/

Lapchick, R (2009) Latino Influence Shapes Action Sport. *ESPN*. Posted 29 September. Downloaded 30 July 2022 https://www.espn.com/espn/hispanicheritage2009/columns/story?columnist=lapchick_richard&id=4516693

Lawton, C (2020) Can Skateboarders in Nottingham be Good Partners to the City Without Being the Shock Troops of Gentrification. In (Eds) Callen-Riley, T and Holsgens, S, *Urban Pamphleteer #8 Skateboardings*, pp 36-38. Downloaded 18 July 2022: http://urbanpamphleteer.org/skateboardings

Lay, R (2019) Life Lessons from Being a Pro Skater. *Jenkem Magazine*. Posted 24 October. Downloaded 23 July 2022: https://www.jenkemmag.com/home/2019/10/24/life-lessons-pro-skater/

Lefebvre, H (1991) *The Production of Space*. Oxford: Blackwell.

Liu, B (2018) *Minding the Gap*. Kartemquin Films, USA.

Lombard, K. J (2010). Skate and Create/Skate and Destroy: The Commercial and Governmental Incorporation of Skateboarding. *Continuum: Journal of Media & Cultural Studies*, 24(4), 475–488. https://doi.org/10.1080/10304310903294713

Lupine, G (2015) Skateboarding: The Latino Effect, *Cali Strong*. Posted 15 February. Downloaded 30 July 2022: https://www.cali-strong.com/skateboarding-latino-effect/

Mackay, D (2022) USA Skateboarding President Resigns, *Inside the Games*. Posted 2 August. Downloaded 7 August 2022: https://www.insidethegames.biz/articles/1126506/usa-skateboarding-president-resigns#:~:text=Gary%20Ream%20has%20resigned%20as,at%20the%20national%20governing%20body.

Martínez, D (2013) From Off the Rez to Off the Hook!: Douglas Miles and Apache Skateboards. *American Indian Quarterly* 37(4):370–94.

Miles Snr, D (2022), Desert Rider: Under the Hood - Douglas Miles (ep. 01), interview for *Desert Rider Series Installation*, Phoenix Art Museum, Downloaded 13 May. URL: bit.ly/UTH-Miles

Moldof, Z (2022) Nazi Skaters in Sweden, Every Anti-Semite is an Anti-Seminte. *Stoke Much*. Posted 2 November. Downloaded 18 November 2022: https://medium.com/@stokemuchmag/nazi-skaters-in-sweden-every-antisemite-is-every-antisemite-477a98c05d0a

Mull, C (2017) Manramp: The Follow Up. *Thrasher Magazine*. Posted Downloaded 4 August 2022: https://www.thrashermagazine.com/articles/the-follow-up-manramp/

Murrell, A (2018) Skateboarding Icon Jason Jessee is Under Fire for Use of Swastikas and Racist Remarks, *Vice*. Posted 25 May. Downloaded 31 July 2022: https://www.vice.com/en/article/59q343/skateboarding-icon-jason-jessee-is-under-fire-for-use-of-swastikas-and-racist-remarks

Murrell, A (2019) How a Sexual Predator Infiltrated Atlanta's Skate Scene. *Jenkem Mag*. Posted 5 November. Downloaded 6 August 2022: http://www.jenkemmag.com/home/2019/11/05/sexual-predator-infiltrated-atlantas-skate-scene/

Nemeth, J (2006) Conflict, Exclusion, Relocation: Skateboarding and Public Space, *Journal of Urban Design*, 11:3, 297-318, DOI: https://doi.org/10.1080/13574800600888343

NHS Inc (2022) From Pro Skater to Running Krux Trucks - Alex White, *NHS Skate Direct*, Posted 30 July: https://www.youtube.com/watch?v=BbObkOntBUM

Nolan (2003) The Ins and Outs of Skateboarding and Transgression in Public Space in Newcastle, *Australia, Australian Geographer*, 34(3), 311-327, DOI: https://doi.org/10.1080/0004918032000152401

Nut Daily News Team (2018) Park Local Waiting for Woman Meme, *Nut Daily News* Posted 29 June at: https://www.instagram.com/p/Bklv1i8Fddi/

Nut Daily News Team (2019) Local Skaters Day Made Meme, *Nut Daily News* Posted 16 January at: https://www.instagram.com/p/BsqyEfcFf7I/

O'Connor, P (2020) *Skateboarding and Religion*. London: Palgrave

O'Sullivan, S (2021) The Colonial Project of Gender (and Everything Else), *Genealogy*, 5(67): 1-9. https://doi.org/10.3390/genealogy5030067

Pape, M (2019) Expertise and Non-binary Bodies: Sex, Gender and the Case of Dutee Chand. *Body & Society*, *25*(4), 3–28. https://doi.org/10.1177/1357034X19865940

Pappalardo, A (2020a) Skateboarding Shames Victims, Artless Industria, Posted 11 July 2020. Downloaded 6 August 2022: https://anthonypappalardo.substack.com/p/skateboarding-shames-victims?fbclid=IwAR0jka5iMIHmpUZuZ61i77W5xOsr4FjqPyKaHKA6DkbUFxvg%2D%2DhopLtUcUo

Pappalardo, A (2020b) Skateboarding Has an Education Problem, *Artless Industria*. Posted 21 July. Downloaded 2 August 2022: https://anthonypappalardo.substack.com/p/skateboarding-has-an-education-problem

Pappalardo, A (2022b) Gator, Mark Oblow and Apologies, *Artless Industria*. Posted Downloaded 17 July 2022: https://anthonypappalardo.substack.com/p/gator-mark-oblow-and-apologies

Pappalardo, A (2022c) Skateboarding Needs to Listen, *Artless Industria*, Posted 6 August. Downloaded 6 August 2022: https://anthonypappalardo.substack.com/p/skateboarding-needs-to-listen

Plage, S, Willing, I, Woodward, I, and Skrbiš Z, (2017). Cosmopolitan encounters: reflexive engagements and the ethics of sharing, *Ethnic and Racial Studies*, *40*(1), 4–23. https://doi.org/10.1080/01419870.2016.1178788

Pushing Boarders (2019) Bad Design is a Crime: Skate Friendly Cities, *Pushing Boarders* Conference website: https://www.pushingboarders.com/talks-2019-watch

Quartersnacks Staff (2012) A Not At All Comprehensive Guide to Prominent Jewish Pro Skateboarders. Quarter Snacks. Posted 23 August. Downloaded 30 July: https://quartersnacks.com/2012/08/a-not-at-all-comprehensive-guide-to-prominent-jewish-pro-skateboarders/

Ramiez, J (2016) The Latinos Who Helped Shape Modern Skateboarding, *Latino Rebels*. Posted 31 July. Downloaded 30 July: https://www.latinorebels.com/2016/07/31/the-latinos-who-helped-shape-modern-skateboarding/

Roechoudt, J (2020) How Rookie Skateboards Shaped Women's Skateboarding, *Quell Magazine*. Posted 21 July. Downloaded 5 August 2022: https://www.jenkemmag.com/home/2021/07/02/rookie-skateboards-shaped-womens-skateboarding/

Rubin, B and Nunes, F (2020) Skateboarding and Mobility: Filipe Nunes Interviewed by Ben Rubin, Eds Callen-Riley, T and Holsgens, S, *Urban Pamphleteer #8 Skateboardings*, pp 8-10, Downloaded 18 July 2022: http://urbanpamphleteer.org/skateboardings

Ruddick, S (1996) Constructing difference in public spaces: race, class and gender as interlocking systems, Urban Geography, 17(2), pp. 132–151.

Ruiz, P, Snelson, T, Madgin, R, and Webb, D (2020). 'Look at What We Made': Communicating Subcultural Value on London's Southbank. *Cultural Studies*, *34*(3), 392–417. https://doi.org/10.1080/09502386.2019.1621916

Sayers, E and Griffin, S (2020) City Mill Skate: Skateboarding and Architecture, Eds Callen-Riley, T and Holsgens, S, *Urban Pamphleteer #8 Skateboardings*, pp 8-10, Downloaded 18 July 2022: http://urbanpamphleteer.org/skateboardings

Sharp, M and Threadgold, S (2020). Defiance Labour and Reflexive Complicity: Illusio and Gendered Marginalisation in DIY Punk Scenes. *Sociological Review*, 68(3), pp. 606-622. https://doi.org/10.1177/0038026119875325.

Singh, D (2020) Racial Complaint and Sovereign Divergence: The Case of Australia's First Indigenous Ophthalmologist, *The Australian Journal of Indigenous Education*, 49(2): 145 - 148

Snyder, G. J (2017) *Skateboarding LA: Inside Professional Street Skateboarding*. New York University Press.

Sueyoshi, A (2015) Skate and Create: Skateboarding, Asian Pacific America and Masculinity. *Amerasia Journal*. 4(2): 2-24

Thorpe, H (2007) Extreme Media, in *Berkshire Encyclopedia of Extreme Sports*, Berkshire Publishing Group. 1-6

Thorpe, H, Toffoletti, K, and Bruce, T (2017) Sportswomen and social media: Bringing third-wave feminism, postfeminism, and neoliberal feminism into conversation, *Journal of Sport and Social Issues*, 41, 359–383. https://doi.org/10.1177/0193723517730808

Thorpe, H, Hayhurst, L, and Chawansky, M (2018) The girl effect and "positive" representations of sporting girls of the Global South: Social media portrayals of Afghan girls on skateboards. In K. Toffoletti, H. Thorpe, & J. Francombe-Webb (Eds.), *New sporting femininities: Embodied politics in postfeminist times* (pp. 299–323). Palgrave Macmillan.

Toffoletti, K and Thorpe, H (2018a). Female Athletes' Self-representation on Social Media: A Feminist Analysis of Neoliberal Marketing Strategies in "Economies of Visibility", *Feminism and Psychology*, 28, 11–31. https://doi.org/10.1177/0959353517726705

Toffoletti, K and Thorpe, H (2018b). The Athletic Labour of Femininity: The Branding and Consumption of Global Celebrity Sportswomen on Instagram, *Journal of Consumer Culture*, 18, 298–316. https://doi.org/10.1177/1469540517747068

Toffoletti, K, Francombe-Webb, J and Thorpe, T (2018) *New Sporting Femininities: Embodied Politics in Postfeminist Times*. Cham, Switzerland: Palgrave Macmillan.

Watego, C (2021) *Another Day in the Colony*. University of Queensland Press.

Weaver, H (2016) Where Wounded Knee meets Wounded Knees: Skateparks and Native American Youth. *Alternative: An International Journal of Indigenous Peoples*, 12(5), 513–526. https://search-informit-org.libraryproxy.griffith.edu.au/doi/epdf/10.3316/informit.523827165207373

Wheaton, B and Thorpe, T (2019) Action Sport Media Consumption Trends across Generations: Exploring the Olympic Audience and the Impact of Action Sports Inclusion, *Communication and Sport* 7(4): 415–45, https://doi.org/10.1177/2167479518780410

Wheaton, B and Thorpe, H (2021) *Action Sports and the Olympic Games: Past, Present, Future*, Routledge

Williams, N (2021) Understanding Race in Skateboarding: A Retrospection and Agenda for the Importance of Being Seen, Dupont, T and Beal, B (eds), *Lifestyle Sports and Identities: Subcultural Careers Throughout the Life Course*, London: Routledge, pp. 284 - 296.

Willing, I (2014) Interview with Kim Woozy, founder of MAHFIA Web TV, *Asian Australian Film Forum and Network Interview Series*, Posted March. Downloaded 31 July 2022: https://asianaustralianfilmforum.wordpress.com/2014/03/03/aaffn_interview2014_with_kim_woozy/

Willing, I (2019a) Real Talk, Real Change: An Interview with Sports Agent Yulin Oliver, *Yeah Girl*. Posted 11 July 2019. Downloaded 31 July 2022: https://yeahgirlmedia.com/real-talk-real-change-an-interview-with-skateboarding-agent-yulin-olliver/

Willing, I (2019b) The Evolution of Skateboarding and Why Pushing Boarders is a Sign of the Times, *Yeah Girl*. Posted 10 October. Downloaded 6 August 2022: https://yeahgirlmedia.com/the-evolution-of-skateboarding-and-why-pushing-boarders-is-a-sign-of-the-times/

Willing, I (2019c) Get By, Get Through, Get Rolling: Pushing Boarders Reflections 2, *Yeah Girl*. Posted 17 December. Downloaded 4 August 2022: https://yeahgirlmedia.com/get-by-get-through-get-rolling-pushing-boarders-reflections-part-2

Willing, I (2020a) Twenty Twenty Skate Visions: Pushing Boarders Reflections 3. *Yeah Girl.* Posted 29 January. Downloaded 6 August 2022: https://yeahgirlmedia.com/2020-skate-visions-pushing-boarders-reflections-part-3/

Willing, I (2020b) 'The Film Kids 25 Years On: A Qualitative Study of Rape Culture and Representations of Sexual Violence in Skateboarding'. *Young,* Special Issue on Skateboarding. Accepted 20 July, 2020. First published 6 November: https://journals.sagepub.com/doi/10.1177/1103308820966457

Willing, I (2021) Book Review: 'Skateboarding and Urban Landscapes in Asia: Endless Spots' by Duncan McDuie-Ra. *Asian Anthropology Journal,* 20(4): 282-283. Preview version August, 2021: 10.1080/1683478X.2021.1968106

Willing, I and Barbier, E (2020) Beyond the Gender Binary: Skateboarding and the Olympics, *Skateboard, de la rue à l'olympisme Conference,* Rouen University, 29 October. Talk posted 2 November 2020: https://webtv.univ-rouen.fr/videos/skateboarders-the-olympic-games-and-re-thinking-and-resisting-the-gender-binary-indigo-willing-et-emanuele-barbier/

Willing, I and Shearer, S (2016) Skateboarding Activism: Exploring Diverse Voices and Community Support, Lombard, KJ (ed) *Skateboarding: Subcultures, Sites and Shifts,* London: Routledge. pp. 44-58.

Willing, I, Bennett, A, Piispa, M and Green, B (2019) Skateboarding and the 'Tired Generation': Ageing in Youth Cultures and Lifestyle Sports. *Sociology* 53(3):503–18.

Willing, I, Green, B and Pavlidis, P (2020) The 'Boy Scouts' and 'Bad Boys' of Skateboarding: A Thematic Analysis of *The Bones Brigade. Sport in Society,* 23(5), 832 - 846. DOI: https://doi.org/10.1080/17430437.2019.1580265

Yochim, E (2010). *Skate Life: Re-imagining White Masculinity.* San Francisco: University of Michigan Press.

Young, A. and Dallaire, C (2008) Beware*#! Sk8 at Your Own Risk: The Discourses of Young Female Skateboarders. In *Tribal Play: Subcultural Journeys through Sport,* edited by M. Atkinson and K. Young, 235–254. Bingley, UK: JAI Press.

6

Wish Lists, Roadmaps, and Recipes for Skateboarding in the Future

© The Author(s), under exclusive license to Springer Nature Singapore Pte Ltd. 2023   **235**
I. Willing, A. Pappalardo, *Skateboarding, Power and Change*,
https://doi.org/10.1007/978-981-99-1234-6_6

Chapter 6 Illustration by Adam Abada

Introduction

Skateboarding can be a highly personal form of expression, and because of this, skateboarders are not always asked to think about the bigger picture or to encourage each other to think about their collective future ahead. Skateboarding is not always carefully planned. Its spontaneous nature is what makes skateboarding attractive to many. What we are good at is being in the "zone" when thinking about our relationship to skating as a "physical culture" (Abulhawa 2021: 62) and "skateboard consciousness" (Vivoni and Folsom-Fraser 2021: 312). For instance, when we are doing a trick, or even just rolling along some flat ground, the world can seem as if it is timeless, and one becomes absorbed into an all-encompassing zone, where nothing but that trick or moment matters. Yet we are also concurrently and externally relating to the intricacies of the urban environment. Skateboarding takes focus and an awareness of minute details: where the cracks in the pavement are in relation to an obstacle, how the geometry of a skateboard deck impacts tricks, or even how the weather will change our bodies or the terrain we are skating. We should also remember skateboarders typically have the tenacity to try new things, test them, practice, and push through difficult stages of progress (Vivoni and Folsom-Fraser 2021).

Skateboarding, as we have outlined in Chaps. 1 and 2, began as a youth culture. In many ways, skaters still embody a "youthful" disposition into adulthood from not losing touch with valuing creative play, and the pursuit of fun (O'Connor 2017; Willing et al. 2019). Such relationality to the world around us can be seen as a hindrance to being "elders" and stewards for a more inclusive, progressive, and evolved future. But something we can reflect on is that when you are in the act of skating, you become timeless or devoid of age. Our bodies will act differently over time but the euphoric feeling of getting the first trick we ever did, and the ones that follow, with that sense of accomplishment, will always feel as exciting as any age. In short, the joy that skateboarding can bring is ageless.

We can also think at an enormous speed about how things will play out ahead of time, using our imagination, to quickly sum up and strategize from errors from the past and execute a course of action to "get" or "get closer" to our trick goal in micro-time. And, through the concept of "radical empathy" (Carroll and Cianciotto 2020; Givens 2022) we introduced in Chap. 4, we are reminded of how skaters can have an open and sharp physical awareness of each other when skating together, leading us to anticipate and respect each other's spatial needs, trick intentions, and lines of action. We can also share a uniting and sometimes an almost electrifying sense of joy or "stoke" when seeing other skaters get a trick, especially after overcoming a significant struggle to land it and roll away cleanly. These skate-related skills, reflexes, and outlooks can also contribute to us having a sense of belonging to a community (Corwin et al. 2019) or even more so, an "imaged community" (Anderson 1993) where like nationhood, people feel a sense of belonging and connection as a community, even among strangers who they may skate with, or never meet.

In this chapter, which is the final one that draws on our interviews, we have some final occasions to think about how skateboarders use these skills and outlooks in ways that can translate beyond physical pursuits over into the social world, through things such as values of openness, ethical reflexive practices, and collective action. We devote our attention to what kinds of things skateboarders anticipate, feel for, and foresee for fellow skaters in terms of their shared needs and interests. This includes developing respectful, safe, and appreciative environments, not just for skating in their immediate circles and communities, but also for new people who follow on. Our inquiry is presented through three main themes: (1) Door Opening and Thinking Forward, (2) Critical Self-Reflection, and Self-Care, and (3) Recipes for Building Skate Futures Together.

As we shall see, some interviewees feel there is a range of things that are actionable in the present. This includes addressing overlooked issues in skateboarding, such as how self-care and self-critique can be built into skate projects as a form of safeguarding and accountability. Others identify and flesh out goals that will only be realized through more awareness, commitment, and tangible forms of support. We pay attention to how landscape they envisage for the future of skateboarding is shaped by particular values and outlooks that promote forms of mutual respect and ethical togetherness. Our aim in presenting these insights is not to be forcefully prescriptive or deterministic, but rather, to offer an antidote to apathy and complicity by sharing pathways, and an expanded sense of possibility.

Opening Doors and Thinking Forward

The skateboarders we spoke with are no longer satisfied with "business as usual" within the "core" side of skateboarding culture. In past chapters exploring their strategies of change, we saw how they push against fatalist and complicit notions of "it is what it is" over to an ethical and action-focused orientation of "it is not what it could be" (Sharp and Threadgold 2020: 618). What this chapter aims to explore are the types of insights they share on "what it can be" and "how we keep making it as it should be."

> One day pro skateboarders will be selected on their ability to work in the community. Nobody's thought about that. I think the industry is behind the times. They're not looking at the social impact that these brands, companies, pros, and teams could have, they have not even begun to scratch the surface of how impactful they could be in America—Douglas Miles Sr. (Quoted in our interview)

When we asked what is the future of skateboarding, the skateboarders we spoke to did not talk of NBDs (never been done) tricks on the largest rails and stair sets, or who is the most popular skateboarder based on their competition titles and wealth. Instead, they emphasized what new ground skaters might cover socially, and for the benefit of the community. For Douglas Miles Sr., this includes shifting the power in skate media, and seeing multiple platforms run by First Nations skateboarders and others pushed to the periphery. He states, "what I predict is we'll have our own skateboard media, our own skateboard channel. We will have our own skateboard publication. We'll have our own given form of support on social media." Miles Sr. also extends this idea, explaining "that way, skateboarders, left outside of the 'norm', the mainstream, or whatever you want to call it, will have a voice." Miles Sr. also sees advantages in moving attention outwards rather than just on "pros" who "have corporations, teams, brand managers, brand owners and so onto please."

The *Black Lives Matter* movement in America was also a groundbreaking moment for an old guard of "skate power-brokers" as Miles Sr. proposes, and he feels systemic racism "has been unmasked and the curtain has been pulled back on it for many industries." The priorities he calls for include that efforts of inclusion should not be token or simply performative for "clout" rather than proper payment, representation, and positions. He warns, "skate brands, now are not the time to parade your one or two minority pros out right now, you should have been hiring them all along." He explains, "Skateboarding is going to change, and it is changing and it's been changing. We personified that with *Apache skateboards*."

In terms of what will keep fueling the plans of *Apache Skateboards* to keep decolonizing and re-engineering the skate culture, he is enthusiastic about the power of the skate team, which includes Douglas Miles Jr., Tasha Hastings, Tray Polk, Brina Adley plus Diné skaters Di'orr Greenwood, Ty Thomason, and others. Miles Sr. states, "I trust them and then they trust me as well. And they are the true revolutionaries, and they are the true history makers." He adds, "they are the true workers, the true revolutionaries. The *Apache Skateboards* team are the true leaders of now."

While maintaining an outlook on Indigenous sovereignty and agency, his vision also enacts a cosmopolitan, anti-racist repertoire. He emphasizes that he hopes to also "inspire People of Color, artists and writers and creatives, and skaters that deserve to be respected for what you do and what you bring to the table." He explains, "we empathize with your struggle and with those battles. We could never understand what it's like to be you, but we empathize because we've been the subject of numerous wars and violence and American militarism." He adds, "we're using skateboarding as the platform that it was meant to be used for, to talk about societal change and bring about positive cultural information in a country that is made up of Native, Black, Latino, Chicano and Asian people."

Patrick Kigongo places a similar emphasis on restructuring rather than accessorizing White-dominated areas of the skate culture such as the industry and businesses, which he felt he made a dent through the support given to *The Black List*. He states that "the next step of taking skateboarding forward would be for someone to start communicating and talking about setting up their own distribution channels." To describe the impact of his initiative, he offers a sports metaphor, "If we can think about it like boxing, the first round of the fight is to put money in people's pockets. We won that. No problem. That was a knockout."

When thinking about going into the future, for him, "The next round, the next card, I would say the main event even, is smashing white supremacy within the skateboard industry." He explains that this means "the warehouse workers, the accountant, the person who becomes a shoe designer, that's gonna be the person who becomes a team manager. And that's going to be the next crucial step." He feels encouraged by the launching pad *The Black List* offers and its combining a DIY approach with an approach that is business and profits focused, stating, "It's very easy to put together *The Black List*. That was the whole point. It was an easy lift. You want to get money in people's pockets." Kigongo also offers the advice that "if you want to effect some real change, you're going to have to stand up with something more and new to dismantle those structures." He warns, "skateboarding still being what it is, I do not anticipate it is going to start letting in folks who look like me in large numbers. To be doing everything behind the scenes, we'll have to do it ourselves." Instead of seeing the responsibility resting on individuals, he encourages a community-driven approach and that "collective brainstorming will get us there."

Offering insight into steps for bringing in a more inclusive skate media, Timothy Ward expresses that it needs to meet the needs of people who appreciate a more holistic and diverse look at what is going on in skateboarding. He states that for many skateboarders, "I think that what is different now is that the focus isn't as much on 'who's the best!' etc. which I also believed is the reason why so much the marginalization happened in skateboarding." He feels that barriers that need to still be removed in the future include, "that there are still people in the industry that want only to see the hardest and gnarliest skating, and they think that all skaters want that too." He also explains how industry also needs to look beyond men to define and appreciate what "good" skateboarding looks like, giving the example, "I want to see the best switch kickflip ever, and that happens to belong to Alexis Sablone."

Denia Kopita feels that men's attitudes toward "non-traditional" skaters also need to be reset in a way that they are aware their skills are not the bar to measure other genders, an issue some men are becoming more reflexive about as highlighted in Chap. 5 in the section on the power of humor as a form of critical self-reflection. Kopita also provides an example of how men need to relate to women in a way that is genuinely appreciative rather than simply benevolent and based on an assumption about their level. She urges, "everyone to treat women skaters the same. I don't want to do an ollie and everyone be super pumped only because dudes think that's all a woman can do." Her example indicates how good intentions can mask patronizing assumptions, while also still placing men in a position of superiority, explaining "it's like a very thin line. I mean, it comes from a good place."

A more equitable way to relate in Kopita's view is through a shared sense of joy any skater feels for each other, which we explored in Chap. 4 in the section on skater's values and outlooks. Moreover, joy can help establish the act of recognizing what a skater fully brings, rather than a projection of what they are about and treating them as deficient. Kopita's critical reflections on how men can interact with other genders also open the door for another consideration. This is the importance of finding ways to establish the grounds for relating through mutual respect of who a person is, rather than from having the exact same skills or doing tricks "even they can't do." Kopita states, "I want you to show that you're supporting me. I want you to cheer for me. Like when it comes from a genuine place of 'oh, she did that. And it was cool…it was stylish and she rocked it." She explains, "I want people to kind of like treat women the same as men. When it comes to skating and skate tricks, I think that's achievable. I believe in equality. So everyone is the same. And we should just go for that."

Izzi Cooper also frames the future as one that can improve by appreciating who skateboarders are and what they do outside of a dynamic where masculinity is dominant and considered superior. She offers for instance that, "the 'cool guy' attitude of many skaters needs to change." She encourages skateboarders foster a duty of care for one another as part of this process, with attentiveness to differences. She states, "Skateboarding is vast and this diversity needs to be celebrated at all levels of skateboarding. Skaters also need to reach out to those that are marginalized and make sure their needs are being met in the community." Cooper also suggests making pathways for newcomers to "become a skateboarder" that resists pressures to conform to rituals and practices used to gatekeep. Her advice is that "we should be welcoming newcomers to the community and not making fun of them for not knowing the proper terms or ways to hold the board. None of that matters as long as people are having fun." She also emphasizes how this can promote unity, stating, "Skateboarding can teach us a lot. Just like how skating brings people together."

In terms of the media, Christian Kerr feels that exchanging pedestals and hero-worshipping with the idea of ambassadors who promote inclusion is a constructive way forward. He proposes, "I think that the kind of 'elder statesman' that we're trying to sort of elevating." Providing more explanation of a conservativeness that can gain traction that ends up being exclusionary he states, "there are some original legends of skateboarding who are right-leaning and White, which feeds into this idea that the origins skateboarding and seeds of its culture are from White America, which I don't think is true." By way of example he points to "the Jason Jessee thing where they're trying to elevate him as an important historical figure for skateboarding for some reason when he has like a long history of pretty negative associations." Kerr's proposal is that:

> Skateboarding does not need a single narrative or idols. But I do think that it's really important that we have articulate skateboarding ambassadors, from a variety of different identities, who can explain to the outside world what is unique, special, and worth preserving within skateboarding, culture, and our history. (Christian Kerr quoted in our interview)

The development of a more nuanced and diverse skate history that balances formal and DIY approaches is important to Kerr. He feels this can involve "the creation and archiving of history in skateboarding with the *Hall of Fame*, and long in-depth oral history projects, kind of like the *Nine Club*, with depth interviews about skateboarders and what they were thinking at a certain time." His rationale is that "I think all that's important for just the preservation of whatever skateboarding is now, and for the stories, we want to create in the future."

As skateboarders, we also emphasize that it is important to remember what we do requires being spatially aware and reliant on the built environment as well. And here too innovative roadmaps for the future begin to unfold through what Steven Flusty (2000: 153) called the "skater's eye" view (quoted in Vivoni and Folsom-Fraser 2021: 312, also see McDuie-Ra 2021). For instance, Tom Dupere of *Duty Now* has been building and refurbishing parks for over 20 years, and his view of skateable architecture focuses on collective rather than just individualistic benefits. It can also be intergenerational. Now aged fifty, he states, "it's been rad, I've got to work with some great dudes, and we've got some younger dudes in the crew now too so I get to pass on knowledge to them and they're stepping up" (quoted in Murphy 2018). For Dupere and his crew, the thrill of skating is not just personal. It is also, as we have pointed to at the beginning of this section, about "sharing the stoke." In this case, from building something, then seeing other people experience it for the first time. Ricky Oyola (Epicly Later'd 2013) also brings insight into skateboarders' relationships to spaces and DIY. This includes that for him, the idea that finding a spot or building a spot is actually a part of the trick. Oyola's motives are often more personal and reflect his approach to how he skateboards. But it is interesting to observe a philosophy with the DIY skate spot scene that part of the trick in skating is not just "doing it yourself" but the joy in sharing a DIY or even a spot you found, and documenting the journey and experience.

In Chap. 2 we discussed some parallels between surfing and skateboarding. Of course, skateboarding has many distinctions that deviate from surfing, particularly as the latter relies on tides and a changeable terrain. In contrast, skateboarding takes place on land, but this does not mean skateboarders defy needing to adapt. The conditions of what allows a spot or skatepark to emerge, then stay or are banned or dismantled, can change. And it is why skaters in New York or other major cities are also creative thinkers because random street spots can change every day. They are also attuned to seeing opportunities and using them to the fullest. Moreover, the things skateboarders use to skate can be adjusted in budget and resources. For instance, the curbs in front of a house or a car park can go from their practical use to a gateway for fun and collective joy.

In the field of skatepark advocacy, Alec Beck emphasizes the importance of building toolboxes and paying things forward to continue such pathways for joy, some planned, some found, and some spontaneously created, and is influenced by how he was mentored when he worked on campaigns for Stoner Park and the West LA Courthouse. *The Skatepark*

Project has developed freely accessible guides on its website with a focus on helping communities start from the ground up and often with no experience to start lobbying for skateparks. With insight into a reflexive process that draws on his own experiences, Beck states that "there's a bit of privilege when some people have the opportunity to advocate." He emphasizes how "a lot of people don't have the time or space to advocate, but still do it anyway because they see what needs to be done." In response to this issue, he explains they launched a BIPOC Fellows Program in 2022. Their goal is to offer practical, material assistance so people can build up expertise and lead within their communities, rather than just drawing knowledge from the top down. He states, "we are paying advocates, we're saying, look, you're spending time on this. We want to make sure you have what you need, to spend the time to get this done."

At the beginning of this section, we proposed that skateboarding has a particular quality of spontaneity to it that encourages a thought-making process that can be rapidly applied and is youthful in its openness to learning, but not necessarily focused on the big picture and long-term plans. However, in the discussions above we see a kind of "maturing" or occasion for a purposefully forward-thinking application of all the qualities and skills that can be drawn from their skating habits and ability to think about community betterment, rather than just individual successes and goals. Part of this includes that many of the skateboarders are Millennials in their 30s or part of Generation X in their 40s and 50s. This age demographic is also reflected in the overall group we interviewed. However, younger change-makers such as Izzi Cooper and Chris Giamarino who were in their 20s when interviewed convey similar values and outlooks.

It is not surprising that these individuals have similar dispositions, especially as we employed a purposive and expert sample for our research. However, the group is also a part of the evolution consisting of the "*détournement* or the turnaround" (Vivoni and Folsom-Fraser 2021: 313) observed in skateboarding that is reflecting the increased numbers of diverse skateboarders now engaging with and influencing the culture. The value of the discussion here is that it has thrown more light not just on where people who are change-makers feel skateboarding should be heading, but also on the roadmaps and resources they feel are crucial to get there.

Critical Self-Reflection and Self-Care

In this section, we explore the idea of "agitation" taking inspiration from Simone Fullagar et al.'s (2020: 30, also see Pavlidis and Fullagar 2016) qualitative study that encourages an active and reflective process of critique throughout their reading and analysis of interviews. What this means for us is that despite both ourselves and our interviewees being skateboarders who value the idea of being change-makers, we needed to do more than just activate conversations about problematic things done by people with the most power. We also need to be agitators, creating an occasion to turn our critical research gaze back on ourselves, our skate scenes we actively participate in, and the progress we feel we are achieving, both in our line of questioning and presentation of the findings.

The skateboarders we talked with provided many critical reflections, looking back onto themselves in terms of how they actively shape skateboarding, but also, how it shapes them and not always gently or without some negative impacts. Timothy Ward for instance describes how "skateboarding is for better or worse, my life. It means more to me than most things and that is why I critique it…I love skateboarding so much that is why it's important to speak up about its flaws." Even when he feels the rest of the community is celebrating its progress, he reveals "I'm the one starting side chats about how this 'progress' is too little too late. Some of my friends get bummed on me for taking those stances." He adds, "I think that it's part of my very real love for skateboarding and my hope that it can and will continue to get better for people that aren't like me. I believe the critics are the true optimists."

Adam Abada illustrates how even ordinary skateboarders can be privileged and disempower others. He gives the example of skate videos people put on social media and includes footage of unhoused people in the same spots, sometimes who are clearly distressed, without their consent, and without compensation. Abada explains how "I'm pretty vocal about using homeless people. I'm experiencing homeless people a lot on the streets. It's true that skaters interact with people living on the streets more than a lot of other people that's just the fact." One of the issues he wants skaters to address is "the way homelessness is depicted in skateboarding culture is ridiculous, given how astutely aware of it skaters are—it's mean. And there's a lot of what we experience under the same umbrella, on issues like harassment to move on." For Abada, it is something that he wants to engage with in a supportive way, and also to get others "to get more involved in personally when it comes to social justice because it's all related to sharing public space."

In the context of being side by side with other skateboarders, Hatton highlights what he sees as a common yet distressing, almost self-abusive type of behavior that has been normalized. He states, "I see a lot of skaters that will try and get a trick, not get it, and get angry at themselves. They set up a tense environment and expectation. That 'the trick' is what counts the most. I think that's one of the most damaging aspects of skate culture." This can include swearing, throwing, and breaking their board, and not being aware if that is negatively affecting or intimidating others. The "skate or die" approach is often glorified as a hyper-masculine trait in skating, but it can also produce energy or a "vibe" that others at the skatepark may involuntarily be impacted by.

As a response to that energy, Hatton suggests people and especially men can amplify a different and optional kind of behavior that embodies a type of "alternative masculinity" (Atencio and Beal 2011; Beal 1995). He offers for example, "I try to be a role model, and very intentionally think hard about how I act around and treat people in the skatepark. I treat everyone in the skate park as important and belonging...it all counts." Drawing on his work in empathy building through VR, Hatton also encourages people to also be attentive rather than assume what someone is about at the skatepark. He states, "there's a lot of room for growth for people in terms of just being able to see another person, and being able to identify someone who needs support." He also explains that this includes being more aware of how people can experience the same space very differently, such as if "they're from a minority group, or you can see that they don't have any friends, or that they're just not feeling welcome in the skate park."

Many barriers and distractions can reduce the capacity for empathy, and some are internalized biases and assumptions as well. He states, "there's so much that gets in the way of being able to see that." He continues, "it takes a certain level of awareness that is often just lacking at the skate parks, and it's not necessarily easy to come by that awareness. To just be able to see all the different barriers that people are facing just getting in there." Hatton reflects on his work in VR which gives people the opportunity to virtually experience scenarios of relating to people from marginalized backgrounds on ways forward.

VR helps transform empathy from an abstract concept to values that can be embodied, and provides the starting point for everyday interactions when skating with others. Moreover, for White cisgendered heterosexual men like Hatton, such empathy provides the foundations and springboard to becoming a stronger ally. He states, "I think what we're doing at *Equal Reality* does get into the sort of into the depth of those that awareness processes." The reason he proposes is that "Being able to use Virtual Reality puts you into the shoes of someone else, to see things from their perspective, and to just be able to experience what it feels like to be in someone else's shoes, and look at things from their perspective." In his view, while not everyone can access the technology yet, it is also about encouraging skateboarders to simply spend more time thinking and feeling what it is like to be someone else as an effective way to start building empathy, which can then lead to respect and equality.

On being allies, Mara from *Doyenne Skateboards* demonstrates a common discursive repertoire seen in several other skaters that are based on the idea that no one is perfect, and a need to be humble and critically reflect on one's privilege. She states, "I have a lot of privilege myself and I'm always learning about my White privilege and the many privileges I have." She continues, "I believe it's important to not have like an ego. You know, 'I'm perfect and I already know my stuff. I'm not racist, I'm not sexist.' Be open to the fact that we all live in a society that is. Therefore, there's no way that we're not a little bit, and we need to stay open and always learn how to see." This process for her "is beautiful when you see it because you live your life thinking one thing and then you see something from a new perspective. Some people don't get to experience that. But it's important to do so and kind of learn how to dismantle it." The key for her is "just realizing yourself to be a bit more reflective. Otherwise, it becomes easy to feel you're perfect and nobody's perfect."

Our interview with Kristin Ebeling offers further insight into skateboarders' critical self-reflections. For instance, she states, "I would just say like I'm not immune from sexism, racism, or homophobia just because I'm in the social justice skate world. I fuck up all the time. I'm not positioning myself as some fucking expert or anything." She emphasizes that one of the ethical ways of engaging is "being less concerned about being right and more concerned about moving forward and changing things. I think we have a lot to improve on that as a society." She also is careful not to just internalize all the responsibility or confuse change led from the ground up to suggesting the work is only done by "non-traditional" skaters. In a call to action to industry and figures with more power, she proposes, "you have connections in the skate world and street, you have money from your company, here's what you're going to do with your power. Leverage it and harness your resources."

Patrick Kigongo points out how self-care and healing in the skate community also need to prioritize an anti-racism approach that is attentive to structural issues and the personal impact of racial injustice. He states, "I think now a lot of us have not only the vocabulary to identify what microaggressions are, but also a willingness to acknowledge they are hurtful and have an effect on our psyche, well-being, and mental health because another thing that skateboarding has rubbed up against recently is folks saying, 'why don't you just deal with it?'" Additionally, he expresses serious concern that "something that is actively being discussed in the Black community is the long-term effects of stress that racism creates. 'Black may not crack' but internally, we are feeling it dying from strokes, hypertension, all of these things. The psychological burden of having to deal with that regularly. Imagine that in the thing you love."

Kigongo encourages Black and PoC skaters to take up space at things like events and elsewhere in skateboarding. He explains, "Skateboarding isn't the only predominantly white space that we have to engage with. I believe that energy should be directed at bending those spaces to be more inclusive and accommodating to us." He also feels that while things like Black and PoC-run initiatives within the skate community can be useful, skateboarders should not lose sight of how power must shift from addressing structural barriers. For instance, he explains how "There are a number of podcasts hosted by Black and PoC professionals, and not-so professionals, devoted to mental health. Podcasts are great. I'm a co-host of the *Mostly Skateboarding* podcast. But I'm not sure if we need more. What we do need is more affordable and equitable access to mental health services."

We propose that advice that assists skateboarders at an intrapersonal level is complementary to how they address macro-level concerns. Although her academic and non-profit work is very much focused on both micro and macro issues, Dani Abulhawa also introduced the idea of how being socially responsible must include ways of also channeling our caring back onto ourselves. She states, "We all have the ability to parent ourselves. I think about that phrase a lot. I feel like I parent myself a great deal." Examples she provides include, "sometimes I have reactions to things. I think, 'Oh, I'm not I'm not happy at all with that reaction. But yeah, OK, that's normal,' and finding ways of developing people's sense of being an authority to themselves." Her encouragement to practice this form of reflexive engagement is also shaped by her feelings that, "when it doesn't come externally, it is much more powerful, Let's take responsibility for ourselves." But rather than becoming an exercise of self-absorption, it still has the power to influence and direct oneself to interact ethically with others. For instance, she explains "you're in a space and someone says something that's really offensive, take responsibility for that situation. Think about what are you going to do first. Give yourself advice. You know, that's a nice vantage point."

External support was also raised by the interviewees in the form of learning things from role models and mentors, and how this can also be a way to navigate past or alleviate burnout. This is especially useful for social programs that can get over-stretched. Keegan Guizard for instance explains that with *CSEF* "There is no payroll…So yeah, it can be easy to get burnt out because all seven of us have other hustles." He is enthusiastic about reaching out rather than over-reaching, explaining "the big thing I believe in is when somebody has a good idea and they're getting traction on a project, the dream is to mix and work with them." Guizard also emphasizes that there is a list of people always around to be inspired by. He states, "I guess to a younger person, there are a lot of talented people, with good ideas, that love skateboarding. Just be willing to work with your friends, put faith in the process, and have faith that together you can do something just as influential as people already out there making things happen."

Ryan Lay provides insights from the perspective of a professional skateboarder, which he often leverages to elevate the profile of social projects like *Skate Pal*, *Vent City*, and *Skate After School*. Lay advises other professional skaters that the key to his own activities off the board is to work "on the projects that I'm interested in and that feel good for everyone." Lay's activities include the local nonprofit *Skate After School* in Arizona and overseas work with *Skate Pal* in Palestine, activities which Dani Abulhawa (2021) and Paul O'Connor (2020) both describe as a form of "skate philanthropy." Abulhawa (2021: 83) whose parentage is British and Palestinian recognizes critiques of a philanthropy framework that can "promote hierarchical relationships." However, she feels there is also the potential to foster "discussions around inclusivity and social justice in skateboarding" (Abulhawa 2021: 83).

Going to Palestine to work on skate videos and skatepark projects with Aram Sabbah is one of the projects Lay values highly. He states, "I don't get burnt out very often, because I focused on projects that I really want to do." For him, it is also a good balance and time away from professional demands where "sometimes you get paid to do what you want to do, but sometimes you have to grind through some bullshit." However, he offers some critical reflection about "white savior complex" and about genuinely engaging with people overseas rather than seeing their communities as an avenue for escapism and what he calls "resume building." For instance, he recalls a conversation he had with another skateboarder early in his career who encouraged him to think about how "there are people here who need help. You don't need to go halfway across the world. You need to think if it is something that you're only doing for your own selfish reasons." This reflexive process was influential on his co-founding *Skate After School* in Arizona as well as his work as an ambassador with *Skate Pal*.

Researchers of skateboarding in conflict zones such as Sophie Friedel (2015: 43) propose volunteers are developing a more critical understanding of issues abroad, and to avoid perpetuating colonialist dynamics of "helping the exotic Other" (Thorpe and Rinehart 2013: 20). On his initial interest in volunteering overseas, Lay critically reflected that, "at the early stages, I had a very superficial understanding of my role in this process." As a way to check in on his intentions and the spaces and people he would be engaging with, he explains, "I went through all sorts of political education about how to affect change in the world, and also about charity, mutual aid, and nonprofits." This included not shying away from "just having really tough moments of wondering, 'am I helping? Am I just patching up a broken system, putting a Bandaid on it? Or maybe I'm causing more harm thinking I'm helping?'"

One way we can observe Lay as ethically engaging and in a dynamic of mutual respect is when the spotlight on his own skateboarding is shared with high-profile Palestinian skateboarders such as Sabbah and Maen Hammad, both of who were featured with Lay in an article for *Thrasher* (Lay 2020) that also discussed the work of *Skate Pal*. Lay also emphasizes the value of always being willing to engage with people outside of one's own circles, and being open to learning about new ideas from a younger generation. He explains, "I'm looking at skateboarding with a more critical eye than I ever have. And people seem to be learning faster, we're also seeing changes unfold, as they seem like hyper-educated like they're moving through that process a lot quicker."

Reflecting on how to navigate self-care in nonprofits and skate networks in the US, Ashley Masters reveals how before *Skate Like a Girl* she had "worked in the nonprofit sector for a long time and it wasn't till this job that I truly got to experiment with not burning out, instead of just like talking about not burning out, like how to address it." As a starting point of advice, she suggests where possible drawing on "teamwork in whatever you're up to because it's not sustainable to try to do it all by yourself and wearing multiple hats is often necessary but it's when you are wearing the whole hat rack yourself that becomes the problem. Also it's important to listen to others as bit and powerful. I'm committed to causing other people's leadership; give folks a chance to lead and take on more responsibility."

Another thing Masters feels has been helpful is to implement tangible changes, such as rostering time off for staff and breaks from social media, especially after big events like their week-long skate camps and "Wheel of Fortune" event. For instance, she describes how at *Skate Like a Girl* "when we are doing something large scale, we are making sure that we schedule time to decompress and recalibrate. For folks to be showing up for themselves, and slowing down or taking time off or whatever it is."

Masters also advises that what has been helpful is "just being able to stay focused on what we can control, and what we can't control and being okay with that." She explains how this involves things such as, "we can look out for what's the missing gap—what don't we have access to, or what do we want to see more of, and just figuring out how to create it ourselves, or be mentored, and then share out our best practices." The key issue, in Master's view, is "really normalizing self-care, and being held accountable to show up for ourselves. So we can show for others, and thinking together, as a community, about what does that actually look like in practice."

This section has explored forms of critical self-reflection by skateboarders who do various forms of social change work. The aim was not to go into an in-depth exposure or hardline investigation of each individual to look for prior incidents or instances incongruous with their current mission. Rather, we have seen this as an occasion for what we can all do to keep moving forward rather than hold us back in some way. These occasions have been important for well-known skaters such as Grosso (2020) who in his *Love Letter to LGBT and Queer Skateboarding*, for instance, regretted his use of homophobic slurs like "f*g." Rather than becoming suspended in guilt and unable to do anything because of fear, the ways he worked to improve himself and the thing he loved, which is skateboarding, were by listening to and giving a platform to queer skateboarders. Because he did this "out of his depth" (Beachy 2021: 298) it also reminds us that change has to start somewhere, and often with a sense of surrendering our power to share it (Plage et al. 2017).

The examples above also indicate a sense of surrendering to new things rather than being experts. Sometimes the skaters confess they do not really know what they are doing and have no roadmaps or manuals, and often lack resources. They are creating them as they hit the ground running. And some of the key advice we draw ourselves as skateboarders is that while we can become absorbed in the act of trying to bring social change, we all need to pause to reflect on where we go wrong (Geckle and

Shaw 2022). And that we can also burn out and need to recharge and be aware of our mental health.

Recipes for the Future

Earlier in our discussion of values and outlooks in Chap. 4, we introduced the idea of "sharing" rather than "giving" as the basis for ethically encountering and engaging with people who are different from each other (Plage et al. 2017). But the line between sharing power with each other and reproducing power relationships where a more privileged actor is still in control can be confusing, tricky, or blurry. There is also difficulty involved in recognizing and responding to any need for safe spaces without falling into patterns of simply segregating ourselves as a one-stop solution. This raises the question of how we picture a future that is not reduced to a simple "us" and "them" dynamic. And, in our quest to unify, how can we attend to and not erase differences?

Building representation where there is a historical lack is not seen by Sarah Huston as divisive if applied to the realm of skate media. Rather, she conveys how it is like reserving a space to create and appreciate something different. She encourages people to adopt the DIY culture and to "create something for yourself. Tell your story, in your way, rather than trying to fit your story into somebody else's platform." She also feels by doing so tells others, "it is OK to not be like everyone else." We propose that media with a specific target audience can indeed be a process to let difference have space, while also empowering women and "non-traditional" skaters to have exposure. We see this as a way to keep up the work of sharing the "symbolic resources needed to identify them as action sports participants, despite idealist views of action sports as subcultures inclusive to all regardless of gender, sexuality, race, ethnicity, class, ability or age" (MacKay 2016: 301–302).

Brennan Hatton feels an effective way to interact at the micro-level, such as down at the skatepark, actually requires a deeper and more careful level of attention to differences. He states, "There needs to be a lot of work that goes into awareness of different people and their backgrounds and their experiences and what it takes to help them feel included." He also encourages a future where we interact through the act of asking, and observing rather than projecting what someone is about or wants. He feels, "it's not necessarily an easy thing. There's a lot of depth to it. Skateboarding has a long way to go." One way forward that he encourages is to pay attention to "how so many people are drawn to skating because of mental health. It's their chance to escape from a battle they have, and being able to create a safe space for that." In his view, "this is kind of where the culture of skating is heading towards, largely from cases where people have come in here to get away from something and to feel connected." This also includes the digital and virtual worlds, including technologies like VR. Most skateboarders will not have the technical training to create programs, but they can facilitate and co-design experiences for people, elite athletes, brand managers, and industry people as part of their training. He states, "we can learn a lot from how LGBTQIA+ and Black and other skaters navigate their own issues with what they're dealing with, while also creating a safe space for other people to do the same."

There is a degree of serendipity that Ashley Masters feels is a large part of helping skateboarders build stronger and more inclusive communities through skate networks that hold meet-ups and other programs. For her, it is also a combination of showing up, committing, and applying experiences of the physical act of skating to social issues and problem-solving. She states, "I feel grateful every single day. I catch myself getting these reminders that I really am at the right place at the right time, and doing the work that I'm meant to be doing." Her advice is that skaters tap into their ability to be quick thinker, creative and spontaneous, and other things they learn on the board in that, "we are often creating and learning as we go, rewriting culture and being resourceful. We're folks reimagining the world and it's about getting out and of the stands and being on the court." And rather than foresee an ongoing need for programs like Skate Like a Girl in a way that is empire building, she views it as something temporary stating, "you know, we're looking to end our job" meaning that equity is established and for her "that's always gonna come from a skater brain, which is just all about creativity."

At the level of community, Kristin Ebeling sees a brighter future that can ensure diversity is constantly being normalized rather than as a spectacle that is constantly being pointed out. She describes a shift in power dynamics that can be achievable through collective efforts, stating, "I really want to get to a point where there's more solidarity in skating. For me, the ultimate space is where everyone is just perfectly free to be seen as a whole and complete person—where everyone is welcome."

Having solidarity and being able to be a whole person when skateboarding for Ebeling requires an attitudinal shift where there is "none of this, people are good for a girl or fill in the blank. Let's arrive at a place where people are just existing and skating together." She also feels that progress is being made, and she has "faith that skateboarding as a microcosm could create that within my lifetime—that it's not weird if you're a girl or trans or any gender." The emphasis she makes is that "the ultimate freedom is to just come and show up and just be yourself in a safe space."

Ebeling adds that she wants the culture to be at a point where "people aren't like, 'oh my god! Yay! You're so good for a girl!'" Ebeling is also critical of men comparing women's skills to their own, saying things such as "oh I couldn't even do that! I'm always like, that's not a compliment." These sentiments are clearly the inspiration for the self-reflection that the men who started *The Nut Daily News* creatively embraced. Ebeling's frustrations can also be seen as shared back where we present Kopita's frustration over being applauded for doing an ollie when she can do more advanced tricks. In short, we can see again the need for skaters to develop mutual respect for each other, rather than the appreciation that can be benevolent and patronizing. But the act of raising awareness about this is not to "call out" but to "call in." She proposes that:

> The next steps are fucking building solidarity with each other, and finding ways to connect with different people and at risk of sounding like I'm a fucking cheesy line, I do think skateboarding could be a space at some point where people can see past human differences, and be a microcosm for anti-racism, and this progressive, inclusive space. I've been in sessions where I'm skating with a fucking seven-year-old and a 47-year-old and we're trying the same trick together and we make it work.

Key ingredients for change and achieving this shift for Ebeling include that skaters need to "build a community of like trust and, you know, consent and support and inclusion and to exist and be themselves and feel safe, and I think we can all be a part of that." Men are integral as allies, but also as recipients of these shifts too. Ebeling explains, "I really truly believe no one benefits from racism, sexism, homophobia, none of that...men lose more from sexism too." Solutions include keeping building up more inclusive spaces where people can actually see how to identify and remove toxic behaviors, and "creating spaces where people can be educated."

The need to avoid creating another insular world is important to Ebeling, who explains, "I don't want to recreate the same power structures with a different label, I don't want to create the same exclusive bullshit gatekeeping." Instead, she states, "I am actually looking for human liberation and community inclusion and safety and I don't think you get that by recreating harm and recreating bubbles." She recognizes that boundaries in events, for now, are needed, describing how "I've been a part of creating a lot of bubbles and that was for good reason. We didn't have a girls' contest so we fucking made one." And for her, the "goal for the rest of my life is going to be, 'how can I make that girls' contest fucking fun and awesome celebration, but not like crucial,' or maybe I can even make it (girls' contests) irrelevant in my lifetime."

Alex White is both honest about the past and optimistic about the future of skateboarding. Her feelings are based not on wishful thinking or abstract sentiments but on seeing actual change including that, "what trips me out is the way that I internalized the sexism and homophobia around me in skateboarding over the years." White now has a front row to industry, and big competitions like the *Olympics*, as well as having spent years in the DIY and non-traditional skate scene. Her work includes as an industry person paid to promote women and non-binary skaters, advocating for LGBTQIA+ skaters across media, and taking up space in the previously men's dominated world of sports such as at the *Olympic Games*. Describing this evolution she sheds light on how sometimes skateboarders do not have a grand plan, and may even be holding themselves back, but if they just keep doing the work then change can happen, stating:

I can say as a blanket statement, never would I ever have imagined we'd be like sitting here having this conversation about skateboarding at this point. I never had any expectations when I was starting skateboarding that there would be any place for me or that there would be. If we just don't accept things the way they are, we can grow so much. (Alex White quoted from our interview)

We conclude this chapter by highlighting the thoughts of Peggy Oki. Now aged 66, she is the oldest individual in our interviews and one of the most dedicated and energetic change-makers in her activism, most notably with the *Origami Whale Project* (https://www.origamiwhalesproject.org) which started in 2004. Throughout the writing of this book, she was actively focused on lobbying and getting petition signing done to free whales and dolphins from captivity and protect their lives in their natural habitat at sea. She was also a supporter at *Standing Rock* and has done numerous charity events.

Oki was asked what she wants the future to look like and her responses call people in rather than call them out. Her approach mobilizes and encourages younger people to get involved in bringing change without controlling where they place their passions and energies. It is also an invitation to participate without conditions or need for prior experiences or training. She states, "what I want everybody to do is exactly what I'm doing. Not necessarily for whales and dolphins. I mean something that's fulfilling. Something that might be very challenging." In her conservation work, she describes how "we've got high odds against us but it is something that matters deeply to me. With that mindset, we can do so much good out there in the world."

Oki also emphasizes that people who have a public platform can use that to share positive messages, stating, "as with some of my *Zephyr* skateboarding teammates, I never sought fame but thanks to the documentary [*Dogtown & Z-Boys*] I have been utilizing my celebrity status as a voice for the things that matter to me. In this way the skateboarding community has an opportunity to become more aware." She also adds that, "it's been wonderful to share—through public speaking—my journey from skateboarding with the *Zephyr* team to my activism for Cetaceans [dolphins and whales]. It's fulfilling for me to inspire and empower people to follow their passion and to be of service for the things we care about."

There is no singular recipe for change in Oki's view. It can be creative and affect any level of power rather than always be of the most sizeable proportions. What she does encourage is for "everyone to just pick something. Maybe you are watching the Internet, and you see something that's terrible and, you think, 'that bothers me.'" The next stage is to then commit. She gives the example of grassroots change campaigns and activities such as, "instead of just yelling at the TV…start out as a volunteer and if you want, try starting your own organization. See how that feels and where it takes people. We need people to be doing something now—everybody can do something to make this world a better place."

This chapter explored what kinds of wishlists, roadmaps, and ideas for change skateboarders have for the future. We traveled through a broad range of areas, selecting examples that more broadly reflect the overall interests and outlooks of the interviewees. This includes changes people want to see made at the grassroots in the industry and the broader skate community and culture. It is important to acknowledge there are power differences among the interviewees across ages, genders, races, ethnicity, sexuality, and class. A cisgender White heterosexual man and a queer person or PoC for instance will be affected by intersectional points of oppression. But we also need to remember our own agency and how power is a part of our lives, therefore we need to keep thinking about what ways we operate it and position our own practices and subjectivities.

Returning to the application of Michael Foucault's theories of power applied in skateboarding and also feminist sports studies, Thorpe (2008: 200) in particular reminds us that while power can be constraining, it can also be "enabling and productive." Within this theoretical framework, everyone has the power to be a change-maker. The conversations now presented in this book provide important windows that we can all benefit from as we move into the future. The aim is not to "win" control and horde power, but rather, to achieve equity and mutual respect and to co-exist in ways that we feel constitute forms of ethical togetherness.

References

Abulhawa, D (2021). *Skateboarding and Femininity: Gender, Space-making and Expressive movement*. London: Routledge.

Anderson, B (1993) *Imagined Communities: Reflections on the Origin and Spread of Nationalism*, Verso.

Atencio, M and Beal, B (2011). Beautiful losers: the symbolic exhibition and legitimization of outsider masculinity. *Sport in Society, 14*(1), 1–16.

Beachy, K (2021) *The Most Fun Thing: Dispatches from a Skateboard Life*. Grand Central Publishing.

Beal, B (1995). Disqualifying the official: An exploration of social resistance through the subculture of skateboarding. *Sociology of Sport Journal, 12*(3), 252–267. https://doi.org/10.1123/ssj.12.3.252.

Carroll, T, and Cianciotto, L (2020) Towards Radical Empathy, Eds Callen-Riley, T and Holsgens, S, *Urban Pamphleteer #8 Skateboardings*, pp 11–12, Downloaded 18 July 2022: http://urbanpamphleteer.org/skateboardings.

Corwin, Z, Maruco, T, Williams, N, Reichardt, R, Romero-Morales, M, Rocha, C and Astiazaran, C (2019) *Beyond the Board: Findings from the Field*, Pullias Center for Education, University of Southern California.

Epicly Later'd (2013) *Epicly Later'd: Ricky Oyola*, YouTube video posted 4 April: https://www.youtube.com/watch?v=iW6asj6gojc.

Flusty, S (2000) Thrashing Downtown: Play as Resistance to the Spatial and Representational Regulation of Los Angeles. *Cities, 17*(2): 149–158.

Friedel, S (2015) *The Art of Living Sideways*. Masters of Peace. Springer.

Fullagar, S, O'Brien, W and Pavlidis, A (2020) *Feminism and a Vital Politics of Depression and Recovery*. Palgrave Macmillan.

Geckle, B and Shaw, S (2022). Failure and Futurity: The Transformative Potential of Queer Skateboarding. *Young, 30*(2), 132–148. https://doi.org/10.1177/1103308820945100.

Givens, T (2022) *Radical Empathy*, Bristol: Polity Press.

Grosso, J (2020) Loveletter To LGBTQ+ | Jeff Grosso's Loveletters to Skateboarding, VANS, Posted 12 June: https://www.youtube.com/watch?v=kqD4xfNwd6k.

Lay, R (2020) Well Spring: Ryan Lay in Palestine. *Thrasher Magazine*. Posted 14 April. Downloaded 11 August 2022: https://www.thrashermagazine.com/articles/wellspring-ryan-lay-in-palestine-article/.

MacKay, S (2016) Carving From Out of Space in the Action Sports Media Landscape: The 'Skirboarders' Blog as a 'Skate Feminist' Project, (eds) Thorpe, H and Olive, R. *Women in Action Sport Cultures.* London: Palgrave Macmillan. pp 301–308.

McDuie-Ra, D (2021) *Skateboard Video: Archiving the City from Below.* Palgrave Pivot.

Murphy, (2018) Duty Now for the Future Artisan Skaters, *Juice Magazine.* Posted 1 September, Downloaded 21 August 2022: https://juicemagazine. com/home/duty-now-for-the-future-artisan-skateparks-tom-dupere/.

O'Connor, P (2017) Beyond the Youth Culture: Understanding Middle-aged Skateboarders through Temporal Capital, *International Review for the Sociology of Sport*, 1–20 Preview copy.

O'Connor, P (2020) Skateboarding and Religion. London: Palgrave.

Pavlidis, A and Fullagar, S (2016) *Sport, Gender and Power: The Rise of Roller Derby.* London: Taylor and Francis.

Plage, S, Willing, I, Woodward, I, and Skrbiš Z, (2017). Cosmopolitan encounters: reflexive engagements and the ethics of sharing, *Ethnic and Racial Studies*, 40(1), 4–23. https://doi.org/10.1080/01419870.2016.1178788

Sharp, M and Threadgold, S (2020) Defiance Labour and Reflexive Complicity: Illusio and Gendered Marginalisation in DIY Punk Scenes. *Sociological Review*, 68(3), pp. 606–622. https://doi.org/10.1177/0038026119875325.

Thorpe, H (2008) Foucault, technologies of the Self, and the Media: Discourses of Femininity in Snowboarding Culture, *Journal of Sport and Social Issues.* 32. 199–229.

Thorpe, H, and Rinehart, R (2013) Action Sports NGOs in a Neo-Liberal Context: The Case of Skateistan and Surf Aid International, *Journal of Sport & Social Issues*, 37(2), 115–141.

Vivoni, F and Folsom-Fraser, J (2021) Crafting Cities for All: Qualitative Inquiry of the Street and the Spatial Practice of Skateboarding, *Cultural Studies ↔ Critical Methodologies.* 21(4) 311–318.

Willing, I, Bennett, A, Piispa, M and Green, B (2019) Skateboarding and the 'Tired Generation': Ageing in Youth Cultures and Lifestyle Sports. *Sociology* 53(3):503–18.

7

Stick With It: Legacies, Inheritances, and New Windows

© The Author(s), under exclusive license to Springer Nature Singapore Pte Ltd. 2023
I. Willing, A. Pappalardo, *Skateboarding, Power and Change*,
https://doi.org/10.1007/978-981-99-1234-6_7

Chapter 7 Illustration by Adam Abada

Introduction

In the opening chapter of this book we drew attention to how skateboarders are taking a stance, and in this concluding chapter we want to highlight the sentiment below by Edmund Bacon, a renowned city planner and designer of Love Park. He states in the 2006 film *Freedom of Space: Skateboard Culture in Public Space* by Steve Olpin and Tim Irwin that:

I think sometimes that skateboarders are even a little bit modest about themselves and I think that they must realize that they are at the edge of a new perception of life for the young. And that in the long run they're absolutely bound to win because that's the way history works, there are a bunch of jerks that can't see the new vision at all and it scares them…you really are the revolutionaries in sport and culture you should be proud of the resistance you've created and you must stick with it. You must not let the stick in the mud prevent you from continuing the great process that you've initiated. (55.30 mark (quoted in 2017: 207)

The resilience and determination of skateboarders to "stick with it" such as with a trick until they accomplish and master it are advantageous, as they can also embrace it as a broader approach to their lives and the world. As we also highlight at the beginning of our book, we are living in an era of rapid and remarkable social upheaval, where protests and resistance to power have been ignited across the US and the world. Far from being removed and distanced from this, skateboarders are mobilizing, making calls for action, and deploying new ways and solutions to work toward equity and progress. The above confidence and faith in the statement by Edmund Bacon amplifies the potential skaters have to be leading social change in sport and culture rather than just swept up in broader movements of resistance. With his wisdom with age as an elderly man during the interview, he also reminds skateboarders to ignore "the jerks" in the way of their vision, and that part of the power they have is in their youth to see new ways of doing things.

We share Bacon's belief and enthusiasm for our potential as skateboarders. As a community and culture, we can be innovative, free-thinking, and transgressive, as well as successful in whatever we choose, and ushering in progressive new ways of thinking in the process. However, as our historical overview and then our interviews with change-makers in our study reveal, the world of skateboarding has brought with it both positive and negative legacies and inheritances. Skateboarding has remained creative, and artistic, and kept many of its best innovations like adapting the built environment to keeping skater-led media and skate videos that new generations enjoy, "riff" with, and contribute their own styles and approaches. Yet within the interviews, the challenges our interviewees feel are prominent still in their lives demonstrate how far we sometimes still have to go. We can sometimes actually be "jerks" to each other.

Additionally, we are no longer just youthful outliers, and instead, skateboarders are now multigenerational and have an expansive social and cultural history (Borden 2019). There are more adult and middle-aged skaters than ever before (O'Connor 2017, Willing et al. 2019, and this includes "elders" who are icons such as from teams such as Powell Peralta's *Bones Brigade* (Willing et al. 2020) who have had a certain level of time to reflect, be open to progress, share wisdom and their accumulated power and resources to influence others. These skateboarders are joined by new generations sharing their own perspectives on how to turn things around, and rapidly change things. And we will keep learning from younger generations who harness the ever-changing technologies and advances in communication like social media to call out injustices and to create their own networks, businesses, cultural productions, and pathways. Accordingly, as skateboarders, we have to combine our celebrations alongside the need to critically but also openly assess where skateboarding is at and where it is going. Furthermore, we need to be more open to those who may have useful strategies and advice from other subcultures, sports, industries, academic areas, and beyond.

The research questions we started our exploration with were: What type of people are leading social change in skateboarding? And, what lived experiences of skateboarding and personal outlooks, as well as strategies and skills, do they develop and bring into their activities focused on social change? Our goals were also to gain insight into their perceptions, feelings, and reflections on what taking a stance involves, and where others can help or hinder their efforts. Furthermore, we aimed to explore what lessons can be drawn from their stories to keep creating change for now and in the future for skateboarding. In this final concluding chapter, we reflect on how our research findings respond to these questions and aims. We begin by summarizing key insights from our research and then evaluate some of the strengths and limitations of the scope of topics and typologies of change-makers we were able to cover. We also consider how future studies can continue to generate insights on what barriers in skateboarding still hold people back, and how they can be removed, reshaped, and unsettled. Finally, we share some of our own thoughts on where skateboarding is at and what is next.

We present our discussion within the following themes and sections: 1) Key Findings and Contributions to the Research Field, 2) Limitations, Significance, and Future Recommendations, and 3) Some Final Thoughts: Skateboarding Now and Where to Next. Before we begin, we want to emphasize that this study has not had the goal of investigating and becoming stagnant in blaming individuals for past mistakes or conversely, acting to absolve past errors, harms, and wrongs. We also want to emphasize that the individuals and members of the skateboarding community who have lived experiences of the topics we covered are always best positioned to lead initiatives for change that will directly affect them. Instead, our aim is to "stick" with the goals to explore a recent "ethical turn" in skateboarding where there is a boom in change-makers, and more broadly thinking about how, as skateboarders, we all can keep on improving together. As part of this, our study highlights certain legacies, wisdom, inheritances, and new windows on "being a skateboarder" that we feel are constructive foundations to keep shaping the culture of skateboarding.

Key Findings and Contributions to the Research Field

In this section, we discuss key findings and contributions that our research makes to the field of studies of skateboarding, action and lifestyle sports, youth cultures and subcultures, and related areas in the social sciences. To begin, our study confirms that the continuing commercialization of skateboarding within the skate industry and its incorporation into the formalized sports competitions provide horizons where skateboarders can become elite athletes, business people, and ambitious entrepreneurs, supporting observations in other research (Williams 2022, Snyder, 2012, Snyder 2017, Thorpe and Wheaton 2011, Wheaton and Thorpe 2019, 2021). We expand on existing knowledge by exploring what contemporary meanings "non-traditional" skaters and men who are activists and allies attach to these growing opportunities today.

Key findings include that many skaters are willingly embracing rather than resisting commercialization and incorporation, but not unreflexively, and sometimes with frustrations and regret at the limitations still in place. Importantly, in light of the discussions of decolonizing and decentering established power in Chap. 5, we also emphasize that "non-traditional" skateboarders are far from passive recipients. They have always had agency, be it turning down offers due to subpar conditions or implementing better and new ones into their collaborations and partnerships. Priorities include their representation and participation on their own terms, in ways that reflect their own artistic visions and cultural lenses, and with expectations of reciprocity, better representation, and with a focus on equity.

The discussion of the *Olympic Games* by skateboarders who were strategists, community builders, and breakthrough figures like Kim Woozy and Amelia Brodka for instance offers insight into how skateboarders can harness the weight it has to push for social change. This includes speeding up the pace in commercialized and large skate competitions to include more than just men's divisions, building pay parity into prize structures, and gaining more sponsorship and other forms of support for independent competitions too such as *Exposure Skate*. Brodka also sheds light on the ways skateboarders can change the *Olympics* rather than the other way around through their ability to prioritize their appreciation and support of fellow competitors despite differences or medal results.

However, skateboarders such as Leo Baker and Mimi Knoop, who withdrew their involvement in *The Olympic Games* and *USA Skateboarding* during the period we were writing this book, also remind us how formal sporting bodies also have a long way to go before ensuring equity for "non-traditional" skateboarders and the communities with whom they belong. At the same time, in Brodka's experiences of seeing participants like Alana Smith, a non-binary competitor, and the inclusion of Alex White, Ashley Masters, and other "non-traditional" skateboarders in non-competitive roles, we catch glimpses of how skateboarders can still make a positive impact on *The Olympic Games* and may be able to unsettle and reshape it more in the future. The presence and the inclusive outlooks they bring to the games, albeit as minorities, already help in terms of reflecting the actual diversity that exists within their own sport, mainstream sports, and also society.

The icons, iconoclasts, and breakthrough skateboarders we spoke to also demonstrate that they prioritize having an ethical outlook and progressive stance within how they build their careers, teams, and company, brands, or business ventures. This is in contrast to how corporate sponsorship dollars in mainstream sports are often seen as the end goal. For example, Douglas Miles Sr. and Douglas Miles Jr.'s interviews, with their emphasis on Indigenous representation and independence from "core" skating through artistic work on their boards, murals, films, and other innovations, confirm and extend observations of how Native skateboarders challenge colonialism and racism in skateboarding (Martínez 2013; Weaver 2016). The standpoint in the artistic work of *Apache Skateboards*, which emphasizes everyone in the US is skating on Native Land, also offers important insights into how Native skateboarders work with industry on their own terms which are founded upon Indigenous sovereignty that sets clear boundaries on how others should engage.

The attitudes of other icons, iconoclasts, and breakthrough skateboarders we listened to were also socially engaged, such as Tommy Guerrero, Peggy Oki, Cindy Whitehead, Atiba Jefferson, Amelia Broda, Kristin Ebeling, Alex White, Ryan Lay, Karlie Thornton, Lynn Kramer, L Brew, and Latosha Stone. We have illuminated how all are involved in forms of activism and social change projects as part of their outlooks and values rather than just for occasional events, marketing "clout" and "virtual signaling." Some reflect Dani Abulhawa's (2020) observations in her study of skate philanthropy where there is an element of altruism balanced with cosmopolitan feelings of being global citizens with a duty to care. Some add to Nefttalie Williams' studies of skate activism and the experiences and careers of skateboarders that connect to legacies and inheritances of Black Power and new ways of skate diplomacy (Williams 2021, 2022). Others advance the feminist, gender-based, and LGBTQIA+ rights activism scholars have observed by "non-traditional" skaters trying to advance across the years (such as Beal 1995, Geckle and Shaw 2022, Toffoletti et al. 2018).

Our interviews with Karlie Thornton and L Brew from *froSkate* and Latosha Stone from *Proper Gnar* also provided more understanding into brands engage with the women's, non-binary, and LGBTQIA+ skate scene and how they also navigate intersectional issues of racism and the strengths and constraints of being seen as representatives for Black skaters. Their insights also confirm scholarship that argues for a need to look beyond just White masculine interpretations of the culture. Moreover, they point to a revolutionary shake-up in market power regarding what types of skateboarders are now able to get sponsored, be offered brand partnerships, and shape marketing decisions, and also how rapidly this can happen if their image, mission, and message capture freshness and vibrancy in skateboarding rather than something stale and contrived.

For instance, we can observe how brands can make decisions to collaborate on shoe lines with skateboarders who are comparatively new to skating like in *froSkate*. In the promotional video launch of *Nike SB* #AllLoveNoHate *froSkate* Dunks shoes the group explains how they wanted to capture aspects of skateboarding that were not about advanced tricks. Instead, they are about validating forms of lived experiences, identity, and belonging, in which they explain:

> It was also incredibly important to us to ensure this video was inclusive for all levels of skateboarding and de-stigmatizing what a "real skater" looks like…We're blending Black, Femme & Queer culture with skateboarding in a way that's never been done before, and paying homage to our people throughout it all. To showcase that through a Nike SB video is definitely something folks have never seen before. (*froSkate* post on Instagram, 9 August 2022)

We talked to skateboarders from a variety of backgrounds across the typologies we developed, and the reflexive processes skateboarders navigate, which can include being aware of racial and gender privilege. In Chap. 4, for instance, we drew attention to how some skaters could be "complicit" or "defiant" (Sharp and Threadgold 2020) such as internalizing negative attitudes when they were first "becoming skateboarders." Yet as our analysis of the interviews progressed in Chaps. 5 and 6, we were also able to explore how they can change over time. Lay for instance exhibited the reflexive process of growing his awareness of his positionality as a White man from the US, and his thinking through the risks of perpetuating what he described as a "White savior complex." Kevin Pacella's discussion offers some insight into what motivates White men to decide to take action against racism and how they can use their social networks to encourage more potential allies to take a stance that shifts from complicit to actively defiant, such as protesting on the streets. And with "Mara" who is a White cisgender woman from *Doyenne Skateboards*, we are reminded that while she too reflects on her own racial privilege, her lived experience is also shaped by gender and disability, and this influences assumptions and micro-aggressions in skating she wants to challenge and communities she and her co-founder "Giulia" want to work with.

Our study of change-makers who we described as storytellers, creatives, and provocateurs also charts how their increasing sense of responsibility and awareness of power is complemented by their appreciation of subcultural resistance (Borden 2001, 2019; Callen-Riley and Hölsgens 2020). We have also argued that their attitudes and stances of resistance should not be seen as static and that their opposition can be shifting and flexible (Dinces 2011; Lombard 2010). Worded differently, skateboarders can be many things, including ambitious, entrepreneurial, subcultural, resistant and oppositional, independently creative, subversive, and transgressive. This has led to many vibrant expressions of the culture that can be progressive.

There is also still a sense of freedom of expression within skateboarding to just get things done without having to obey any overarching governing body, official rule books, or sports authorities. We demonstrated how this can be seen in the DIY approaches in alternative and DIY style zines, skate magazines, and media platforms that give "non-traditional" skateboarders and their allies room to thrive and be showcased. For example, we highlighted shows such skaters have been creating spaces to bring under-recognized and under-represented stories, experiences, images, and ideas to light such as in *Heal Flip*, *The Skate Witches*, *Quell Magazine*, *Yeah Girl*, *Skateism*, *Mess Magazine*, and podcasts like *Vent City*. And we have also shown how a genre of humor in skateboarding has often featured over-the-top videos and elements of satire, but is now joined by more self-aware and accessible ways to reflect on masculine tropes and assumptions men make about "non-traditional" skaters. This includes the *Manramp* project and *The Nut Daily News*.

Skateboarding is always shifting and we have shown how ethical road-maps are emerging, but it is also on a journey where everyone needs to keep working at it. Our study has also shown that there is a wide variety of people who can become change-makers. This diversity is important as it opens the doors for people with various skills to become involved in shaping the culture rather than gatekeeping skateboarding to people with the highest level of tricks. In addition, we have drawn attention to the types of values and outlooks that are also being brought into the culture. As introduced in early chapters, some of these foundational values and outlooks include an everyday cosmopolitanism where skaters have a willingness to be open and engage with people who are different from them (Hannerz 1990; Lamont and Aksartova 2002). Enhancing this outlook is that skaters can also embody a type of radical empathy (Carroll and Cianciotta 2020; Givens 2022) that promotes ethical engagements that prioritize sharing over possessing power (Plage et al, 2017) and being defiant rather than complicit (Sharp and Threadgold 2020) to formations of power in skateboarding that can discriminate and exclude. This is crucial to note as the culture of skateboarding cannot become more inclusive and achieve equity without skateboarders paying attention to how power operates, including their own.

We argue that the change-makers we interviewed are likely to "stick" with the challenges ahead in collective ways too. This is because, despite differences, they all expressed feeling a sense of love for skateboarding and were committed to keeping the culture joyful, fun, social, creative, and progressive. Yet the skateboarders we spoke with are far from naive or "romantics." In the conversations we explored it is clear that they do not view skateboarding as a utopia and that they can often struggle, both internally and externally, to nurture the types of attitudes, relationships, resources, and environments where everyone can thrive. But more importantly, all have demonstrated they utilize their own strengths, time, networks, and resources to address social issues to ensure power is shared and equity can be achieved for others, not just themselves.

We might think of skateboarding as a type of post-traditional or detraditional "family" (Beck-Gernsheim 1998) and "imagined community"

(Anderson 1993) whose ties and affinities can be strong or weak, and elective rather than firmly bounded. At the same time, the concept of "crews," which resembles the idea of "neo-tribes" in post-subcultural theory (Bennett 2011), is also helpful, as they can be loyal to each other and share an identity but in ways that are porous to new members and flexibly aligned to other duties, interests, and significant others. These "non-traditional" crews and families for skateboarders can be ignorant, divided, and conflicted over each others' needs, and become harmful in the process. But our study has also now outlined that there are constructive legacies and wisdom that skateboarders in each generation inherit from the past, and with younger generations adding their own new ways of doing things which the next generation after them can "grow up" with.

Limitations, Significance, and Future Recommendations

Our interview data emerged from lines of questioning designed by skateboarders, to generate conversations with skateboarders. The research was therefore informed and influenced by a type of auto-ethnographic tradition that sees the value of "insiders" doing research. We offered assessments not from a vantage point separately above what is happening, or within a vacuum. We are also living within the rapid and unprecedented social changes we were exploring from 2019 to 2022. This includes our being in awe, anguished, and stunned by seeing things like police violence, and our energies being poured over into rather than contained separately from the upsurge of protests in the US and globally.

While designing and conducting research, we too joined people around the world experiencing new levels of isolation, introspection, and anxiousness from lockdowns, illnesses, and personal, emotional, and financial impacts stemming from the global COVID-19 pandemic. And we also both celebrated the new doors of opportunities opening to "non-traditional" skateboarders, such as seeing the most diverse lineup so far of change-makers calling for, guiding, and implementing various forms of change in skateboarding, from important incremental steps to conditions of remarkable contrast. We have discussed how this impacts our research, our process of balancing researcher bias, and the strengths we felt we brought to our roles as "insiders."

However, it is important for us to also recognize what limitations exist in terms of lived experiences we do not have. This includes our being cisgender and not transgender, non-binary or gender non-conforming, not Indigenous, or Black for instance. Our efforts to be mindful of these differences in the people we interviewed included drawing on writings and literature by people from these populations but we cannot and do not claim to be able to fully know or understand their subjectivities and lived experiences of discrimination. Our aim was to create conversations with transparency around our own subjective positions as authors including a cisgender woman who is from an orphanage and migrated to the West as a Vietnamese refugee, and a cisgender man who is Italian American, and both being fellow skateboarders who were willing to be open to listening to rather than claiming authority over others. We recommend more studies by other individuals from diverse communities and populations to improve their representation.

We also recommend that future studies on change-makers include an increased sample size across the variety of skateboarders we interviewed and beyond both for qualitative and quantitative research. We did not aim to be representative in a statistical sense and explained the strengths and limitations of our own sample and typologies in Chaps. 1 and 3. We aimed for depth over breadth and felt for our own qualitative study, with an interest in themes such as reflexive thinking, empathy, and openness, reached theoretical saturation with our final numbers. But we propose the field of skateboarding studies and other relevant areas will also benefit from future studies that include larger numbers of all the populations we spoke with. Moreover, there is a need for more studies by scholars with lived experience to join valuable studies by non-skateboarders whose research will be shaped by other strengths and limitations. This includes studies by researchers who are under-represented, such as Indigenous, LGBTQIA+ skaters, and individuals who are disability researchers and strategists, including WCMX, and adaptive skaters. We were also unable to provide substantial attention to topics such as how people's religion, class, geographic locations, and from non-English language backgrounds contribute to their facing discrimination and how they navigate it to become change-makers.

In terms of our methods, our use of interviews over zoom allowed us to have in-depth conversations and cover all of our research interview questions. We were also thankful to the interviewees for speaking so generously, with interviews sometimes going well over an hour. However we were unable to gain the extra benefits of in-person communication and being in a shared atmosphere, so things like visual cues and body language and having moments for spontaneity were less possible. An opportunity to add insight into what people say by being able to go visit their local scenes in person was also not able to be included. We recommend future research include mixed methods such as participant observation and site visits.

Our study is able to offer some interesting parallels between change-makers in skateboarding, and athletes in mainstream sports who are activists or make political protests. This includes the powerful statement individuals can make by walking away from situations that continue to oppress, exclude, and marginalize remains, as well as boycotts. The skaters we interviewed also provide valuable contemporary windows on how to "pay it forward" and "give back" in ways that can be both educational and complementary to athletes in mainstream sports. Skateboarders are savvy social media users including how they use it for things like campaigns and building alliances. Importantly, skateboarders' DIY culture, particularly in their media, provides examples of how other athletes from sports can change who creates narratives and improve the representation of individuals who are pushed to the periphery.

We used a broad brush approach to covering change-makers in skateboarding rather than focusing on specific populations, roles, or occupations. The advantage of this reach is that while specific biographies, identities, and histories matter, skateboarders can be conceptualized as a community with some shared legacies, inherited tactics, and capacities to open new doors, and can be the source of collective power. This study can assist larger social movements and campaigns to see skateboarders as potential contributors and collaborators. Moreover, we have also shown how skateboarders are well positioned to be hired by industry and formal and corporate-run competitions to act as consultants and in leadership positions in the areas of improving diversity, inclusion, and equity. Extending on this, we have also highlighted the professional skills that skateboarders have acquired such as in business, arts, media, architecture and urban planning, product design and fashion, non-profit organizations, and academia. Skateboarders are accomplished in areas where they can be hired, funded, and supported to make changes "from below" and from skateboarders' perspective rather than under directions from powers "from above" and translated through outsiders.

In the area of social change, we have delivered a picture of how things have not always been inclusive and that skateboarders are not only taking a stance but are actively working to change things. As possible ways forward, we propose actionable things such as removing barriers around gender in competitions, conducting "health checks" for how skateboarding businesses in the industry are performing across the areas of diversity and inclusion, and more information gathering and community consultations. But this should not be done at the cost of losing skateboarding's punk and subcultural approach of less managerialism and more DIY approaches and organic changes. For instance, community skate jams mixed with workshops and zine making to express issues and solutions in the community can be rolled out side by side with more traditional surveys and focus groups.

Creatives can also be funded to create more transparency and improve the culture. This might be done in collaboration with traditional researchers, through things like interviews but also with skaters' own input in the tradition of participatory action research. Methods could include getting them to contribute visual content similar to TikTok videos and other creative ways to document and share things they think help them and their peers. In short, skateboarders can harness the creative freedom and rule-free ways they skate and socialize and apply that to exploring, evaluating, and improving social issues that are still a part of the culture. We will now conclude with a final collection of thoughts on the big picture. We also cast our thoughts over to issues in skateboarding that linger, remain under-examined, and require more concentrated attention.

Some Final Thoughts: Skateboarding Now and Where to Next?

The world of skateboarding may see itself as an underdog compared to mainstream sports and even other subcultures like surfing, but it has been one of the gold standards of cool in the US for decades and an increasing amount of people hope to somehow monetize that cool. Whether in high-end fashion and multinational shoe companies, gaming and new technology, social media platforms, lifestyle and athletic markets, or *The Olympics*, it is clear throughout our interviews and research that skateboarding has a cultural currency that extends further than most realize. We do not deny that similar dynamics exist in other subcultural scenes and creative pursuits that attract innovators, risk takers, and visionaries in pursuit of fun, style, and some form of artistic and athletic progression. However, there are certain combinations of things brought together in skateboarding that make it different from most other sports and creative and cultural disciplines. Its lack of organization or formalization can both fuel and quell its creativity. And, unlike many other cultures, skateboarding is able to change in real-time.

First and foremost, it is a physical practice that is not entirely predictable or rules based. It is also dependent on people of all kinds of backgrounds "doing their thing" often "for and by" their own communities rather than having the aim to be generic, predictable, and easy replicate en masse. Skateboarding is not like learning to be an actor and then performing a classic play in a theatre company for instance, or like a song or a painting that can be catalogued into a set genre once it drops in the airwaves or hits a canvas. Skateboarding is something more spontaneous, diverse, open, flexible, and fluid and skateboarders are becoming less easy to categorize, but this is to their advantage now more than ever.

Skateboarders can of course teach lessons, compete in events, and sign up with companies to use their image and videos, or make and sell products like skateboards and clothes. These are all things that they are able to sustain a living from. However, it is the intangible, temporal, and impermanent things about the act of skating, including how skateboarders look on their board, what they accomplish on it, and what they find cool and fun to do, often defiantly in the face of what "they should do" that creates a mystique and allure around them, producing notions of cool and archetypes that then become marketable.

An important point to glean from both skateboarding as a culture and the research we have done for this book is that "cool" in skateboarding is now rarely defined by ability, especially in the modern era where the level has risen so high that beginners are routinely performing tricks that many pros from the decades prior could not execute at their athletic peak. "Cool" in skateboarding is not static. It is shifting, evolving, and defined by individuals, as well as skateboarding's collective consciousness, yet there is no metric for it, and no clearly defined guidebook for deeming who is cool.

In a sense, skateboarders just by being themselves and doing what they love have generated a legacy of cool, and this has become something desirable that others across generations now want to have a piece of and absorb. These intangibles are what makes skateboarding precious to those devoted to it and gives it an allure to those also mystified and attracted to it. The idealized skateboarder as a figure of cool, independence, freedom, and skill is where they have had their greatest influence. You cannot replicate the feeling skateboarding gives like re-playing a song, although many people try to get close to that feeling, such as in skate video games, by watching movies about skating and adopting some of their images in shoes and clothes. And as video games and fashion brands have shown alone, the market is sizeable.

In the past money has seldom been "put in the pockets" of skateboarders, with the exception of a handful of well-known figures and successful brands but things are rapidly changing. There are more blurred rather than hard lines between "core" and "non-traditional" skateboarders, the grassroots and industry, and what is subcultural and what is mainstreamed and monetized. And this is not a one-way process. Corporate athletic brands have become less enamored with competitive skateboarding and have pivoted to collaborating with artists, organizations, and those on the more creative side of skating.

We are now well into an era where skateboarders of all kinds are "bankable" and a source of profit. We are also now at a time in history where there are more products and capital being given to skateboarders who the public wants to connect, if only through what they buy. The *Nike* with *froSkate* collaboration creating a shoe, for instance, and *Pop Tarts USA* and *Proper Gnar* bringing out products together are recent examples. Many of the people we spoke with understand they have a labor and market value, and may even know how to put a price tag on it. It will be interesting to see how much these business arrangements will lead to sustainable change, both personal or culturally for "non-traditional" skaters. At present, the doors are opening and it appears these change-makers are taking people in with them and giving others a way in. In other words, they are not just trying to be the "first"; they are ensuring they are not "the last" with a seat at the table.

Others have created a whole "new table," in the form of spaces such as skate shops and skateparks. At the time of writing this book, queer skateboarding companies *Unity* and *There* were opening their own skateboard shop in San Francisco, and with the *DLX* distribution company placing them into their "family" of older "legacy" brands that have been innovative yet also lagged on being inclusive to "non-traditional" skaters. This is an enormous move forward from the low-budget beginnings less than ten years ago of *Pave the Way*, the first queer-run skate company in the US. Such skateboarders can provide useful lessons for mainstream sports and their industries to open more pathways and doors and to let appreciative audiences and markets build up rather than assuming they do not exist. We have reached an era for instance where one can observe there are more openly gay and queer, and as well as other "non-traditional" skateboarders who are sponsored by teams, companies, and by brands than most men's major sporting leagues in North America for instance. This includes how such role models are still rarities in sports such as the men's National Football League, National Basketball Association, Major League Baseball, and National Hockey League.

We can also now easily observe progress and breakthroughs such as more skateparks being funded and built by First Nations leaders in skateboarding like Douglas Miles Jr. at San Carlos Reservation and Whiteriver, the latter with *The Skatepark Project*. There are also other First Nations skatepark projects happening including in Pine Ridge, South Dakota, one by Lakota Skaters with support by groups such as *Salad Days of Skateboarding* which Keegan Guizard is involved with. Alongside and often with these communities, projects like *The Skatepark Project* continue to evolve and seek ways to work for communities who want to take a local approach, and have themselves lead how skateparks are built in their area. The ethics in such projects is one that rejects "top-down" approaches and is often shaped by the wisdom of what community activists in the past have experienced including how to get funding and resources and be persuasive to officials. In a sense, skateboarders are sharing certain inheritances with each other as both a local solution and a broader, long-term strategy for skateboarding's growth and longevity for all.

While there are more skateparks devoted to skateboarding than at any other time in history, it is important to note skateboarding mostly still exists in public spaces. And the creative force and progression of skateboarding have long been in the streets than in contained, designated areas. However, the interaction skateboarders have with the public can still be an issue and requires plenty of strategic and creative thinking. There are few subcultural activities that happen spontaneously in a public space, and for skateboarders, things they regularly negotiate include clashes with authority, harsh public policies, their skating activities and social behavior being stigmatized, and a lack of a say in urban planning that often results in hostile private and public architecture. And, when skateboarders do become a welcomed presence by cities, they need to understand whether they are contributing to a form of gentrification that selectively rezones areas for those deemed creative, rather than more equitable use of public and common space for all, including other still stigmatized people.

In many ways, skateboarding shares parallels and a trajectory with graffiti, whose earliest provocateurs were teenagers in urban areas leaving their mark on public spaces. As industry became involved, commercialized brands and products were targeted specifically for the graffiti world, graffiti writers became re-imagined as marketable artists, zones in cities started to welcome their presence, and even museums began displaying their work. Like skateboarding, graffiti artists are also involved with brand collaborations and marketing. And one of the more frustrating parallels is that there is an entire industry devoted to removing graffiti from public spaces just as there is one centered on "skate-stopping" structures to discourage skateboarders from using them.

Skateboarding is embedded within societal structures and one has to navigate through them in order to exist and thrive. From running a company to building spaces, skateboarders learn to participate in, use, and sometimes subvert and convert existing societal structures and rules in order to continue to pursue what they love. And, now that larger corporations from sporting goods manufacturers, lifestyle brands, tech companies, and couture brands are investing in skateboarding, it remains unclear what do those skaters want to invest in, and is there an end game other than securing more revenue? These are questions for the future and perhaps some of the ways forward will be influenced from outside the culture as much as from within it in order to keep things fresh, inclusive, open-minded, and progressive.

What skaters seldom do is look at how others may navigate similar issues and succeed, from similar subcultures and lifestyle sports or even mainstream sports and industries. One of skateboarding's tendencies is to be insular and to view skateboarding as such a unique activity that it does not need guidance and influence from outside itself. Yet skateboarding could be more resourceful in learning from others on tackling a number of issues, such as the issues of inclusion and equity discussed in our book, but also many other under-explored and less-talked about areas including but not limited to access to mental health support, work entitlements and health insurance, salary increases and ethical work conditions, environmentally aware and sustainable products, and codes of conduct for professional skateboarders on teams and in competitions. Many conversations are happening and we are enthusiastic to see what future researchers observe. There have also been so many recent and rapid advances in skateboarding going on that were not possible to document within the scope of this book. Numerous breakthroughs and turnarounds were happening in real-time as we typed our words onto the pages.

We conclude with our belief that skateboarding remains an interesting case study to explore how power operates, and can be changed both within and beyond its own world. This is because it is ever-evolving and often an enigma, including how its relationship with authorities remains precarious, even while it is becoming increasingly legitimized and commercialized. It has also found ways to survive, monetize, and legitimize what it does while preserving a sense of autonomy, authenticity, agency, and capacity for resistance. And in relation to mainstream sports, while skateboarding's lack of a universal governing body can make its path forward less clear, that same lack of organization allows it to change rapidly. And the tenacity skateboarders have when facing their own challenges, matched with their capacity for a radical kind of empathy when watching others face theirs, is perhaps some of their greatest "super powers." Skateboarding is reaching an era where it needs to be owning its influence while sharing its wisdom, inheritances, and visions of opening up more doors for more people than ever before.

References

Abulhawa, D. (2020). *Skateboarding and Femininity: Gender, Space-making and Expressive movement* London: Routledge.

Anderson, B (1993) *Imagined Communities: Reflections on the Origin and Spread of Nationalism*, Verso.

Beal, B (1995). Disqualifying the official: An exploration of social resistance through the subculture of skateboarding. *Sociology of Sport Journal, 12*(3), 252–267. 10.1123/ssj.12.3.252

Beck-Gernsheim, E (1998) On the Way to a Post-Familial Family: From a Community of Need to Elective Affinities, *Theory, Culture & Society, 15*(3–4), 53–70. https://doi.org/10.1177/0263276498015003004

Bennett, A. (2011) The Post-subcultural Turn: Some Reflections 10 years on, *Journal of Youth Studies, 14*(5), 493–506. https://doi.org/10.1080/1367626 1.2011.559216

Borden, I. (2001). *Skateboarding, Space and the City: Architecture and the Body.* Oxford: Berg.

Borden, I. (2019). *Skateboarding and the City: A Complete History.* London: Bloomsbury Visual Arts.

Callen-Riley, T and Hölsgens, S, 2020 (Eds) *Urban Pamphleteer #8 Skateboardings*, pp 36-38. Downloaded 18 July 2022: http://urbanpamphleteer.org/skateboardings

Carroll, T, and Cianciotta, L (2020) Towards Radical Empathy, Eds Callen-Riley, T and Holsgens, S, *Urban Pamphleteer #8 Skateboardings*, pp 11 - 12, Downloaded 18 July 2022: http://urbanpamphleteer.org/skateboardings

Dinces, S (2011) Flexible Opposition: Skateboarding Subcultures under the Rubric of Late Capitalism, International Journal of the History of Sport, 28, (11): 1512–1535.

froSkate (2022) Caption with photograph, Posted 9 August. @froskate Instagram, https://www.instagram.com/p/ChA6soqMLsx/

Geckle, B and Shaw, S (2022) Failure and Futurity: The Transformative Potential of Queer Skateboarding. *YOUNG, 30*(2), 132–148. https://doi.org/10.1177/1103308820945100

Givens, T (2022) *Radical Empathy*, Bristol: Polity Press.

Hannerz, U (1990) Cosmopolitans and Locals in World Culture, *Theory, Culture and Society* 7(2): 237–251. doi:https://doi.org/10.1177/026327690007002014.

Lamont, M and Aksartova, S (2002) Ordinary Cosmopolitanisms: Strategies for Bridging Racial Boundaries among Working Class Men, *Theory, Culture and Society* 19(4):1-25. https://doi.org/10.1177/026327640201900.4001

Lombard, K.J (2010). Skate and create/skate and destroy: The commercial and governmental incorporation of skateboarding. *Continuum: Journal of Media & Cultural Studies, 24*(4), 475–488. https://doi.org/10.1080/10304310903294713

Martínez, D (2013) From Off the Rez to Off the Hook!: Douglas Miles and Apache Skateboards. *American Indian Quarterly* 37(4):370–94.

O'Connor, P (2017) Beyond the youth culture: Understanding middle-aged skateboarders through temporal capital, *International Review for the Sociology of Sport*, 1-20 preview copy.

Sharp, M, and Threadgold, S (2020). Defiance Labour and Reflexive Complicity: Illusio and Gendered Marginalisation in DIY Punk Scenes. *Sociological Review*, 68(3), pp. 606-622. https://doi.org/10.1177/0038026119875325.

Snyder, G (2017) *Skateboarding LA: Inside Professional Street Skateboarding*, New York University Press.

Thorpe, H, and Wheaton, B (2011). 'Generation X Games', Action Sports and the Olympic Movement: Understanding the Cultural Politics of Incorporation. *Sociology, 45*(5), 830–847.

Toffoletti, K, Francombe-Webb, J and Thorpe, T (2018) *New Sporting Femininities : Embodied Politics in Postfeminist Times*. Cham, Switzerland: Palgrave Macmillan.

Weaver, H. N (2016) Where Wounded Knee meets Wounded Knees: Skateparks and Native American Youth. *Alternative: An International Journal of Indigenous Peoples*, *12*(5), 513–526. https://search-informit-org.libraryproxy.griffith.edu.au/doi/epdf/10.3316/informit.523827165207373

Wheaton, B, and Thorpe, T (2019) Action Sports Media Consumption Trends across Generations: Exploring the Olympic Audience and the Impact of Action Sports Inclusion, *Communication, and Sport* 7(4): 415–45, 10.1177/2167479518780410

Wheaton, B and Thorpe, H (2021) *Action Sports and the Olympic Games: Past, Present, Future,* Routledge

Williams, N (2021) Understanding Race in Skateboarding: A Retrospection and Agenda for the Importance of Being Seen, Dupont, T and Beal, B (eds), *Lifestyle Sports and Identities: Subcultural Careers Throughout the Life Course,* London: Routledge, pp 284 - 296.

Williams, N (2022) Before the Gold: Connecting Aspirations, Activism, and BIPOC Excellence Through Olympic Skateboarding, *Journal of Olympic Studies,* 3 (1): 4–27. https://doi.org/10.5406/26396025.3.1.02

Willing, I, Bennett, A, Piispa, M and Green, B (2019) Skateboarding and the 'Tired Generation': Ageing in Youth Cultures and Lifestyle Sports. *Sociology* 53(3):503–18.

Willing, I, Green, B and Pavlidis, P (2020), The 'Boy Scouts' and 'Bad Boys' of SKateboarding: A Thematic Analysis of *The Bones Brigade. Sport in Society,* 23(5), 832 - 846. DOI: https://doi.org/10.1080/17430437.2019.1580265

Coda

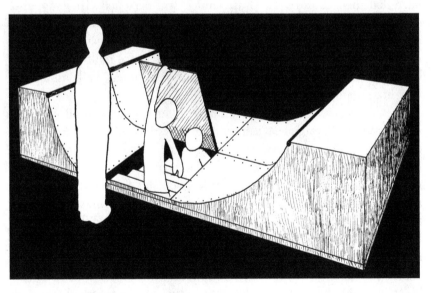

Coda Illustration by Adam Abada

Indigo Willing

I have never met a skateboarder who does not have an incredible life story to tell. Listening to, reading about, and seeing the stories of fellow skateboarders out in the world is my second favorite thing about skateboarding, after skating of course. Many people you meet in skateboarding can tell you about fun-filled adventures of hanging with wonderfully unique and vibrant people, taking risks to do fun and impressive things, but also with openness and a humble way about them that can include some laugh-out-loud moments. Very often, these very same individuals who were able to take up skateboarding are also carrying the weight of traumatic and challenging circumstances and life experiences. This includes people who are unhoused and homeless, have lived in a conflict zone, or have fled their country, or whose land is still occupied. There are also skaters I know who have survived all kinds of harmful interpersonal and domestic situations on top of facing social discrimination and exclusions. And I also have met many skateboarders who balance multiple responsibilities and are constantly seeing to the needs of others while asking for very little if anything for themselves.

The sanctuary that skateboarding can offer people with all kinds of stories and lived experiences cannot be underestimated, but I do not raise these points to evoke pity or to suggest all skateboarders have gone through extreme hardships, although many have. My point is that along with skateboarding being able to thrill, fascinate, entertain, and soothe us, it is also a way to realize, nurture, and mobilize one's power and agency. A common thread that is observable across many different people I have met in skateboarding, and also with Anthony through doing our research for this book, is that no matter what they faced in the past, where they are now, or even where they feel they may be heading, all will burst into life and be filled with enthusiasm when you ask them what they love about skateboarding. As part of this, they will have stories of pushing themselves to accomplish things they never dreamed they could do, from rolling smoothly with confidence from A to B to learning a new trick. They also have stories of innovation, whether creating, improving, modifying, or adjusting something out of necessity to meet specific needs or achieve certain goals.

When you extend that conversation further, most emphasize that they will also do all kinds of things to share the joys of skateboarding with others too. This might be through the remarkable projects we have outlined in this book, but also through ordinary, everyday things such as informally teaching others how to skate down at the local skatepark or giving away spare parts of skateboards to total strangers or helping them set one up for their first time. It can also be through sharing time to build a DIY skate spot or a donation to build a skatepark somewhere well across the other side of the world that people they do not even know will also get to use. Through the lived experiences of skateboarding and "falling in love" with it, anyone can develop the capacity to make a positive difference for someone else and are also able to share that power within a team, group, community, or larger social configurations like an alliance. We also have the power as skateboarders to make changes within ourselves, drawing on the tenacity and fine-tuned skills of evaluation we build up through our failures as well as our progress.

No study of skateboarding will ever be complete because skateboarders are so diverse and we are still learning so much about ourselves and our potential to bring about change, not just from within our culture but also beyond it. And even the most seasoned skate communities and professionals who have been doing what they do for decades have to navigate sometimes highly unpredictable and shifting social, cultural, and political environments. As skate researchers and writers, what is important to us is to keep creating spaces where skateboarders can document and witness our progress and share our multiple and ever-expanding skills, creative strategies, and wisdom from lived experiences. In doing so, we are able to grow healthier scenes and positively channel our instincts to push ourselves in skateboarding over to also pushing the culture forward, and with greater awareness and overdue respect of where we roll, who with, and on whose land.

Anthony Pappalardo

My goal in working on this book was to expose the patterns and structures that have been present in skateboarding since its initial rise in the 1970s, so that there is not only a historical record and reference for others but also a roadmap to changing it for those who are struggling or at odds with what skateboarding is as an industry and culture.

Skateboarding is liquid and living. It expands and contracts with the economy and popularity and even authority, but none of those factors has been able to "end" it. Some similar cultures such as Freestyle BMX or even Rollerblading saw similar plateaus but were never able to rebound. For whatever reason, skateboarding is resilient and perhaps that's because it's always been aware that it relies on itself.

Regardless of its warts, the companies driving skateboarding as an industry are now a mix of heritage brands and independent brands. There are few corporate drivers in the actual industry of skateboarding. Sure, the corporations have massive influence, but the "core" companies are skateboarding's pulse and the corporations know that. Moreover, those corporations are too large to know or even address skateboarding as directly and need to collaborate with smaller, leaner brands that more fully reflect what skateboarding is today. Believe me, if they could they would. It's not worth wondering if that's positive or negative, instead, skateboarding should embrace that power.

The brands that many still view as "small" have now operated longer than the original brands that started skateboarding. Pro skaters have longer careers and relevancy than the originals. Skateboarding equipment is better. Parks are better. Media has been democratized to a degree with social media. There are more organizations supporting skateboarders and their lifestyles than ever before. There are more skateboarders than at any time in history and the people skateboarding are more diverse than at any time in its existence.

And skateboarding even has a holiday. Yes, "Go Skateboarding," "Go Skate," or "Whatever the Fuck Day" every June 21, the longest day of the calendar year. The Summer Solstice.

That's great and all, but maybe, instead of a day encouraging you to do the thing you already do or a day that urges you to buy skateboarding products you already will, perhaps skateboarding just needs a day to celebrate itself and all that it's achieved. Rather than focusing on commerce, skateboarding needs more attention and love for its culture.

Actually, we all know a holiday isn't going to do shit. So yes, come June, please ride your skateboard if you're so inclined. Skateboarding doesn't need a single day, it needs to constantly be conscious of what it is, what power it has, and how to leverage it to make more people skateboard. That's it.

From rocks and cracks to inequality and representation, everyone rolling is thinking about what skateboarding is as they push. Skateboarding should think about the people who are going to fill the parks they are fundraising to build, or the people buying the skateboards and clothing they plan seasons out, before making more things because skateboarding can exist and has existed without all those things. If the industry crumbled, there would still be a group of diehards figuring out ways to make and ride skateboards. And there will still be problems because skateboarding is a mirror of the culture, society, and structures we deal with every day.

How can skateboarding be one of the most influential activities globally but also be an underdog? The answer is not simple and clear-cut. I am reminded of Blind Skateboards' *Video Days* released in 1991 and directed by Spike Jonze, with artistic and conceptual input and influence by Mark Gonzales. *Video Days* is arguably the most influential documentation of modern skateboarding put to tape. Before Gonzales' part in it, there is a brief clip spliced into the footage from *Willy Wonka & the Chocolate Factory*, directed by Mel Stuart at Paramount Pictures in 1971. In that clip, Wonka, played by Gene Wilder, interrupts Veruca Salt's character, played by child actor Judy Dawn Cole. He offers her the following insight: "we are the music makers. And we are the dreamers of the dreams." Clever juxtaposition or artistic irreverence? Perhaps it's an analog and reminder of skateboarding's power, told from an adult to a child unaware of their influence.

The challenge is not making or selling products, generating enough money to make a living riding a skateboard, or even creating physical spaces to ride skateboards. History has shown us that skateboarding will exist and maybe even thrive without those "luxuries." The luxury we don't have is to allow the historical injustices and inequalities in skateboarding to fester and impact future generations. We can't control skateboarding, but we can influence the community around it by how we act, speak, and share the feeling that got us all hooked on this thing in the first place.

Appendix

List of Interviewees

Adam Abada
Dani Abulhawa
Thomas Barker
Kyle Beachy
Alec Beck
Lisa Berenson
Kaily "Bayr" Blackburn
L Brew
Amelia Brodka
Rhianon Bader
Izzi Cooper
"Mara" Doyenne
Kristin Ebeling
Paul Forsline
Bethany Geckle
Chris Giamarino

© The Author(s), under exclusive license to Springer Nature Singapore Pte Ltd. 2023
I. Willing, A. Pappalardo, *Skateboarding, Power and Change*,
https://doi.org/10.1007/978-981-99-1234-6

Brian Glenney
Tommy Guerrero
Keegan Guizard
Sarah Huston
Brennan Hatton
Norma Ibarra
Atiba Jefferson
Christian Kerr
Patrick Kigongo
Adrian Koenisberg
Denia Kopita
Lynn Kramer
Ryan Lay
Ashely Masters
Douglas Miles Senior
Douglas Miles Junior
Peggy Oki
Kevin Pacella
Ted Schmitz
Latosha Stone
Karlie Thornton
Timothy Ward
Alex White
Shari White
Cindy Whitehead
Kim Woozy

Index

© The Author(s), under exclusive license to Springer Nature Singapore Pte Ltd. 2023
I. Willing, A. Pappalardo, *Skateboarding, Power and Change*,
https://doi.org/10.1007/978-981-99-1234-6

CPSIA information can be obtained
at www.ICGtesting.com
Printed in the USA
LVHW011752210723
752877LV00002BA/79